Drawn to the exoticism and mystery of names on a map of Iran – Isfahan, Shiraz, Meshed, Kerman, Khorassan – Michael Carroll embarked on a journey that took him through the heart of the country, from the Taurus mountains to the Gulf of Oman. He travelled during a relatively calm, but nonetheless pivotal period in Iran's recent history – in the years following the CIA-led coup of 1953. Carroll spent much time in the bustling tea houses of Isfahan, where he observed the richness of Iranian life in microcosm and visited a Tehran that would be unrecognisable today – a sleepy town pushing towards modernity with its shiny 1950s American cars and social elites exploring the lifestyles of a newly discovered West. From the Zagros Mountains to the Caspian shore and Persepolis to the holy city of Qom, he explored countless mosques, tombs and palaces, went in pursuit of an elusive dervish, bargained for Silk Road jade and forged strong and lasting friendships with his Iranian travelling companions. Carroll's beautifully written narrative is adorned with colourful episodes from Iran's long and momentous history and enriched with anecdotes from his travels. A forgotten gem of travel writing, *From a Persian Tea House* is a literary period piece and a luminous portrait of a country that has since changed beyond all recognition.

Michael Carroll was born in England in 1935. He was educated at Harrow and Cambridge but spent much of his early life in India. He is also the author of *Gates of the Wind*, the story of his time spent on the Greek island of Skopelos.

'Carroll is a born traveller. He is hungry for strangeness. He is tough without being coarse; amused and unpretentious. Above all he can write.'   *The Observer*

'The romance of the book is the traditional romance of a perceptive young man, happy to soak himself in the life of a foreign country and evoke it with rich, descriptive writing.'   *The New Statesman*

'He has a natural gift for writing and especially for translating the observations of a quick eye into a telling phrase.'
                                                    Times Literary Supplement

'Describes all he saw and experienced in the most entrancing detail and with great good humour. A lovely, gracious book.'
                                                    Press and Journal

'A travel writer of rare charm and perception. His travels reveal observation combined with sympathy, persistence with humour.'
                                                    Western Mail

Tauris Parke Paperbacks is an imprint of I.B.Tauris. It is dedicated to publishing books in accessible paperback editions for the serious general reader within a wide range of categories, including biography, history, travel and the ancient world. The list includes select, critically acclaimed works of top quality writing by distinguished authors that continue to challenge, to inform and to inspire. These are books that possess those subtle but intrinsic elements that mark them out as something exceptional.

The Colophon of Tauris Parke Paperbacks is a representation of the ancient Egyptian ibis, sacred to the god Thoth, who was himself often depicted in the form of this most elegant of birds. Thoth was credited in antiquity as the scribe of the ancient Egyptian gods and as the inventor of writing and was associated with many aspects of wisdom and learning.

FROM A PERSIAN TEA HOUSE

Travels in Old Iran

Michael Carroll

TPP

TAURIS PARKE
PAPERBACKS

Published in 2007 by Tauris Parke Paperbacks
an imprint of I.B.Tauris and Co Ltd
6 Salem Road, London W2 4BU
175 Fifth Avenue, New York NY 10010
www.ibtauris.com

First published in 1960 by John Murray
Copyright © 1960, Michael Carroll

Cover image © Mark Daffey/Lonely Planet Images

ISBN: 978 1 84511 500 5

A full CIP record for this book is available from the British Library

Printed and bound in India by Replika Press Pvt. Ltd

Contents

❈

1 TEA-HOUSE IN ISFAHAN   1

2 NOMADS AND RUINS   34

3 DESERTS   65

4 THE ART OF BARGAINING:
  CARPETS AND BAZAARS   101

5 TEHRAN AND THE CASPIAN   125

6 DIVERSION TO THE GULF OF OMAN 145

7 RETURN TO ISFAHAN   170

8 EPILOGUE: TEA-LEAVES   202

v

Illustrations

From photographs by author, except where otherwise acknowledged

Sketch Map by John Woodcock

Courtyard of the *Madraseh* in Isfahan

Autumn Migration: Tribe on the move near Kermanshah

Kurds: A ploughman; and woman and child★

Naksh-i-Rustam; Shapur I receiving the homage of the
    captured Roman Emperor Valerian

Tomb of Xerxes

Persepolis: Bas-relief

Persepolis: the Great King holds court

Tribute-bearers from all the Empire

An independent camel in the mountains south of Yezd

Hand-loom in a Baluch village

The bus we rescued near Guk★

Down the rapids on the way to Charbahar

We shall leave to-morrow, *Insha'allah*

Young and old in Baluchistan★

A street in Kerman†

Across the Elburz†

A *Mullah* at Isfahan

★ *From photographs by David Gaunt*
† *From photographs by Martin Berthoud*

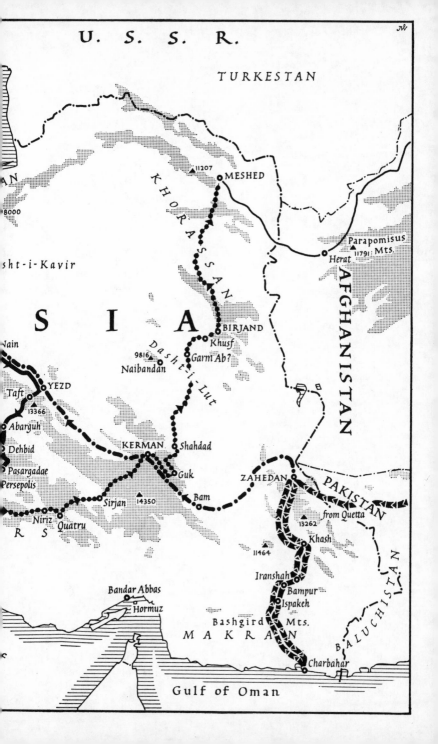

For
DAVID GAUNT

I

Tea-house in Isfahan

❄

It was the time I loved best in the tea-house, the chill early morning when the sunlight streamed like thin smoke between the pillars, filling the vast room mysteriously; when the air was sharp with the tang of a wood fire, and the few customers sat alone and withdrawn to themselves, and the only sound was the click of glasses and the rhythmic sweep of the boy's brush on the floor.

There were not many in the tea-house at this hour, breakfasting off sweet strong tea and flaps of unleavened bread; not more than a dozen, mostly solitary figures hunched cross-legged and shivering upon the threadbare carpets, warming their hands over the little charcoal braziers that the attendant had brought to each one.

I leaned back against the wooden pillar and changed the position of my legs. There were no chairs or tables, but low trestles spread with carpets set up in lines down the whole length of the room. Two rows of dark worm-eaten oak pillars, still pockmarked with traces of green paint, propped up the roof, a crosswork of beams blackened with age and smoke, with cobwebs sagging from their corners.

The attendant stood with his back to the sun, balancing a brass tray on his arm. Motionless in the sea of pale light that broke around his body, he seemed for a moment transfigured, some fallen spirit suddenly redeemed. The collarless shirt that hung loose over his stained rolled-up trousers, curling slippers broken at the heel, became the gilded vestments of an archangel; the thin unshaven head, vacant-eyed, became the haloed face of ineffable

Tea-house in Isfahan

wisdom, the tea-tray flashing on his arm the insignia of heaven, God's gift to mankind. Reverently I handed him my glass: 'More tea, please.'

A boy kneeling below me bent across the pool and rinsed his hands. Water bubbled from the snub, bronze fountain-snout and slid into the blue-tiled basin. When the sun leaves the pool, I decided, I shall get up and go; until then . . .

It was evening in late summer, not long after my arrival in Isfahan, when I drew aside the curtain of blue beads hanging across the doorway and stepped into the tea-house for the first time. The benches on each side of the passage were full. I walked uncertainly on into the central room, looking for a place to sit. The place was full of smoke and people. I stood by the pool, accustoming myself to the dim light and the clamour of voices, evading the attendants who jostled me as they hurried by, circling round the water. A few naked electric bulbs were stuck on the sides of the pillars, oil lamps hung from the ceiling rafters; their light, hardly penetrating into the farthest corners, between the shadows of the pillars, made the room look larger, the smoke and medley of voices rising from the men crowded shoulder to shoulder on the carpeted benches only made the scene more confusing. I turned, about to go, when someone touched my coat and spoke to me in Persian. I looked round at a little man with a smiling face, a brown skull-cap cocked at a jaunty angle on his head. He was clearing a space for me, pushing aside the others on the trestle who made way willingly enough, and waved an authoritative hand to a human tea-trolley that was passing by. In a moment I was sitting awkwardly on the edge of the carpet, a glass and saucer of strong brown tea in my hands.

A boy was dropping lumps of sugar into the glass. When it was half full and the tea overflowed, he glanced at me in surprise and moved on. I hadn't told him to stop. My host laughed and offered me a cigarette. As I turned to accept the match a figure brushed past, dropping a spoon into the glass. We sat for a short time without speaking. We introduced ourselves. His name was Hassan; and seeing that my Persian was very inadequate he broke into a sort of English, picked up, he told me, when he worked with a British oil company in the south. Hassan was out of work and had been for more than a year. The suspension of the oil concern had meant the end of his job, and so he had drifted back to Isfahan, where he was born. He seemed to enjoy talking English. No, he had nothing against the English; in fact he was still living on the money they paid him. And when that finished? Well . . . And how about another job? Hassan was shocked: Impossible! Where could he work? Besides (with relief), he was too old. He grinned cheerfully and waved to the tea-boy. Our empty glasses and saucers were whisked away and immediately replaced full. He asked me if I was married, and when I said no, he looked surprised; and then considered a little, nodding to himself as if he thought my decision, after all, had been a wise one. As for him, he was with his second wife, living with his parents-in-law. It appeared that the arrangement was not altogether satisfactory. Had he any children? He shrugged and replied airily that he had one or two. Later I discovered that he had two daughters. But no one in Persia is proud of having daughters. It's the sons that count.

How did I like Isfahan?—'Isfahan the city most beautiful in Iran.' I agreed. But had I seen everything, Masjid-i-Shah, Maidan . . .? Only part, I admitted. He seemed pleased. Good, well he had a friend, a great scholar who spoke very fine English. He would show me everything. He looked round the crowded room; usually he came in the evenings. Perhaps if I waited . . . This friend of his, 'wise man, his name Ibrahim', had a beard. Hassan stroked his stubbly chin by way of further clarification.

I decided to wait. I was beginning to enjoy myself. The atmosphere of the tea-house was stimulating; nowhere in Persia had I seen so much life and movement concentrated in one place. I could understand little of what was being said round about me, only the widespread comments of Hassan sometimes gave sense to the gesticulations and raised voices on every side. Hassan would nudge me and cock his head in the direction of a group of young men who seemed to be on the point of blows.

'Politic . . .' and added, 'What difference will it make?' Or, casting an eye towards a huge man, bald, with black hairs sticking out round his ears: 'He has lorries, trucks—he want to buy that man's also . . .' 'That man' was a thin little fellow who sat crushed up against a pillar, his legs neatly folded under him, an expression of acute misery on his face as he looked up at his giant adversary. Hassan sensed where my sympathy lay, and chuckled. He tapped his head knowingly: 'Clever man, my friend; good price, or not sell!'

I wasn't so sure. The big man had changed his tactics. Words like black treacle flowed from a mouth twisted into the parody of a smile. His tea glass was enveloped in a mighty paw. Such was the violence straining in that hand that I felt the glass would be ground to pieces. The little fellow, caught suddenly by a friendly blow on the shoulder, rocked so that he spilt his tea. He seemed on the point of tears. But Hassan's smile was full of satisfaction. He rubbed his thumb and forefinger together: 'Best price!'

Not everyone in the tea-house was arguing. An old man on the other side of Hassan sat with bowed head chewing the end of his long white moustache, talking quietly, but to himself. Many simply sat, exchanging an occasional word or greeting across the crowded room, smoking cigarettes, or water-pipes.

There must have been at least forty of these pipes bubbling in the tea-house, thickening the air with clouds of sweet blue smoke. Hookahs, or hubble-bubbles as they are called in India; *kalians* in Persia. There was a special attendant, I noticed, whose sole duty was the supply of *kalians* to customers in the tea-house. He padded round the low, heavily laden trestles, a pipe in each hand, the charcoal glowing on the tobacco, long coloured piping stems hanging over his arms. As soon as a pipe was ordered he would disappear into the background to set about its careful preparation, a job which though outwardly simple is held to require consider-able skill and experience. In India the *hookah-burdar* (pipe-carrier) was an essential functionary in the entourage of every Raja and

4

would accompany him even while out hunting. Persian nobles used to set as much store by their pipe-fillers as the Parisian by his chef.

I persuaded Hassan to call the attendant and get him to show me how it was done. I followed him into a dark cellar-like room at the back of the tea-house, where a small half-naked boy was puffing and blowing over a great tray of red-hot charcoal. The tobacco was stored in stone tubs round the wall, the leaves ground to a certain fine consistency. I watched as with deft fingers he measured out the tobacco and packed it into a metal cup supported on a carved wooden stand. The stand was screwed into a glass jar half filled with water, one of many prepared and waiting on the shelf. He sprinkled a little water over the tobacco, and the boy was ready with the charcoal, laying it with tongs upon the top. He showed me how to use the pipe, how the smoke is drawn, down through the water and by way of the stem, deep into the smoker's lungs. The smoke is purified by being passed through the water, and cooled; further cooling depends on the length of the stem, which is sometimes as much as three yards. In the tea-house the stems and mouth-pieces are washed after each smoker, and are brought in dripping with water. But I noticed that some of the men prefer to bring their own wooden or ivory mouthpieces, and occasionally even their own tobacco—a practice which Hassan strongly recommended. Tea-house tobacco was always poor, he said. Pigeon-dung, he called it.

Hassan tried to dissuade me from ordering a pipe. He coughed hoarsely; a *kalian* would choke me. But he was already complaining of a sore throat after a couple of my English cigarettes; besides, I had smoked a *kalian* once before, though not very successfully. Hassan was impressed by my performance, but I was smoking the pipe too quickly, perhaps because I was afraid it would go out; a humiliating experience at any time, and especially at that moment when my efforts were attracting considerable attention. A pipe can last from twenty minutes up to an hour, depending on the energy with which one attacks it; the more experienced nurse it as long as possible. There is a major difference between *kalian*-smoking and any other in that the smoke must be completely inhaled; only in this way can the pipe be made to function; but contrary to what is generally thought I have found the tobacco to be exceptionally mild, milder than a cigarette—perhaps because of the water? And certainly the effect is most satisfying, a sense of gentle intoxication in which the mind floats in the air as a bird above a lake of deep calm . . . the water bubbles soothingly, the smooth smoke curls blue in the jar. There was a radish floating in my water jar. Sometimes the Persians put flowers.

A tall man in shirt-sleeves, coat slung across his shoulders, was making his way across the room exchanging exuberant greetings with friends scattered about the benches. He clapped Hassan on the shoulder, and when he saw me, bowed and shook my hand. He was called Ashaf and appeared to be a sort of travelling salesman dealing with a strange combination of merchandise: rice and tobacco. He had just come back from the north, the Caspian. Hassan was determined to show off his English.

'Your trip good?'

Ashaf nodded, teeth gleaming under his short dark moustache: 'Resht——' he shrugged; 'Isfahan ——!' He raised his arms as if to embrace the entire tea-house in the pleasure of his return. He grabbed the passing tea-boy playfully by the hair and pretended a great rage because his tea was not ready. Hassan said that he had been waiting for him for days; but Ashaf's bus had broken down at Qum. He made off towards the far corner, the tea-boy trotting obediently at his heels, towards a group of men sitting round a wild-eyed fellow with a tilted cloth cap and a cigarette hanging out of his mouth who was holding the attention of his audience with some tale evidently full of suspense.

Hassan poked a thumb in his direction and said, 'That man come back from Tehran yesterday,' and catching a few words across the room hazarded a guess at the subject of the story in progress. 'Women,' he said, and shook his head wisely. 'New lies, every trip.' We watched Ashaf and the raconteur, who stood up to meet him, embrace each other noisily. Hassan knew everybody in the tea-house. 'Always go—always come back.' Hassan patted the old carpet on which we were sitting and nodded with satisfaction.

It seemed that Ibrahim would not be coming in to-night. There was a disturbance across the pool, at the corner where the passage entered the room. Someone coming in had knocked against the corner of the sugar-cutter; lumps of white crystal went bouncing on to the floor, one had even plopped into the pool. The sugar-cutter was trembling with anger and cursed the culprit for his clumsiness. But now they were collecting the sugar again, fetching out the lumps from under the trestles and putting them back on the cloth. The lump in the pool had dissolved. Hassan told me his name was Mahmoud; he did nothing else in the tea-house but cut sugar and had been doing it for Allah alone knows how many years. Old and white-bearded, Mahmoud sat cross-legged on his little carpet, a figure of concentration poised over his work. Blocks of sugar were piled by his side; the miniature axe in his hand fell rhythmically, neat cubes rolled endlessly on to the cloth spread between his knees to be gathered away by the tea-boys. Customers liked their sugar cut before their eyes.

Over in the corner the glasses were being filled from a towering brass samovar that hissed and steamed upon the ledge. Rows of flowered Japanese teapots (never used as far as I could see) hung from a shelf behind. There is a special ritual in the serving and drinking of tea. First come the little brimful glasses, scalding hot upon clean wet saucers; followed immediately by the sugar, doled out from a bulging apron; in a moment the spoon, dropped neatly into the glass. Usually the tea is too hot to drink straight from the glass; most Persians will delicately tip the liquid into the saucer and drink from that and, instead of stirring in the sugar, will take a lump and, placing it between their teeth, sip the tea through.

Hassan was talking to a man who must have been very hot in a long ex-army greatcoat. When I had been introduced and looked more closely I saw he had nothing else underneath. Persian dress could hardly have improved since Reza Shah and Western influences have been at work. The foreigner expecting an Arabian Nights display of brilliant cloaks, brocades and silk and tulip turbans will, if he stays in the towns, be disappointed; and the Persian who frequents tea-houses is not of the wealthier sort; the tea-house is the meeting-place of the 'common man'. From my position—and I had wormed my way up against a pillar to ease my back—I could count not more than a dozen turbans in the whole room; old men, or just blatant yokels in from the country-side. Mostly the men were bare-headed with the occasional *pahlevi* peaked cap—relic of a Shah's decree, or with skull-caps, like Hassan, or plain battered felts. Patches of white, open-necked shirts without collars; the summer evenings were still very warm. But mostly browns, greys and blacks, remnants of cheap suits, shabby coats above worn striped trousers, down-at-heel black shoes, or slippers. And then, pyjamas, adopted in the hot seasons as the most practical dress, comfortable and cool. Always a surprise to me, the sudden but common apparition of respectable citizens dressed for the street in pyjamas. With its familiar connotation of sleep it never failed to give me the impression that these gentlemen had just got out of bed, an assumption usually confirmed by unbrushed hair and unshaven chins. But Persians have a horror of shaving and do so as little as possible, compromising at once a week, and then as far as possible getting a barber to go about the hideous task for them.

Hassan had already left, apologising half comically; he must get home, his mother-in-law . . . He would see me to-morrow, and he would tell his friend Ibrahim. It was only half-past ten and the tea-house was emptying. Some of the benches were already clear, and here and there a man was preparing to doss down for the night, his shoes and hat for a pillow, a blanket or a cloak round him on the carpet. I got up stiffly and walked round the fountain, still now in the pool, the water fouled by cigarette-ends and bits of paper. At the door I paid. Nine glasses of tea, one *kalian*: the amount was calculated with an impressive mathematical talent upon the abacus at the doorman's side. Less than two shillings, an inexpensive evening. Hassan had already paid for his own. '*Khoda hafiz.*' Goodnight. Someone coming in touched my elbow: Taki, a mechanic on the bus from Kerman that had arrived this morning. As Hassan had forecast earlier, he was going to sleep on a bench here. He always did. He carried a blanket roll under his arm. Everybody came back to the tea-house, some time. Where else was there to go? I stepped through the blue bead curtain into the quiet street. Warm breaths of air stirred the trees, turning their leaves in the moonlight. The jagged line of mountains was faintly discernible under the brilliant sky. I walked back slowly towards the hotel, steering by the minaret of the Madraseh, the fat dome pushing up blackly against the stars.

I had found a place in the shade on the roof of the hotel, over-looking on one side the hotel courtyard, on the other a garden of tall firs, the flat roofs of the city beyond. It was still the middle of the day, when the sun was at its hottest and Isfahan dozed. Straw mattresses and old bedsteads were scattered about my roof; a cat, curled up in their shadow, slept uneasily. I put down my book. Tremors of heat danced over the dun-coloured roof-tops, the firs drooped lifeless, grey with dust. Even the mountains, those bare peaks rimming the city, whose contours never fail to surprise, now leaned pale and characterless, drained of their strength against the colourless haze of sky. The dogs had stopped barking.

Not everybody was asleep. Down in the courtyard below me two buxom women, bulging in their bright full skirts and aprons, slapped and pummelled the hotel washing, up to their arms in soap-filled buckets. Their shrill arguing voices jarred into the per-vading silence. I watched disapprovingly as one took up a pile of clothes and knelt by the pool, rinsing them in the water. It was a large pool, rectangular and tiled in the usual blue, and this morn-ing the water had been comparatively clear. Now a wave of dis-coloured soapsuds moved across the pool; in a far corner a few indignant goldfish huddled away from the flapping and bubbling. Ali, of the light trousers and black waistcoat, who was always ready to push back the big doors in the arch for me whenever I left the hotel, whose head I could now just see resting on his arm by the steps in profound slumber, was always talking about clearing out the pool. I had pointed out to him the dark layer of slime on the tiles on the bottom. He agreed with me wholeheartedly—it was such a pity; the pool could be so beautiful, with those vermilion flower beds on the other side, the plum tree in the corner. He had even gone so far as to lean gingerly over the water and with a broom flick off a few floating dead leaves. But there it had stopped. He must think it over, must ask permission. It would take time. Probably he was wondering which of his fellow servants would do the job best . . . Meanwhile the pool got dirtier. But somehow the goldfish lived; and after all, I thought, the pool was still rather beautiful with the flowers and the plum tree, even though the tiles were less blue, the water not so clear. Besides, Persians have never sacrificed utility to beauty; it would be meaningless; everything must be used, water above all else. The women were hanging up the washing, clipping the wet clothes to the lines across the flower beds. There, at any rate, hanging in the sun, were my pyjamas; they would be dry by to-morrow.

A broad flight of steps led up from the court to the bedrooms, whose doors opened on to a balcony surrounding the yard. Most of the rooms were unoccupied. I had seen part of only one family staying at the hotel; a bristly middle-aged man who had stood at his door in his shirt-tails as I passed along the balcony, standing guard over the dim, fluttering shapes of his wife and children in the room behind. The room next to mine was taken by two elderly gentlemen who smoked *kalians* in bed and spent most of the day playing chess with each other, and sometimes with me. So far, the score stood at two-all. Some Persians claim that chess was invented in Persia, though I believe it was played first in China, and must have come west with Tamerlane. Certainly the game as it is played in Europe owes much to Persia. 'Pawn' and 'rook', for instance, are the Persian words for foot-soldier and fortress, while our 'check-mate' is really the Persian *Shah-mat*: 'the Shah is dead'.

The managers of the hotel, brothers they looked, smooth-faced men in tailored suits who had tried to ask twice too much for my

room, spent most of their time smoking cigarettes and talking to
the bored waiter in the hotel 'restaurant', a room full of mirrors
and clean tablecloths and shining cutlery which no one ever used.
When they had first shown me to my room they had not omitted
to accompany me to see the shower-bath, lately installed; with a
few hours' notice, the water might be hot.

'Ali!' One of them was calling, probably for his tea. Ali woke
up with a start, bumping his head on the step. Jeers from the
washerwomen followed his unsteady flight indoors, one hand
clutched to his head.

They were painting the inside of the courtyard, perhaps with an
eye on the promising future that Isfahan had as a tourist centre.
At the moment wealthy Americans stayed only at the Govern-
ment-sponsored 'Irantour', where the amenities and the prices
more suited their pockets. But with a bit of paint, perhaps another
hot shower, who knows? The Hotel Kasra was progressive. After
all the restaurant was ready, and waiting. There was a solitary
workman in the yard. He had been mixing white paint all day,
stirring it lovingly, and occasionally trying it for consistency on
the paving between the flower beds.

It was a little cooler now, the sun sloping down the sky. Gradually the colours were returning to the fir trees and the mountains,
to the sky. The workman laid down his stick and began to take off
his boots. His trousers followed. Underneath he wore pyjamas.
He spread his coat and knelt down in the corner of the yard to
pray.

Someone was standing by the arch that led out to the street; a
thin slight figure in a neat blue suit, with a short pointed beard
and a walking-stick. I guessed this must be Ibrahim, Hassan's
friend, and stood up to wave. The figure brandished his stick.
Down in the courtyard we shook hands.

'My friend has spoken about you in the tea-house . . .' He
smiled to reveal perfect teeth. A powerful hooked nose presided
over a short moustache; deep-set black eyes smiled at me from
under a head of bushy dark hair. He spoke carefully, with an
almost perfect accent, in a deep, pleasant voice. 'I shall be

delighted, Sir, to show you something of Isfahan.' No, he couldn't stay now, his class was waiting. He was a schoolmaster, a teacher; he moved his hand deprecatingly. But to-morrow morning he was free. Would I care to have breakfast with him in the tea-house, early? We shook hands again, and with a brief bow and a smile, Ibrahim turned and walked out of the yard.

There is a brilliance of light, a purity of air, at Isfahan that reminds me of Greece. Perhaps it is the altitude; as with most of the Iranian plateau, Isfahan is well over 5,000 feet. October had come to temper the blaze of summer, without lessening its warmth. A few leaves of the chenars lining the great avenue of the Charbagh were beginning to turn, splashes of yellow invading the green arches that veiled a pale-blue sky.

Ibrahim and I walked down the broad street. A few stragglers from the gang of beggar boys who knew me only too well were still following from their usual place of ambush outside the hotel. '*Baksheesh, agha!*' Light fingers brushed my sleeve, compelling me to turn. Ibrahim spoke sharply, magic words, and the boys fell behind. We were walking by the stone channel that runs each side of the avenue, stepping round the groups of idlers that had already collected to chat over their newspapers in the early sunshine. Ancient carriages drawn by a single horse rattled by leisurely, the drivers sitting over the faded splendour of their worn upholstery, dangling whips, calling out for their fares. A few cars passed, the water-cart behind, spraying the street. A delicious smell of wet dust. The single-storeyed shops were already open, with blue wood shutters drawn back. The shop-keepers stood at their doorways tempting the passers-by with a wheedling summary of their wares. Clear sunlight lit the mountains, streaking their flanks with blue shadow; so clear were they that I felt that they stood only just beyond that row of low buildings, almost within reach. We turned by the roundabout where the smart policeman conducted a rather thinly attended orchestra, and walked down by the new brightly tiled bank, along the street leading east towards the Maidan.

Ibrahim was taking his position of guide seriously, and flooded me with dates and the names of kings and ministers, wars and sieges centuries ago. He was telling me of Isfahan as it was once, the splendid capital of an empire that stretched from Baghdad to the Hindu Kush. For a little longer than a hundred years, in the seventeenth century, Isfahan was the most glorious city in the East. *Isfahan nisf-i-jahan*: 'Isfahan is half the world'. A boast of its citizens that was confirmed not only by other Persians, but by the few adventurous European travellers who visited the Court of the Safavid monarchs at Isfahan. We stood at the edge of the Maidan-i-Shah, the Royal Square, one of the largest public places in the world. Emerging from the street into this vast space was like coming out of an echoing tunnel into a wide calm of open air. We were standing with our backs to the towering arch of the Bazaar Gate, looking south; the crowd streaming in and out of it seemed to thin and fade away, absorbed inconsequentially into the huge square. Figures of men and donkeys dwindled in the distance to sub-human size; at the far end the people standing and walking looked no larger than puppets. Ibrahim had taken out a bright green notebook and was reading numbers into my ear. '510 yards in length, north to south; 174 yards in breadth.' A double tier of inset arches enclosed the Maidan, a regular façade broken only by the three great buildings, one on each side, that rose above it. Ibrahim pointed down the Maidan: at the far southern end, the shadowed portal and minarets of the Masjid-i-Shah, the Royal Mosque, the sanctuary behind crowned with its dome, the blue surface flashing in the sun. To the left the Mosque of Sheikh Lutf-Allah; and on the right the Ali Kapu, the 'High Gate' or Sublime Porte, the entrance arch and gallery of the Shah's palace.

The Maidan has remained almost exactly as it was built 350 years ago. Workmen were putting the finishing touches to some huge flower-beds in the centre of the square, and a great open tank of water. I narrowed my eyes to take in the complete picture, framed in the blue sky and the line of purple mountains behind the minarets. In Tehran they had said that the flower-beds were breaking up the space, destroying its unity and grandeur. I felt this was not so. The place was big enough to take the flowers and the pool, they were only details. Though of course in its original form the surface of the Maidan had been smooth and open, a fit stadium for the grandiose spectacles, the games and processions witnessed by the Shah and his nobles from the pillared audience hall high in the Ali Kapu.

'Shah Abbas . . . Shah Abbas . . .' Ibrahim was murmuring at my shoulder. The most famous of the Safavid kings, Shah Abbas chose Isfahan for his new capital in the spring of 1598, riding about with his architects around him in the semi-ruins of towns and villages which had filled the site, in a cycle of growth and destruction, for the last thousand years. The date was propitious; it was the bi-centenary of Tamerlane's revenge on the then flourishing but rebellious city. The Safavid revival of Isfahan was to expunge the memory of the pyramid of 70,000 heads that Timur built at the battered gates of the city. Shah Abbas was fortunate enough to live to see the new city he had so ambitiously planned rise before his eyes.

Oddly enough, Ibrahim, for all his eulogies of this distant Persian king, was not really a Persian himself, though he never thought of himself as anything else. He was half Armenian, and had been born in Julfa, the surburbia of Isfahan that is almost a separate town, across the river. The Armenians there are descendants of those whom Shah Abbas forcibly transplanted to his new capital to set an example of commercial prosperity which the townsmen of Isfahan were quick to follow. The Armenians were Christian—though Ibrahim was not; and Ibrahim is a Moslem name. Piecing together afterwards the many improbable stories of his life that Ibrahim recounted to me during the short time I knew him, I gathered that he had no particular religious affiliations, but had dabbled enthusiastically in many, only to be disappointed in each. Besides the Christianity into which he had been born and which he had quickly shed, he had considered Zoroastrianism, Islam, had been for a short while a Sufi, and had for a time thought of joining the Babi sect, the modern Bahais. He had left his home at an early age and had been sent by his father to India, where he spent several years 'in business' in Bombay. There he had been much in the society of the Parsees, who presumably encouraged his weakness for Zoroaster's teachings. He had married in India, and learned English there. His wife was dead. Returning to Persia he had come to Isfahan where he had been living now for six or seven years. He was to tell me a little about Sufism, the Persian mysticism, which had always interested me. 'I am of many colours,' he would say, 'they have made one carpet.' Ibrahim told me he never crossed the river to Julfa where he was born. All his people, he said, were dead. Whether he meant this figuratively or quite literally I was never sure.

We walked down the middle of the Maidan towards the Shah's Mosque, and turned to face the Ali Kapu. Behind the *talar*, the columned hall set high over the square, used to stretch the palaces of the Persian kings. Ibrahim was busy with his notebook. As big as London was Isfahan in the seventeenth century, with a populace numbering 600,000: 162 mosques, 1802 caravanserais, 273 public baths; besides these the innumerable palaces and gardens, mostly situated on either side of the Charbagh, which were put at the disposal of the king's nobles or the visiting Embassies from Europe and Asia that came to fix treaties of war and commerce and pay their respects to the head of a great empire . . .

So Ibrahim taught English and Persian History to the schoolboys of Isfahan. Perhaps his admiration for Shah Abbas was more than simply a historian's appreciation of a great historical figure. I felt that Ibrahim believed he had a personal interest.

Through his Armenian ancestry he considered his own existence to be a direct outcome of that king's policy; he felt he owed the long-dead Shah his own tribute of words, perhaps exaggerated and over-coloured, in return for the shaping of his own destiny. Also, being a widely tolerant person himself, he admired the indulgence of this monarch, extraordinary for that age in any part of Islamic Asia, who welcomed Christians to his country and established them in his capital, allowing missions both Catholic and Protestant to work unhindered in Isfahan. Unhindered—but perhaps the great Shah was wiser than we think; for in spite of the vigour and example of so many good priests who have described so busily and vividly their adventures and impressions in the journals handed down to us, their posterity, there is one subject—that of their actual conversions—on which all information is mysteriously lacking . . .

Père Sanson, a French missionary sent by Louis XIV to convert the Persians in 1683, spent several years in the country, learnt the language, and was one of those who have left a written account of their experiences. He was lucky in being allowed to attend many of the Court functions, and describes how on days of public audience the Shah sat on his throne before a marble fountain, in a hall big enough to take a hundred people, and watched between the gilded pillars the festivities in the square below, where Ibrahim and I were standing. Still in position at both ends of the Maidan are the stone goal-posts where sometimes 300 horsemen would play polo before the king: 'The young Persian Lords exercise themselves in this place with playing at Mall [Polo] on horseback, throwing the lance and then catching it again before they quit their stirrups; and by drawing the Bow behind 'em at full speed, according to the custom of the ancient Parthians. They shoot at a Mark in a Plate of Gold which is fix'd to a Pole rais'd in the Middle of the Market.'

Ranged in front of the palace Sanson observed a number of cannon which Shah Abbas, with the aid of an English fleet, took from the Portuguese at the siege of Ormuz in 1622. 'But,' adds the missionary, 'they are at present so ill mounted that they are altogether unfit for service.' In 1870, the guns were taken to Tehran, where they adorn the Maidan Sepah. Shah Abbas had a partiality for Englishmen, and his two most distinguished visitors, the Sherley brothers, he put to good use. The younger he made generalissimo of his army, and employed his military talent in the construction of new cannon foundries and the drilling and equipment of musketeers, with whose aid the Turks were finally defeated, and many Persian provinces recovered; while the elder brother he sent as his ambassador to the Royal Houses of Europe.

That morning Ibrahim had shown me, among the lurid prints and posters of Shiah saints and mythical heroes that were stuck on the tea-house walls, two small paintings which displayed an oriental monarch holding a great drinking-vase and surrounded by over-dressed courtiers weighted with colossal turbans. The central figure, Ibrahim averred, was none other than Shah Abbas.

Certainly the fragments of pillars showing behind the courtiers might have been the representation of the *talar* of the Ali Kapu, and the strange animals prancing below may have been taking part in the spectacle of beasts and games often arranged for the Safavids' entertainment in the Maidan. The paintings were crudely done and I guessed they were comparatively modern; but although I had suspected that Ibrahim's descriptions of the Shah's entourage and habits were over-coloured, here was evidence of a sort which supported his assertions, and Father Sanson, at any rate, should not have lied.

On these state occasions, Sanson tells us: 'All the Riches of the King's House is exposed in its greatest lustre. The King is served out of a Vessel of pure Gold, of more than Three Foot diameter . . . and they carry this Vessel with Ceremony upon a sort of Hand-Barrow enrich't with Plates of Gold. The Entertainment is serv'd up whilst the King is giving Audience, and tis then that he gives Wine to the Lords of his Court. The Bottles and Cups they drink out of are also of Gold enammel'd, and set with Precious Stones. They are rank'd all about the Marble Bason, which is in the Middle of the Hall, and at whose corners are plac'd four small Golden Casks, and four of Silver, each of which is about the weight of a Man. These, together with the Perfume and Flower Pots which are also of Gold, make a very agreeable Symmetry.'

In the galleries over the Bazaar Gate, on the north side of the Maidan, the royal musicians used to play whenever the Shah was in residence. Their hours of music-making were somewhat unusual: at noon, again at sunset, the final performance being at two o'clock in the morning. What the townspeople thought of these midnight concerts is not recorded. Father Sanson, accustomed as he must have been to the refined airs of Cambert and Lully, took a very poor view of these musicians' performances, for he adds that 'on Festivals they continue their Jargon all Day and Night. I call it *Jargon* because there are sometimes Sixty of 'em playing together, without either Time or Measure. Some beat great Drums, other Tymbals; some play upon Hautbois, and others bawl with loud Voices in their sort of Speaking Trumpets . . .'

The French priest, often invited to attend the royal audiences held in the Ali Kapu, was careful to note the etiquette followed at these splendid ceremonies. The Shah sat always, 'crosslegg'd on a rich Brocaid Bed within gilded Balisters, leaning upon a noble Pillow which there's none but he can have in Persia: Nor is any Body else permitted to sit after the same manner, but the Lords always place themselves on their Breech, that Posture looked upon as being more respectful. The Children of the *Haram* are always about him, two of 'em continually refreshing him with long Fans made of Peacocks' Tails. The rest have all some Office near his Majesty. One presents him his Cup, the other his Tobacco, Coffee and Tea, and a third the Bason to wash after he has eaten . . .'

In spite of the Islamic prohibition of alcohol, the Safavid kings were great wine-drinkers, and when, after Shah Abbas, more degenerate monarchs sat in the throne-room above the Maidan, the wine-tasting developed into drunken orgies, at which the few high-principled nobles who abstained came in for a bad time. Chardin has many a sad tale to tell of the then Grand Vizier, an old and respected servant of the crown, who had wine flung in his face, was drugged with opium, and once had his beard cut off by order of the Shah, enraged at his refusal to get drunk with him.

Sanson says that the King 'does it to divert him; for one of his greatest Pleasures consists in seeing 'em carried out from his Table dead-drunk. He works them up to what degree he pleases; for he makes 'em drink in a sort of Goblet made in the fashion of a Ladle, and which holds at least a good *Paris* Pint . . .' All this too on empty stomachs, at Audiences 'when there is nothing serv'd up but Sweetmeats and Fruits'.

A Sable Cap

Drunkenness, however, when not by royal command was looked upon in a very different light. On one occasion Chardin was present at an Audience held for foreign ambassadors and noticed with surprise that although the courtiers drank wine at the banquet none of the ambassadors was offered any. He asked one of the noblemen near him the reason for this, and was told the following story.

Some years ago two 'Muscovite' Ambassadors Extraordinary had arrived from the Czar and at the audience before the Shah 'drank so excessively that they quite lost their Senses'. The Shah had drunk the Czar's health, and it was the Russians' turn to pledge this worthy toast, 'in a Cup that held about Two Pints. The second Ambassador, not being able to digest so much Wine, had a pressing Inclination to vomit, and not knowing where to disembogue, he took his great Sable Cap, which he half fill'd. It is well known that the Muscovites wear large and high Caps. His Colleague, who was above him, and the Secretary of the Embassy, who was below him, enrag'd at so foul an Action, done in the presence of the King of Persia and of the whole Court, reprimanded him and jogged him with their Elbows to remind him of going out. But he, being very drunk, and not knowing either what was said to him nor what he himself did, clapp'd his Cap upon his Head, which presently cover'd him all over with Nastiness.'

The Shah, and the whole Court, was convulsed with laughter 'which lasted about half an Hour, during which time the Companions of this filthy Muscovite were forcing him by dint of Blows with their Fists to rise and go out'. The Shah broke up the assembly and left after having made some extremely unpleasant remarks on the subject of Muscovites in general; but the result of this unfortunate but historic incident was that never again was wine risked in the hands of any representative of the Russian state.

Ibrahim and I walked down towards the Masjid-i-Shah to examine the polo posts. Of course when not used as a stadium or a parade ground the Maidan belonged to the townspeople. It was really a market-place, and on special days the whole area would be covered with stalls and tents set up for the day. Every trade, including prostitution, was represented, each with its own line of booths. Nowadays there is no necessity for this overflow from the main bazaar. The population of Isfahan is less than half of what it used to be, and the business of the market has ample room to flourish in the labyrinth of vaulted tunnels that stretch for nearly a mile behind the Bazaar Gate.

Ibrahim was anxious for me to see the Shah's Mosque before noon, so as not to collide with the service held at that time; for it is only lately that the mosques have been opened to Europeans, and even now the sanctuaries at Qum and Meshed are still forbidden. At Isfahan, however, one may go where one pleases, even with a camera.

He led the way into the shadow of the portal, where the burning sunlight of the open square was suddenly cooled in the curved lustre of blue faience. It was dark in the vestibule. I walked upon a polished floor of jade-green tiles under the tall dome, flower-traced, and out into the sunshine of the great court. Four double arcades, each broken in the centre by a towering arch, look inwards upon a large still pool which faithfully reflects in sun and shadow the magnificent colouring of their tiled surfaces. Dark blue, yellow, green; not an inch has been left unpainted or unglazed; a shining almost garrulous splendour—truly the king's mosque, dominated above the sanctuary by the blue dome poised between two minarets.

In Persia it is quite usual for the mullahs to call the people to prayer not from the top of the minarets but from the outer wall or gate of the mosque. There was a structure erected for this purpose above the northern arcade. Ibrahim was unable to explain this departure from the normal Islamic custom; but Father Sanson, rather surprisingly for him—though perhaps with a tinge of professional jealousy—says that the Persians make their mullahs chant from this reduced altitude 'for fear they should ogle their Women in the Gardens. But sure they ought to be of a very large size, or these Criers should have extraordinary Perspectives, to have any reasonable View from so great a distance . . .'

The Mosque of Sheikh Lutf-Allah

If he was thinking of Isfahan he may well have been right, for the minarets of this mosque must have overlooked the palace gardens of the harem, behind the Ali Kapu; and however extraordinary the perspective, the Shah would certainly not have approved. Ibrahim had to leave me for his classroom, so I crossed the corner of the Maidan and entered the Mosque of Sheikh Lutf-Allah alone.

The mosque was begun in 1603, built by Shah Abbas in pious memory of the Sheikh, his revered father-in-law. However beautiful the exterior of the dome, pale chocolate crossed with arabesques of blue-black and white, it can give no hint of the glories which lie within. Deep grills, high in the spacious octagonal dome chamber, diffuse the light softly upon the blue gloss of a thousand gleaming surfaces. Upon arched panels of faience mosaic, roped with turquoise, bold white letters of calligraphy start out from shining pages of darkest blue. Overhead swims a great shallow dome, turquoise, threaded with the gold rays of an exploding sun. I stood in a blue twilight far under the sea, where the mind floats smoothly and at peace, disengaged.

An inscription proclaims the self-effacement of the architect, the 'poor and humble servant Muhammad Riza Ibn Usted Hussein of Isfahan;' signed, and dated: 1618.

After that first evening when I met Hassan, I became a regular customer at the tea-house. It was pleasant to be recognised when I went in, to sit down without embarrassment and to be served my tea without asking for it, with a special number of sugar lumps that the attendant never forgot. My pipe would follow immediately, with a cheerful grin from the *kalian*-boy. Now that I had mastered the technique of smoking it, the gurgle and bubble in the jar that sounded from my piece of carpet against one of the pillars by the pool no longer attracted attention. I had learnt how to sit, drink tea, and smoke; and I enjoyed doing all these things.

And although I had no illusions about 'being taken for a Persian' or anything of that kind, at least I was accepted for what I was: something of a novelty perhaps, but harmless. Persian manners are such that no one ever hinted at my intrusion.

Perhaps Hassan enjoyed showing off his tame Englishman, if only to impress his friends how well he could speak English; but though it was clear that I was, comparatively, a millionaire, neither he nor anyone else took advantage of this. Whenever I insisted on a round of tea at my expense Hassan accepted, unwillingly enough, but the next round was on him; and several times when I went to the door to pay I found that most of my teas had been already paid for by mysterious benefactors whose names I never knew. So eventually I fell back on what seemed, on a long evening, to be the general rule, each one paying for himself.

Tea had not always been the staple drink of the ordinary Persian. Coffee was discovered in Arabia during the ninth century, and its immediate popularity and low cost carried it all over the Middle East. Tea was known, but at that time must have been difficult to obtain as it had to be brought so far from the East, and was therefore expensive. To-day the positions are reversed, and though coffee is obtainable in Persia, the ordinary man's drink is tea. It seems that this liquid revolution took place during the nineteenth century, when the demand for tea in Europe was growing, matched by the increased production of China and especially India.

Persia has always been a middle-man country, always ready to take over for herself whatever was passing between East and West, at the same time impressing it with her own particular stamp. So it must have been with the custom of tea-drinking. It is said that the habit first spread from Russia; certainly the Russian type *samovar* (retaining its original name) is universally used in Persia. But it is more likely that the peaceful relationship with India, that grew as the British strengthened their hold, had as much to do with it. The small quantities that came with the caravans through Turkestan on their long journey from China were gradually superseded by the wholesale exportation of cheap tea from India, borne on the backs of camels through Baluchistan, or by the short sea-route to the Persian Gulf.

In any case it was only a matter of changing the liquid in the Persian's glass. Tea-houses, or coffee-houses as they were in the old days—and oddly enough they are still called by the old name, *kahve-kahneh*—have always existed in Persia, and whether it is coffee or tea, or, as has been maliciously forecast, pepsicola that is drunk in them, for the average Persian there must always be this place of friendly refuge, where he can sit and talk and drink at leisure his favourite and most inexpensive brew.

Sir John Chardin makes a very brief but to the point mention of the coffee-houses of that time: 'These Houses were hertofore very infamous Places, they were serv'd and entertained by beautiful Georgian Boys, from 10 to 16 years of Age, dress'd after a Lewd Manner, having their Hair ty'd in Wefts, like the Women. They make 'em Dance there, and Act and say a thousand immodest Things, to move the Beholders, who caus'd these Boys to be carry'd everyone where they thought Proper; and this fell to the lot of those who were most beautiful and engaging; in such sort, that these Coffe-Houses were nothing else in Reality but Shops for Sodomy, which was very terrible to Wise and Virtuous People.'

Gone are the Georgian Boys and gone, incidentally, is the coffee. The passage is worth quoting if only to reassure those who still doubt that in the eternal struggle between good and evil—a very Persian concept, after all—right will always triumph. The Georgian Boys were duly suppressed, and the disappointed Isfahanis had to make do with coffee unsweetened; and no doubt doubled their daily dose of opium to make up for the loss. A few years ago attempts to turn tea-houses into brothels were similarly crushed, much to the contentment of all Wise and Virtuous People; and the prostitutes moved back to their former, less conspicuous, quarters.

One night the even tenor of the tea-house was interrupted in a strange way. I was sitting alone engrossed in my *kalian* listening to the hum of voices around me. I had noticed a group of men occupying a trestle some distance from me, huddled round a very talkative figure the top of whose orange turban I could just make out across the heads of other customers. Suddenly there was an excited stir in the room; the man had got up, and gathering his brown cloak about him, was stepping over the people in his way. Under the cloak I caught glimpses of baggy white trousers; he had left his slippers behind. He was making for the platform where Mahmoud the sugar-cutter sat, by the pool near the middle of the room and, as soon as he had reached it and a space on the carpet had been cleared for him, he stretched out his hand for silence.

While he had been striding like a giant through the tea-house, everyone had turned to look, murmuring and setting themselves more comfortably, and some had shouted out something. Now that he stood there on the platform with arm imperatively outstretched the whole room fell quiet. A few people in the far corner who were still talking were hissed into silence. The dervish began to talk, softly at first, and then as he roused himself, with greater energy, accompanying his words with wide, sweeping gestures. He seemed to be reciting in verse, in a sort of sing-song chant, occasionally interrupted by a fierce outburst of passion, his bearded face contorted into an agony of rage; and then the voice would fall to no more than a whisper, a moan, and the tea-house was never more silent, and I could hear the gentle hiss of the samovar.

He made an imposing if fantastic figure, standing there high above the sea of motionless heads, with his black beard and brilliant turban and glittering eyes, caught for a moment in the glare of the lanterns or thrown into the shadow of a pillar, as the smoke curled up before him between the blackened rafters. The effect on his audience was remarkable; several had tears in their eyes. One powerful-looking man, whom I took for a mechanic, was sobbing into his hands. The dervish finished as suddenly as he had begun, his arm sinking to his side. He was helped down from his position and led, almost carried, to a trestle only a few feet from me where he was immediately surrounded by an eager but respectful ring of admirers.

At that moment Hassan came in. I could see he was irritable about something; probably because when the dervish had been speaking the passage and door of the tea-house had been blocked with people and he had been forced to wait outside. He came and sat down by my side and unconcernedly ordered some tea. My pipe had gone out. Hassan cocked his thumb in the direction of the orange turban and whispered under his cupped hand: 'Very holy man.'

Seeing that I was interested, Hassan immediately swivelled himself round, and tapping the shoulders of those squatting in the way begged them to move over. Being introduced to a dervish was not quite what I had expected. He looked a quite different person now, exhausted after his oration, and simply sat there looking at nothing. It was difficult to attract his attention, but when Hassan shouted and I was pointed out to him he put out his hand. With great difficulty we shook hands across several pairs of shoulders and I did my best in my cramped position to bow. The dervish nodded his head solemnly and said something, which brought a murmur of agreement from everyone round him. Then the ring of shoulders closed up again; the interview was over. 'Yes, sir,' said Hassan, as we sipped our tea, 'very holy man.'

The next morning Hassan came early to the hotel and woke me up, chattering incoherently as he hustled me along the white-washed arcaded walls of the Madraseh—the College of the Mother of the Shah—which stood near the hotel in the Charbagh. As we pushed through the great silver-panelled doors into the court I tried to extract some explanation of this wild rushing about, before breakfast, too.

It appeared that we were looking for the dervish. Hassan had always boasted that he knew everyone, but it seemed that the dervish was the only dervish he knew, and as Hassan felt that it was his duty to introduce him properly, we were going to look for him. Word had reached him that the dervish had gone to earth in the Madraseh.

As soon as we were inside Hassan left me, sternly admonishing me to stay where I was, and darted through an archway on the left.

I found myself at the head of a long channel of water that glided across the court between stone steps. The Madraseh was originally intended to combine a mosque, college and caravanserai, and was built in 1706 by the meek and pious descendant of Shah Abbas, Shah Sultan Husein, whose vacillations brought about the fall of Isfahan to the Afghan invaders sixteen years later.

A lovely dome the pale blue of sparrows' eggs, chased with black and yellow tendrils, floated over the branches of dark cypresses and white pollarded chenars that lined the water's edge. Two minarets soared, one on either side, as if anchoring the dome to the earth, brilliantly inscribed with green and yellow Kufic lettering upon a deep-blue ground. Behind the walls and inset arches surrounding the garden were the cells of the students, deserted now; but under the blue arch rising above the trees a mullah sat, a semi-circle of six or seven young men cross-legged around him. He was reading monotonously from a book in his hand. The morning sunlight played lightly upon the bowed shoulders and uncovered heads of his rapt listeners.

I watched a man in a long, brown coat and white turban lean over the long pool by the arch, filling a metal jug. Hassan emerged suddenly from a doorway arguing excitedly with an old man who must have been the doorkeeper of the Madraseh, judging by the huge bunch of keys that dangled from his waist. The doorman was trying to make Hassan lower his voice and waved his hands frantically. Hassan hurried me outside, his little moustache blown out with rage. The doorkeeper's request for a tip was dismissed with a scornful gesture. Out in the street Hassan's fury suddenly evaporated; he looked dejected, and I tried to cheer him up. But no, the dervish was lost, gone for ever; and he was the only dervish Hassan knew . . .

Ibrahim was supposed to take me to the *Masjid-i-Jami*, the Friday Mosque. By nine o'clock I decided to wait no longer—he must have forgotten. So, with an antique map of Isfahan in my pocket, I left the tea-house and set off to find the mosque myself. I entered the bazaar through the great arch on the north side of the Maidan. In five minutes I was lost. The bazaar was not crowded at this hour, the stalls, most of them, were in the throes of opening; the shopkeepers unbarring shutters, arranging their wares, festooning the doorways with pieces of clothing, kettles and silk. Donkeys laden with melons jingled by, and a camel, groaning with displeasure, strode gloomily past, huge bundles of firewood swaying on its back.

I plunged on with failing confidence through the brick vaulted tunnels; in some places where the stalls were deserted or still closed there was no light at all, and I could hardly see my way between the thin bars of sunlight that pierced the vaults at intervals along the way. A growing uproar of echoing hammerstrokes told me I was near the copper-market. I consulted the map and turned left, stepped down into a courtyard where crates and sacks lay piled and untended; through a doorway, through another, and immediately I found myself in open sunlight in the quiet of a narrow back street where a few tiny, half-naked children played with stones against the wall.

A lorry was backing slowly down the street, its wooden sides barely scraping the walls on either side. At the same time, from the opposite direction, came an old bent woman wrapped from head to foot in a black shawl and driving two donkeys, with bulging saddlebags, before her. The lorry driver called out and wrung his hands in despair. The old woman saw nothing but kept on, her head lowered and invisible in the shawl, until the donkeys came up against the back of the lorry and were forced to a standstill.

Angrily and muttering curses she laid about them with her stick, the silver bangles jingling on her thin wrist. The driver edged out of his cab and along the side of the wall, talking volubly and clapping his hands. The old woman, at last seeing the cause of the hold-up, fell into a quivering and incoherent rage and began to beat the driver, who fled back to his cab, while the children screamed happily and pelted the donkey's legs with stones. Flattening myself against the wall I followed the driver round to the front of the lorry. The engine had stopped and, with a face red with anger, he was trying to turn the starting handle.

'Masjid-i-Jami?' I enquired timidly. He shook his hand up the street. At this moment a frantic shriek broke out from behind, followed by the braying of donkeys and excited cries, yells of pain from the children. The driver and I exchanged glances and simultaneously ducked down to look back underneath the lorry. A pyramid of little golden nuts was rising from the ground. One of the donkeys, driven wild by the children's stones, had torn its sack on the mudguard. A little boy lay spread-eagled among the nuts, desperately clutching handfuls of them, while expressions of delight at having captured the nuts and anguish as the old woman's blows rained down on his bare back chased across his face as he tried to escape wriggling under the lorry. The driver flung down his starting-handle in desperation. I walked off quickly and rather guiltily up the street.

One could hardly call them streets, lanes would be a better description. High walls of dull yellow mud-and-straw, uneven dust-covered cobbles or bare earth between, with hardly a window and only occasionally a heavy door set back in the wall under a crumbling brick arch. Very few people were about. Women enveloped in dark blue shawls scuttled close to the walls like mice afraid of the open. Three little girls in red-and-black petticoats sitting on a doorstep fled inside as I went past the rickety wood door, banging it shut behind them.

Through one of these wickets, half open, I caught a glimpse of a small courtyard with a dusty stunted tree growing in the middle; chickens pecked about in the straw. As the sun rose the heat in the close lanes became oppressive, and I was grateful for the cool stretches of vaulted tunnelling that sometimes spanned the walls. I didn't really know where I was going, and there seemed to be no one to ask. I had had enough of the lanes and their interminable twisting. I felt shut out, an enemy. People were living all around me. I could hear their voices, sometimes children crying.

Seljuq Domes

People passed me in the road, intent and hurrying, with hardly a glance. I was shut out, a stranger who could see nothing. The high blind walls, locked doors and gratings, smiled secretly; a life stolen and impenetrable, sealed. An assortment of tame mongrels, mangy and starved, followed me at a distance, suspiciously. I went down some steps, a dark tunnel ahead, an open arch and bright sunlight at the end of it. I walked through, the map useless in my hands. And then I saw that I had arrived. I was standing in the court of the Friday Mosque. A hundred pigeons rose from my feet in a thunder of beating wings.

I walked across the burning court and took refuge in a shadowy forest of columns. Except for the pale tiling about the court there was little to remind me of the brilliant splendour of the Safavid monuments round the Maidan. The Masjid-i-Jami was built 600 years earlier, in the eleventh century, though its foundations are even more ancient. Instead of the soft lustre of tiling, the overwhelming impact of colour, here the prevailing shade is brown. The principles of line and shape, rather than colour and surface are strikingly evident in the mosque's construction.

Two bare brick domes balance marvellously over their stucco chambers. The smaller is considered the most perfectly designed in existence, a more masculine masterpiece of an earlier race of kings, the Seljuqs: Alp Arslan, the victor of Manzikert who made Isfahan his capital, his successor, Malik Shah, and his renowned Vizier, the Nizam-al-Mulk. I have seen the tombs of Seljuq princes on the shores of Lake Van; simple structures of perfect proportion, and I was glad to see this dome also, small by measurement, but to me beneath, as large as the mind could make it. It inspired me with a sense of simplicity and beauty that suddenly made me want to forget the shiny façades of the Royal Mosque, the painted China domes, inverted tea-pots: gloss and superficiality.

Here, I thought, was demonstrated the real expression of true religion, simplicity and strength, the fine economy and balance that came nearest to a man's sense of the infinite. I am ashamed to say that as soon, a day later, as I looked up once more into the deep swimming circle of the dome of Sheikh Lutf-Allah my fierce convictions of that morning were drained away; I was a prisoner once more of those incomparable curved blue surfaces. But something of the impression remains.

It was midday, the mosque was filling up. Although men and women can pray under cover of the halls and flanking chambers provided in every mosque, most Persians prefer the open air. The great court holds a vast congregation; everyone kneels together in one direction, facing and in view of the *mihrab* and the mullah in his pulpit leading the prayers. This togetherness seems to me to be a great principle of the faith, and therefore the courtyard of the mosque becomes a most important expression of Islam, originating from the simple yard of the Prophet's house at Medina.

The mosque belongs to everyone, and in it all men are equal. Ordinary citizens will kneel in company with the highest of the land, at its gates sit the beggars. The outside world is excluded by the high walls; the court and the pool at its centre stand for this isolation, a perfect solitude and calm. And the dome represents another doorway to it, a further dimension. I wonder if I am inferring too much from the structural differences between, say, a Gothic cathedral and a mosque. The Christian church is the 'House of God'. The mosque is no more than the best place to pray. There is no place within it that is holier than another. The soaring architecture of a cathedral leads inspiration *upwards*, it points to the sky, away from oneself. There is no such signpost to heaven in a dome. The curve and circle of its sides may fill the contemplative with an exultation which is more than himself, but if the dome points at all, it points everywhere; the sweep of its direction is universal and concludes by resting inescapably upon the worshipper within.

The integration of Islam with daily life is nowhere more clearly demonstrated than in the position of a mosque, and the old Friday Mosque in Isfahan is a perfect but common ·example. From the noisy tunnels of the bazaar it is but a single step into the peaceful court. The hovels and packed streets of the town lie immediately surrounding it; on one side of the wall the mosque, on the other a warehouse or a shop. It has always been the focal point of everyday life, a meeting-place for friends and even business men, the place where government proclamations were read, a centre for rulers as much as the ruled. Besides being a place for prayer and thought, the mosque has always been an educational institution, with its own library, and often the only school in town. It can be used as a prison, at the same time as being an inviolable sanctuary for criminals; part of the mosque at Isfahan has for a long time been a morgue. To Moslems religion is not a thing set apart; it is a way of life, an attitude, so deeply ingrained in the vast majority of Persians that it influences them, perhaps unconsciously, in their every thought or action.

I came across a workman among the columns where some repairs were being carried out. He had made a little fire by one of the pillars and was heating up some rice for his lunch. At his side stood a donkey, its head buried in a grain sack. The brass bell round its neck tinkled rhythmically over the sound of shuffling feet passing in the court and the quavering cry of the muezzin calling Isfahan to prayer.

The summer was drawing on, it was time to be moving. David Gaunt had returned from Tehran, the Land-Rover was being finally serviced. We must leave Isfahan; all Persia waited. I walked down the Charbagh with Ibrahim, towards the bridge of Allah Verdi Khan. Ibrahim seemed to want to say something, but was prepared to take his time. He was restless. He began to talk about India, then Isfahan and his rather tedious life here. He also felt the need to be on his way. Perhaps it was the delicate change that was becoming apparent in the air, the leaves hesitating, about to turn. Sometimes at night the wind was cool, great gusts shaking the dust down from the trees, whirling in eddies along the street. By day these hints of impending change vanished with the sun, blazing as ever in the cloudless sky. But the feeling was there. On the carpets of the tea-house the maps were spread out. With Hassan and Ibrahim at our elbows we pored over them, gratefully accepting from each of them in turn advice which the other immediately contradicted; and while they argued—Hassan's 'Why travel? What's the point? Stay still and be thankful' with Ibrahim's 'Of course they must travel, they are young, they must find out'—the others in the tea-house who sat near us came over to breathe down our necks, tracing with their blunt finger-tips roads across the length and breadth of Persia, slowly spelling out the letters, offering sage comments, warnings and mild encouragement. Strange-sounding names of cities, deserts, mountains were spoken almost in whispers; pieces of paper jotted with notes and routes, mileages, lay scattered about our rooms. We would go south, keeping pace with the summer.

Ibrahim was depressed and struck the dust with his stick irritably as he walked. There was Turkey, he said, and Iraq. He had visited Baghdad as a child; he would go there again. And Europe, some day he must see Europe. But there was a snag to all this. He looked at me a trifle slyly, his little black beard jutting forwards as he cocked his head. It was difficult for him to get a passport, and expensive. But we had a car. How easy it would all be if he came with us! I began to feel nervous. I told him hurriedly that we should be a long time in Persia; in any case we were travelling in the wrong direction. After Persia there would be Afghanistan . . . I knew he hated the Afghans, they were savages, they had sacked his beautiful Isfahan in 1723. Or if it hadn't been quite *sacked*, very nearly so.

He had enjoyed telling me of the terrible siege, how the starving Isfahanis had been forced to eat cats, men, sometimes even dogs. And the Safavids, descendants of the illustrious Shah Abbas, had been finally dislodged, humiliated beyond repair. The Afghans were unspeakable. Ibrahim frowned, and sighed. Well, then, perhaps when we came back? Yes, I agreed, we could talk about it then. I was relieved. For a moment I had had a horrible vision of trying to smuggle him out of the country, bluffing the customs with Ibrahim rolled up in a carpet in the back of the car.

We leaned on the parapet over the Zayand river, admiring the graceful lines of the bridge. Thirty-three arches. Ibrahim's good humour, tinged as always with nostalgia, was returning. The bridge of Allah Verdi Khan, Shah Abbas's greatest general; built with three separate passageways, the central one wide enough for caravans entering the city. It was, as Ibrahim remarked with satisfaction, as sound to-day as when it was finished, over three centuries ago. We looked back, past the metallic shining statue of Reza Shah, down the great avenue of the Charbagh. When laid out by Shah Abbas it stretched for three miles. Rows of plane-trees lined the triple roadways, with rose bushes and hedges of jasmine between. Fountains marked the four descending levels of the gardens, channels inlaid with onyx and coloured marble fed the pools on either side. When the Shah went hunting with his ladies, riding in brilliant cavalcade down the avenue, the palaces and gardens of his nobility overlooking it on each side, his guards were drawn up, lining the road, facing outwards; and eunuchs watched the guards so that no man should turn and see the mounted harem as it passed. Heralds had gone before warning all men to get off the streets and shut their windows. The penalty for any male above the age of seven caught in sight of the procession was immediate execution. To-day, the palaces are gone with the fountains and the roses. White chenars still stand, but between low rather shabby shops; and there is asphalt on the roadways.

They were washing carpets in the river. Three or four men, arm in arm with trousers rolled up above their knees, stamped on the carpets in the water, singing in time together. As we strolled down the river's edge—the water reduced to a yellow trickle in this drought season—the trees were bright with multicoloured carpets hanging to dry in the sun. Men stretched out in their shade, smoking. Across the river, to the south and east over the mountains, the sky was turning a dull orange. A dust-storm, thought Ibrahim. I began to remember with a new excitement the names read so glibly off the maps: Shiraz, Kerman, Meshed, Fars, Khorassan . . . soon to be something more to me than names.

2

Nomads and Ruins

❀

To anyone travelling eastwards from Europe the first sight of the Asian plateau must come as something of a shock. Perhaps it will be at the end of the long climb inland above Trebizond, up from the lush timbered slopes of the Black Sea; when far above the tree-line at the top of the pass—the same spot where Xenophon's soldiers, marching in the opposite direction, first glimpsed the sea—the mists fall back and the great barren hogs' backs, edged with range on range of blue peaks, break into view. Farther east across the Taurus Mountains, in Persia proper, the landscape is even more astonishing. As the snow-capped cone of Ararat sinks behind the horizon the long burnt plains, crossed by chains of smooth hills, unfold, rolling it seems for ever in waves of bare brown and yellow until they wash the feet of yet another line of mountains whose purple spikes, sharp as dogs' teeth, melt into the sky. Never a tree or a house or the sight of a man; only the thin white thread of dust road unwinding over the plain. As the sun swings west-ward the colours deepen, turning the sea of burnt grass to gold, flushing the peaks to pink and orange, while huge shadows creep out from the hills to swallow the land. Stop, and let the dust settle on the track. Standing so small in so gigantic a scene, the silence made more enormous by the thin pipe of a bird fluttering in the grass, there comes a sense of desolation that is almost painful; a loneliness appalling and yet exultant. Night shuts out the earth; the camp-fire flickers a faint answer to the cold brilliance of the stars.

❀

From Tabriz, the first large city that greeted us on our entry into Persia, we had driven south, on roads scarcely marked on the map, following the summer that was already beginning to fail on those northern highlands; south by the marshy shores of Lake Urmyia, up on to the windswept plateaux of Kurdistan. Tiny villages nestled in tiers of mud roofs in the shelter of valleys watered by streams green with watercress. By one of these streams we came upon a group of women in long flowered petticoats of scarlet and black, baggy dark pantaloons clipped tightly above their bare feet, with untidy bands of black lace wrapped loosely round the oiled ringlets of their hair. They were sitting by the water's edge, with their babies in little sacks on their shoulder, sorting the heaps of golden grain on bright cloths spread on the grass. We approached, rather nervously, to photograph them, and the women hid their faces and turned away, while the children playing round them fell into each other's arms in an excess of embarrassment. A few men came out of the village and gathered round encouraging our camera work, grinning at the shyness of their womenfolk.

In some villages the men were winnowing, tossing the corn with forks into the blue sky, the grain floating in a mist of gold in the light breeze. Walking round the winnowers I was once startled by a thin curl of smoke that rose between my feet, only to find I was standing on the roofs of cottages. Below, the women worked, with chickens pecking greedily among the cornstalks; a white goat stood tethered in the midst of a shining array of brass pots and beakers. Alone on a slope high over the valley a man was ploughing, leaning heavily on the old wooden haft; the sweat ran down from under his black turban, while the team of oxen grunted and swayed over the red earth. Round his waist was tied a brilliant blue-velvet cummerbund, spangled with brass, a proud ornament to his patched working rags. Sometimes I would catch sight of a horseman galloping in a cloud of dust in the plain, or above us on the hillside, reining in his horse as we passed. Lean, dark-faced men, the Kurds, as wiry as their ponies; and easy riders, good to watch, with their ragged black turbans fluttering loose in the wind.

The Kurds have always been something of an international

35

problem. Two millions occupy the mountains of eastern Turkey, a million live in northern Iraq, and another million in western Persia. Their homeland is spread across those inhospitable ranges where the frontiers of the three states intersect. Fortunately for the governments concerned most of the Kurds have given up their nomadic ways and have settled, it seems quite peacefully and successfully, as farmers and herders of sheep. Nevertheless they have always been the despair of diplomats whose duty it has been to divide and neatly apportion the tribesmen's territory among their own respective nations, celebrating their agreement with soft drinks far away in the offices of their capitals, the new red lines, carefully traced upon the wall maps, confirming the success of their work. The Kurds have always failed to understand the importance of these fine distinctions so earnestly applied to their mountains, and stubbornly refuse to notice the difference between one side of a valley and another. It is almost impossible to control these frontiers effectively, and the Kurds, who are by nature a family-loving people, insist on their right occasionally to visit friends and relatives in whatever 'country' they happen to be; and naturally, to sweeten their visits—slipping across at night under the noses of the frontier guards—will take with them a little of the contraband, whatever is in vogue at the time, that will be most acceptable to their hosts.

Quite lately, after the last war, there was an abortive attempt, sponsored by Russia, to create a Kurdish Republic, which, if it had been successful, would have very effectively thrown that section of the Middle East into disorder. Communist-inspired agitators are at the moment doing their rounds among the villages and pasturages, and oddly enough the new republican government of Iraq is putting out a propaganda line of 'Kurds Unite!' Though it is felt that this is done more because it is in keeping with that country's own nationalist principles, and through a desire to demonstrate to the Kurds that Iraq at least has taken their best interests to heart, rather than out of any real wish to put the unlikely plan into practice.

❀

Maps and Policemen

Two new principles have emerged ready-shaped from our late experiences. Bartholomew in his *Middle East* on small roads in north-eastern Persia is very much out of his depth. We should have brought larger-scaled maps, and are surprised that we didn't. Second, policemen. Persian police in these wilds are bored. The sight of a Land-Rover driven by two foreigners it might seem aimlessly along almost non-existent roads is enough to excite their worst suspicions. The long rigmarole with passports—usually given, and held upside down—is pointless and of no real value either to them or to us. From now on we ignore the police, though politely. To the blue-coated figure waving his rifle from a hill-top we wave cheerfully, and drive on. If one bars our way demanding an explanation, we smile disarmingly and never understand. The worst construction that could be put on our behaviour is that we are insane; but it is comforting to know that in Islam the mad have special protection.

After breakfast this morning, marred only by David falling through his new collapsible chair, a strange man with a potato fork appeared from over the brown hillside, and as we drove off seized upon our discarded melon rinds, tearing them hungrily with his teeth.

We lunched in an eating-house set solitarily in the middle of a dusty plain; a long, dark room whose only furniture was a long carpet that would have graced a London drawing-room. We sat down on it and ate the rice and stew with our fingers, served by an old man whose existence alone in that wilderness remained a mystery. I remembered the first meal I had in Persia, in Maku just inside the frontier, with its pleasant contrast with the Turkish food and manners which we had just left: after a long wait the beautifully served dish of saffron rice, chicken, and bowls of vegetables; the quiet courtesy of the other customers in the room, how in the Persian manner they adjusted their seats so that none of them should sit with their backs to us; also, of equal significance, how it was only after having driven several miles that I realised how much we had been overcharged . . .

Somewhat to our surprise we reached a village which turned

37

out to be Saqqiz; the map is not altogether useless. After refreshment of tea, watched with interest by a crowd of villagers, we
bought more petrol and joined the women waiting at the well for
water. Among the elderly ones I noticed a very pretty girl waiting
her turn with two brown babies strapped on her back. By her
face I guessed she could be no older than sixteen. Her red petticoat
was open at the front and revealed her breasts, withered and
drooping, that might have been an old woman's. There is a new
law in Persia, difficult to enforce, which says that no girl may
marry before she is fifteen.

An uneven track led through mountains striped like a tiger's
skin, yellow grass between rocks black with lichen; by the edge
of a gorge that dropped hundreds of feet to a blue snake of river
winding between hedges of tamarisk and smooth sand-dunes.
There were no camels in these mountains, but mules and donkeys.
I saw one other car, and a lorry broken down. In the streets of
Sinneh they were selling bread, huge flat loaves of it, carried on
the heads of hawkers. Outside a shop a carpet was spread in the
street; donkeys, men and women tramped over it, kicking the
dust into the bright weave. We sat in a dingy room dipping bread
into bowls of gravy. An odd noise in the dark corner behind my
bench made me draw back a curtain of sacking to disclose a little
boy, his big eyes streaming with tears, peeling onions. We returned to the car, carrying melons, to find a group of children
standing with suppressed excitement by the wall. Inspired, we
looked under the car; sure enough, before each wheel there had
been carefully placed a large nail. The children ran off with wails
of disappointment.

In Kermanshah it was warmer; we were off the plateau, come
down between tall red-and-grey cliffs, into the plains again. Our
arrival in Kermanshah coincided with a puncture. While it was
being mended we went to the bazaar and emerged triumphantly
an hour later, David with a saddle-bag and I with a small carpet.
Having bought two dozen eggs we were persuaded to put the
saddle-bag to its proper use, and carry the eggs inside. Most of the
eggs might have survived the short journey to the car had it not

been for the passing of an angry camel that stampeded through the narrow tunnels of the bazaar, shedding water melons as it bucketed by, and forcing everyone, including David with the bulging saddle-bag, to flatten himself spontaneously against the wall. . . . But really we had come to Kermanshah to see the Sassanian rock reliefs, six miles east at Taq-i-Bostan.

The walls of two grottoes hollowed from the cliffside portray as if in a tapestry of stone a series of magnificent war and hunting scenes. Every sort of wild beast is represented, with the huntsmen, archers and spearmen, mounted upon camels and elephants or on foot, in everlasting pursuit. The human figures are carved in a rigorous stylism; with the animals the sculptor must have felt himself more at liberty to experiment. The elephants in ponderous motion, the horses, the wild boar pursued headlong but half turned as if undecided as to whether to fight or flee—these are drawn with a realism and fine vigour of which I had not thought the Sassanians capable. It has been suggested, so amazingly detailed are the representations of the animals, elephants especially, that Indian artists were employed.

There is a garden under the cliffs, and the custodian presented each of us with a rose. The place was built originally as a hunting-lodge, the Persian 'paradise' from which our own word derives, by the renowned monarch Khosru, surnamed Parviz, the victorious. 'In his time', writes the ninth-century chronicler al Tabari, 'the prophet, to whom be peace! entered upon his divine mission; that holy personage invited the king to the true faith, which he rejected, tearing in pieces the letter [of Mohammed] . . .'

In his reign, says the historian, Persia arrived at the summit of its glory. Among the king's fabulous possessions, his innumerable harem and household officers, he kept nearly a thousand elephants, which were no doubt the models for the sculptures in his hunting-lodge.

'Whenever he rode forth two hundred persons attended him, scattering perfumes on every side, whilst a thousand water carriers sprinkled with water the roads which he was to pass . . . In his time, white elephants brought forth young ones in Persia. What person, in harmonious powers, resembles his musician Barbud? Or, who in beauty is equal to his mistress Shireen? At last, in the seventh hour of the night, on Tuesday the tenth of Jemad-al-awul, in the seventh year of the Hegira, he was slain by the hand of his son, Shirouieh.' At least he was fortunate enough not to be alive to see his empire collapse not many years later before the invincible armies of that Mohammed whose overtures he had so scornfully rejected.

Ten miles farther east we chose a place to sleep, high on a neck of rock-strewn ridge jutting out from the mountains into the plain. A superb view from our high perch, far across the broad valley, in the failing light, to the gathering hills, crimson-topped, beyond. A river in fine arcs of soft pink gleamed in the darkening plain. Behind, the sheer precipice that marks abruptly the southern edge of the Kurdish plateau towered into the sky. Puffs of air warmed upon the steep rock surfaces blew across the ridge. I looked down upon one of the oldest roads in history, dropping westwards beyond Kermanshah through the passes down to the lowlands of Mesopotamia, and Baghdad; eastwards and north-east across Persia to the Caspian and the steppes of Turkestan, to Samarkand, beyond to China; Flecker's 'Golden Road', the old silk route, manned through thirty centuries by the slow merchant caravans, countless travellers, the baggage trains of armies. How many ordinary people I wondered, each one wrapped in his own close destiny or submerged in the floods of conquerors and fugitives, may have glanced up absentmindedly as they passed towards the bare cliffs, now a deep violet, where I stood?

Darkness: the black precipice above shuts out the stars.

'Did you hear that?'

David: 'Yes.'

(Grimly): 'A wolf.'

David (firmly): 'That was an owl.'

We light the lantern and I come upon a comforting passage in a guide-book: 'The last Persian lion was seen—and naturally shot —by an Englishman, in 1931.'

I woke to find the cliffs and ridge marooned above a sea of

mist, where across the valley the hill-tops rising out of it caught the sunlight. As the sun climbed higher and the mist receded I became aware of a strange and scarcely audible noise ascending from the hidden plain below, a confused murmur of faint cries, the snort of horses, bells, dogs barking. The mist blew apart and except by the river's path vanished. The plain was alive, in movement. Along the white tracks westward streamed a slow disordered train of mules and horses, heavily laden, their cloaked riders perched above the baggage. We watched them through binoculars, a tribe on the move, going down to the Pushit-i-Kuh for the winter pasturage.

Abreast in the plain, herds of sheep travelled with them under steady clouds of dust, the black specks of dogs and men by their side. An hour later we had descended from the ridge and they were still passing, an endless torrent spread out for miles along the route. Now that I stood beside them, watching the procession move by, I saw that the mounted figures were women with multi-coloured head cloths, with shaven-headed babies bundled on their backs. The older children were carried before them, astride, upon bulging red-and-brown saddle-bags, with sometimes a goat tied at the horse's side.

Fleets of donkeys with bells about their necks plodded patiently, almost invisible under loads of tents and carpets, firewood, baskets of fowls, pots and pans, with dogs trotting at their heels. The tribe seemed to be divided into sections, a space where the dust had time to settle between each string of a hundred or more. A striking leader of one division was a woman riding a white horse several yards ahead of the rest, with a high dark headdress and scarlet cloak. The men and boys who were not with the flocks strode alongside slapping the flanks of the animals, driving them on with shouts and whistles. The mules and horses walked with heads lowered to a monotonous steady rhythm, as if they had come a great distance and had a long way to go. As they passed some of the men waved and laughed, and called out to us as if saying, 'Come along, come with us!'

Why not? A strange experience, watching them ride past. I

sensed the difference between us, the ways of nomads and the settled people, and yet from myself felt a disturbing sympathy. This for ever moving, this constant partnership with earth and sky, holds, I am certain, a truth and a vigour of life whose values we have ignored. The settled have built their homes *against* the wind and the changing seasons, have set themselves in opposition to nature; perhaps they have cut themselves off for ever from a source of original vitality whose potency they have under-estimated, and which may be irreplaceable. The nomads travel *with* the changing seasons, in the spring climbing to the mountain pastures, in autumn descending to the warm grasslands of the plains. Their freedom from possessions, beyond those that can be carried with them, must mean a dependence on the elements and on themselves; but really, I think, it is a harmony, an independ-ence, holding a secret that we have for ever lost.

These, we decided, must be Bakhtiari; they and the Kashquais are the two largest of the many nomadic tribes of Persia, physic-ally a fine race of people who have their Turki blood for the most part pure, without intermingling with the sedentary population of the towns and villages. They look fine, too; perhaps it is partly the clothes; mostly, and in spite of relaxed government decrees on the subject, they maintain their ancient and more suitable oriental dress. The turbans and headclothes of varying shades, the em-broidered waistcoats and dark cloaks and all the colourful para-phernalia of rugs and saddlebags that is the tribesman's usual equipment make for overwhelming contrast with the average villager or townsman, with his pitiful drab uniform of semi-western rags, wardrobe of the most destitute clown. After all, the nomad's dress is the long-awaited answer to the romantic traveller's dreams of the 'magic east'. But there is something in clothes, and certainly a great deal in manner.

The tribesman's bolder bearing and air of manly independence is a good thing to see after the insipid faces and obsequious atti-tudes of the mass of townspeople crowded in hovels in the suburbs of the big cities. The women go unveiled, and several I noticed on the march near Kermanshah were remarkably good-looking. The tribesman wears his poverty without shame, without cringing; he is strong in the knowledge that he is part of a great family where loyalty and mutual assistance are the first principles. The best of the Persian army is recruited from the tribes. In spite of attempts to disarm them, most tribesmen still keep their rifles. A few years ago an army of Bakhtiari marched on Tehran and forced the government to remove from the cabinet four Tudeh Party (communist) ministers. The danger of a tribal rising can never be ruled out of possibility by any party in power; and in some quarters it is felt that this slumbering force will for long be a healthy check on any too undemocratic or revolutionary movement in the capital.

In Persia about two millions, or one tenth of the total population, are nomads. The knowledge that huge masses of closely co-ordinated people are constantly on their peregrinations back and forth across the country is enough to make any politician nervous, though modern weapons have reduced the tribal threat to comparative insignificance. It is really a question of possible disorder. But it is well known that the tribes are loyal to the Shah; it is also well known that their first wish is to be left alone. Unfortunately there are other factors involved. There has always been a mutual hostility between the nomads and villagers over whose lands they pass. Incidents of pilfering by stragglers have been numerously cited from the past. Now, however, the khans have realised the necessity for some resemblance to discipline among their followers; the routes to be taken on the spring and autumn journeys are carefully chosen to avoid friction by the crossing of cultivated lands and the grazing grounds have been fixed, not without considerable difficulty, their limits exactly defined.

Of much greater importance is the attitude of the Persian government itself. A principle is at stake. Nomads are out of date. Modernisation (westernisation) has been the foremost ambition of every middle-eastern state for the past seventy years. The funds necessary to implement this transformation must come from abroad, and Persia has been lent and given huge sums for this worthy purpose, mostly from the United States. But in order to attract foreign investment, to persuade the West that its money is not simply being poured into a bottomless void, there must be clear results, visible for all to see. Somehow a curious confusion of reasoning caused emphasis to be laid on the most ludicrous aspects. Gone, fortunately, are the days when turbans were replaced at bayonet point by 'western' Pahlevi caps, when soldiers tore off women's veils in the streets.

A more reasonable attitude is gradually prevailing, with the realisation that the best things the West has to offer should be taken each one on its own merits, and without any extraordinary suspicion that the wealth and apparent superiority of the westerner has anything to do with the style of his clothes or the way he cuts his hair. I believe that the so-called 'backward' nations are slowly losing their sense of general inferiority, a feeling as illogical as it was unnecessary. Yet the educated Persian feels very strongly that he must be 'progressive'; and the existence of tribes, nomadic at that, to one who cherishes the vision that Iran will one day be brimful of factories, and that every other Persian will drive a shiny motor car, is to him a shameful anomaly.

By any European standard the tribal way of life is primitive in the extreme. Literacy is almost unknown. That the tribesmen have no need to write letters and little desire or time to read the newspapers (but know a great deal about raising sheep, while their women are experts at weaving carpets) is given little consideration, and is regarded as beside the point. Hygiene is almost non-existent. That, in spite of this, their standard of health is remarkably high only makes the whole thing more shocking. So, in the best interests of the tribesmen themselves and incidentally for the sake of the country's international reputation, the tribes must be settled. Some were, for a short time. The enforced settlement of several of these communities in packed shanty towns hastily erected for the purpose brought about results which saddened the well-meaning bureaucrats of the capital. An appalling rise in the mortality rate, revulsion at the squalor and confinement of their new quarters, led to a general unhappiness that was all too apparent in the riots that followed, in the steady stream of fugitives escaping back to the open mountains.

The tribes are still comparatively free in Persia, still keep to their seasonal migrations, holding to a way of life that has been handed down to them through a hundred generations from ancestors who once roamed the steppes of Central Asia. For the moment among the busy planners of Tehran a more moderate attitude prevails. It is felt that the whole problem requires far more care, more time, than was previously thought necessary. Experiments are under way in which schools travel with the nomads on their journeys, medical stations are set up near the pasturages. If there is to be a change, then the standard of life in the villages, among the settled people, must be raised; so that when and if the transformation comes about the tribes will find that the new life intended for them will be an improvement and not a deterioration on their present one; though I believe that until there is produced in the laboratories and factories of the world a substitute for sheep and hand-made carpets, a synthetic panacea that will replace sunlight and space and freedom of movement, the nomads must continue, unprevented, on their way.

By midday the Bakhtiari had passed. The plain lay burning in the sun, bare and deserted as before. The mountains stood immersed in the contemplation of themselves; they were bored, they had seen too much. Five hundred feet above the level of the plain, carved upon the cliff-face of the sacred mountain of Bisutun, Darius the Great stands in triumph, facing a line of yoked prisoners, nine rebel kings. A tenth lies under his foot, begging for mercy. The bearded figure of Darius is life-size; his enemies reach only to his chest. They have been conquered, reduced to pygmies. Their suppression fully occupied the first years of Darius' reign, from 521 B.C. onwards; a detailed account of the revolts, the battles and other achievements of the king is inscribed in the arrow-head cuneiform of three languages upon great panels of smoothed rock below the statues. 'I am Darius, the great king, the king of kings, the king of the provinces, the son of Hystaspes . . . the Achaemenian . . . Eight of my race were kings before me; I am the ninth.'

There follows a list of the nations comprised in the great king's empire, twenty-three in all, stretching from the Indus to the valley of the Nile. The god Ahuramazda rising from a sun disc flashing lightning and gold rays, hovers by the king's head, modestly accepting the tribute paid him by the king: 'Thus saith Darius, the king: Ahuramazda hath granted unto me this empire . . . by the grace of Ahuramazda do I hold this empire . . . Within these lands, whosoever was a friend him have I surely protected; whosoever was hostile, him have I utterly destroyed.' The conquered rebels can bear testimony to this latter boast. Each one, his army defeated, was killed, usually first mutilated, then crucified.

Until the intrepid Rawlinson started to copy and decipher the inscriptions, with the aid of ropes, pulleys and ladders, in 1833, the rock carvings of Bisutun, remote and inaccessible upon the towering precipice, have caused confusion and misunderstanding to travellers through the centuries. The earliest, Diodorus Siculus, in the first century A.D., mistook the figure of Darius for the Queen Semiramis who would have passed by the rock on her journeys from Ecbatana to Babylon. One traveller thought the figure of the sun god was a cross, the statues below it, the twelve apostles; another suggested the figures might represent the twelve tribes of Israel.

The springs that flow from the rock face have made Bisutun a perfect resting-place for travellers. Darius, who wished his achievements to be known to all men for all time, could not have chosen a better place to inscribe them. But the mountain bears the memorial without concern, a fly which it is too lazy to brush off. From the white roadway far below the figures look inconsiderable, hardly to be noticed. The Persians journeying beneath the cliff see no reason to raise their heads.

We found a place on the map rejoicing in the name of Kangovar, and developed a burning desire to visit it. Somehow our ambition was frustrated. Whether it had been swept away, engulfed in an earthquake, or had never existed, we never knew. Perhaps we passed through it without knowing, mistaking the houses for rocks, or a slope of the hillside, the smoke of its chimneys for the dust-devils whirling in the plain.

City of Roses and Nightingales?

A man ran out from a cottage by the roadside, frantically
waving one arm, the other clutched to the swollen side of his face.
He had toothache; would we please pull out the offending tooth?
I tried to explain to him that we were no wandering dentists, and
besides, we had no equipment; our only pair of pliers had been
inadvertently left behind, somewhere near Trebizond . . .

According to the plans laid in the tea-house under the supervision of Hassan and Ibrahim, our ultimate destination on the
southward journey from Isfahan was to be Shiraz. Hassan had
never been there and, being a loyal Isfahani, warned us against
expecting too much. He even went so far as to say that while he
had nothing specific against Shiraz as a city—it might well be
attractive, pleasant to live in—the average Shirazi in his experience
was a low effeminate fellow, amoral, overgiven to pleasure, and
particularly to the drinking of wine. Hassan, for all his affected
cynicism, was a devout Moslem. Hassan admitted that occasionally, when he had a cold for instance, he took a nip of *arak*,
medicinally, in the privacy of his home; and even his friend the
dervish (who had not been found) sometimes joined him—when
he had a cold too . . . but as for *wine*! Hassan turned down the
corners of his mouth in disgust. As for Ibrahim, he was torn between his love of Isfahan above all other cities and his highly
developed sense of colour and romance. Shiraz for him was the
city of roses, of nightingales. He had heard it said that at times
one waded through the streets of the city knee-deep—well, ankle-
deep—in rose-leaves. Our interest was aroused. Hassan sneered;
just what he'd always thought. Of course, Ibrahim added sadly,
roses were well out of season now . . .

Ibrahim applauded our decision to visit Nain and Yezd on our
way south. At Nain, he said, though scarcely more than a village,
there was an old mosque dating from the ninth century and one of
the oldest in Persia. We drove into Nain on the first afternoon
after leaving Isfahan, pleasantly surprised after a morning on

47

bumpy earth roads through brown hills and desert to float on to a hundred yards of tarmac leading to a roundabout with a pool, surrounded by neatly laid flower-beds. A very small place indeed; we walked through it in ten minutes, led by a crowd of schoolboys busily practising their English, enthusiastic if not very intelligible guides—as much our fault as theirs. We entered the venerable mosque through a hole in the mud wall. There was an air of desertion about it, as if no one prayed there any longer.

Before the pulpit and mihrab stood a great number of columns covered with the deeply stuccoed foliage of grapes and flowers, so richly done that it seemed wholly incongruous with the simplicity and austerity that surrounded it, the arid little town on the edge of the desert. It was like suddenly biting on a sultana in a mouthful of rice. In company with our devoted guides we climbed the corkscrew staircase of a tottering minaret, surveyed the desert, and came down again. One of the boys ran ahead twirling a little paper propeller and shouting to clear the way as we recrossed the village to visit a later mosque, attracted by the dome, painted in large diamond-shaped design in a lovely and unusual blue. Inside we were received by a very old mullah with a white beard and an expression of extraordinary benevolence and humility on his lined face. As we left (the interior was disappointing) David presented him with some small change, at which the old mullah piously closed his eyes, intoning over us some sort of blessing. A second and younger mullah joined him at the door. Once outside a fierce altercation broke out from behind. I turned to see framed in the doorway the two mullahs angrily facing each other. The younger one seemed on the point of assaulting the other, whose look of higher things had been replaced by a triumphant and excited grin, as he held the money in his fist, out of reach behind his back.

There are many good reasons for visiting Yezd, but we had come there for a specific purpose. We were at the end of the lane facing the portal of the Friday Mosque. A slender pointed arch rises nearly a hundred feet, faced with blue tiles enscrolled in yellow arabesque and surmounted by a pair of minarets likewise enscrolled. The archway, and the remains of the mosque beyond, were built in the fourteenth century, though the tilework has been repaired quite lately. A beautiful arch, as satisfying a piece of architecture as any in Persia, and the tallest of its kind, with such graceful narrowness of proportion, that I have ever seen.

Robert Byron, in his book *The Road to Oxiana*, had included a photograph of this magnificent archway. David and I had driven to Yezd with the particular intention of seeing the portal for ourselves and photographing it, this time in colour—which was the cause of all the trouble.

At first everything was easy. We parked the car by a pile of rubble outside the mosque, and laden with photographic apparatus stood under the portal admiring the simplicity of its lines. It took us only a moment—the book was in our hands—to realise that Byron had taken the photograph from the only possible place, somewhere high up, presumably from the roof of a house, on the left. Followed by a few idlers we plunged into the network of alleys to the left of the mosque, searching for the steps that must have existed. A fat youth on a bicycle had somehow attached himself to us, and immediately suspected our intentions. He rode along behind or in front calling out, 'No, no. Go back!'

We found ourselves in the middle of the bazaar, and what with our outlandish appearance and the unwelcome and vocal attentions of this precocious youth, were attracting too much attention. I began to feel desperate; there was not much time left, the sun was already setting and in half an hour the opportunity would be lost. We calculated the distance as best we could and dived into an open doorway. An old man cutting up vegetables rose up in surprise from a dark corner of the room, and I tried to dispel his alarm by shaking his hand vigorously and muttering a few polite sentences of phrase-book Persian. Dimly in the corner, steps were visible, leading aloft. We slammed the front door, behind which I could already hear the bicycle-youth declaiming angrily, and made a dash for the stairs. It was exactly right. We came out on

49

the roof studded with the brown mud domes of the bazaar. In front of us rose the portal of the mosque; from behind, the setting sun flooded the rooftops with golden light, shining upon the arch and glittering minarets. It was a beautiful sight, but one which we were not allowed to contemplate for long.

Standing on the rooftop fumbling with the cameras, I realised that we were in full view of a little square below. I looked down upon a knot of people all gazing indignantly up at us. With every moment their numbers, fed from the side-alleys, grew until quite a crowd stood grumbling and gesticulating below. Pushing through the crowd came a blue-coated policeman, summoned no doubt by that infernal boy by his side, wheeling the bicycle. We decided to wait for the deputation, which was not long in appearing. It was a fatal mistake. Six or seven of them, led by the policeman and the boy, clambered out on to the roof. The policeman, shortly joined by another, began to expostulate. The boy took on himself the responsibility of interpreter, but I threw him such a murderous glance that he withdrew to the far corner of the roof, from where he felt safe enough to address us.

The policeman demanded our permit to photograph mosques. We had no permit, and never had needed one before. Then we would have to get one, now. But, we tried to explain, there was no time; the sun was only just above the horizon! It was now or never. I took a quick reading with the exposure meter, and David set the camera. The crowd below groaned with horror and the policeman pushed himself in front of us. It was difficult for him to look dignified balanced on those smooth domes, with a drop of forty feet into the arms of his compatriots below, but he did his best. He waved his hat in front of the camera; the other policeman grabbed my ankle. I took out my wallet. For a moment the policeman hesitated. But common sense prevailed; he could hardly take a bribe in front of his colleague, and he guessed, quite correctly, that the wallet held money enough for one policeman only; besides, the fat youth in the corner was watching our every movement like a hawk. Perhaps he felt also that this was the crowning moment of his career; the spectacular roof-top arrest of two dangerous and blaspheming foreigners. It was no good. At that moment the sun went down, almost with a bang.

A silent procession filed down from the roof. Out in the square the crowd fell back to let us through, and as we passed, closed up again, following behind. Once more in front of the mosque, we climbed into the car. By now there must have been more than eighty people surrounding the car, regarding us in no very friendly fashion. It was time to move on, to shake off the dust of Yezd, I hoped, for ever. But the policeman refused to let us go without him. He was coming with us, he said, to the police station, to get a permit. A permit! It was the last straw. David was in the driving seat, and started the engine; but the door, wedged by the policeman's leg and shoulder, could not be closed. The crowd took the hint and began to pile up blocks of stone from the rubble heap before and behind the wheels. The second representative of the law had jumped on a bicycle and had gone off in a hurry, presumably to fetch reinforcements. I began to feel that they would be needed.

In a Land-Rover such as ours only the passenger's door can be locked from the inside. Mine was fortunately so locked, and I was separated from the grimacing faces outside pressing against the glass. But the doors, once open, can be conveniently removed simply by lifting them off their hinges, and in the ensuing struggle between David and the policeman this is what happened. The policeman staggered back, the door in his arms; the crowd whooped with joy. David, in a fine fury born of outraged ownership, sprang after him, wrested the door from his embrace, and plunged it back on the hinges. At this moment a workman issued out of the crowd bearing a flame-spouting blow-lamp which he waved menacingly in front of the bonnet, a suggestion that was greeted by a unanimous murmur of approval. The tension was so high that I began to laugh, a little hysterically. The faces close to me must have caught my expression—simple, pleasant faces most of them—except when so unreasonably incited, and they also began to smile fatuously. The people in the front grinned, even the vandal with the blow-lamp imagined that the situation held an element of comedy. He bashfully withdrew. David put the engine into low-ratio gears and the car bounded over the rubble. Surprised, the crowd scattered. I looked back as we tore down that lane followed by a few random stones. The policeman, backed by the crowd, stood watching us uncertainly . . .

Anyone who is excited simply by looking at a map, and can see in the dry contours and black lines, in the graded shades of brown and green, a whole world of mountains, plains and rivers start up from the paper will understand our feelings as we knelt over the map laid out on the sand, on the brilliant morning after the Yezd débâcle. The brown walls of Yezd were at our back. Yezd had rejected us; we would forget Yezd. A new world lay waiting, south Persia, just over those purple mountains that reared so abruptly from the desert's surface. The map's advice was clear; by making a long detour to the east the mountain barrier could be skirted. On the other hand a thin dotted line led straight across by way of Taft and Alyabad, between the peaks and down the other side. Raising my eyes from the map, there was Shir Khuh, 13,000 feet; and there Khar Khuh, 11,000 feet. Between the two, most surely, our road lay.

The village of Taft is hardly visible until one is upon it, the cottages built on the hillside in layers resembling the strata of the mountains. The track lay along a sandy ravine cut deep by the winter torrents. Children amused themselves by throwing nuts at the car as we passed, until a blast of the horn sent them bolting behind rocks. Well inside the range on a colourless tableland overhung with crags, we stopped at a village where, by the well, there stood an extraordinary structure, a wooden cage fifteen feet high. By the shoulder-poles sticking out from its base I guessed it must be carried during some religious festival, like the platforms used in the Spanish *Semana Santa*.

An elderly man approached, greeting us courteously, wearing a magnificent green turban—insignia of a *seyid*, or descendant of the Prophet. Beside him was a gentleman dressed comfortably but luridly in pink-and-mauve pyjamas. Seeing that we were curious about the strange behaviour of a little boy who kept bobbing up and down out of a hole, suspended by a wheel erected over it, they led us over. It was a *quanat* shaft, and having heard so much about them I was most interested to see one in action.

The *quanat* system is as old as Persia itself. By it every village receives the water on which its life depends. Except in the middle of certain deserts there are always mountains in Persia. At the foot of a mountain, if one digs deep enough and in the right places, there will be water. The *quanat* is an underground channel connecting this subterranean source with the village, which in some cases may be as much as thirty miles away. When a village decides it needs another *quanat*, the backer of the project, either a single wealthy villager, or a group, goes with the local water-diviner to a suitable spot near the hills. They dig until they reach water, and the *quanat* is begun. Under the supervision of experts hired for the purpose an exact elevation is calculated—for centuries this has been done without benefit of modern instruments—and the underground channel is started, usually from the village end, in the direction of the original source shaft. At intervals of a hundred yards or so auxiliary ventilation shafts are sunk, connecting the tunnel with the surface. At each hole the experts make additional calculations to ensure that the *quanat* is travelling on course and at the correct angle of elevation. Whoever has paid for the construction of the channel is entitled to the profits from the water, which is shared out and sold when it reaches the village. The well-to-do, therefore, have their cottages on the outskirts of their village, nearest the hills, and so receive the water at its freshest. The sight of these mounds of loose earth piled up round the *quanat*-heads, strung out like molehills in line across the desert, is always a sure sign, often a comforting one, of approaching habitation.

We persuaded the old man standing by the wheel to demonstrate. The boy disappeared down the shaft, bracing himself with legs apart against the sides of the hole. After a surprisingly long time a faint voice echoed to the surface; he had reached the bottom. A rope with a bucket on the end was unrolled from the wheel, and in a few minutes was drawn up again to the shrill creaking of the wheel, full of slime and stones. These were *quanat*-workers, a privileged and much respected profession, whose duties are to inspect the channels and keep them clear. As the best combination is a man to turn the wheel and a boy to go down the shaft and creep along the tunnels the work is usually passed down from father to son, who work together. It is a dangerous job; collapsing tunnels or sudden unaccountable floods have made these bold workmen the most superstitious of Persians. The slightest sensation of doubt, the faintest sign, taken as an ill omen, will prevent them from going down those shafts, and no one will dare to press them. I could not help thinking as I gazed down the inky hole that the obvious retort, 'Well, go down yourself, then,' would be enough to deter any criticism.

The dust rose in a cloud behind us as we climbed between towering cliffs pale orange, slate and black, riven with the mid-day shadows. A camel of very independent mind strolled down the track. A few yards behind followed a small boy clad only in a patched grey shirt, brandishing a stick and shouting. He was on the verge of tears. Whenever he ran the camel broke into a trot, when the boy walked the camel walked, keeping always just out of reach, trailing its rope on the ground, an expression of studied innocence on its supercilious face. The last moment that we knew we were still on the right road came at the gateway of a turreted mud fort whose walls were decorated in a stucco geometrical pattern, with pale-blue tiles spaced below the crumbling battlements. The few surrounding acres of cultivation were a brilliant, rich green, such a green as brought from us a gasp of delight after so many miles of bare earth and rock. A sunburnt man with a black skull-cap pushed to the back of his head rested on his fork as we drew up. 'The road to Alyabad?' He nodded sympathetically and waved his hand towards the mountains. His was the last cottage we were to see for a hundred miles.

At the top of the pass, it must have been nearly 9,000 feet, a narrow stream of ice-cold water burst out of the hillside. Naked and shouting with the cold we lay in it for a few seconds, the water breaking over our shoulders in torrents of ice and split sunlight; and afterwards fell asleep in the hot sun. We decided to have a late lunch at Alyabad, which could hardly be more than a few miles on.

Two hours later Alyabad seemed as elusive as ever. The descending track, never very clear at its best, was beginning to fade out between boulders and tufts of shoulder-high yellow grass. Rounding a corner of rock we came upon a square pool of water, a single tree bending over it, with a young woman and a girl in blue shawls sitting by its side, washing clothes. A red scarf hanging from a branch joined its bright reflection in the water below. I put my head out of the window. 'Alyabad?' I enquired tentatively. The woman froze, gazing at us in fearful silence. The soap spread in a slow cloud across the pool. Two pairs of unblinking almond eyes followed our hasty retreat out of sight.

Thoughts of Alyabad and lunch were fading, and were regretfully abandoned. The track seemed to be returning uphill, into the mountains again. Following some tyre marks that had broken new ground ahead, we came out upon a ridge for the first time with a full view of the plain below. We built a fire and drank coffee, sitting disconsolately surveying the landscape. The ridge swept down a thousand feet in gentle folds to the level of the plain, which stretched unbroken to the distant blue rim of mountains. Where the rough gullies, studded with bushes and rocks, came to an end, the mud flats began, a sea of copper dried hard and gleaming in the slanting sun. In the crystal afternoon light I guessed the distance to the far range of mountains as thirty miles; by the map it measured eighty. Continuing after the old tyre marks of our hardy predecessor we descended to the desert level and calculating on the chance of encountering the road from Yezd we struck out on our own across the hard grey gravel that thinly covered the sand. A brief diversion in pursuit of a pair of gazelle that bounded from a ravine and fled towards the sunset led us to a rise from which we watched the sun drop out of sight. On the other side, a few yards away, lay the main road.

At Abarguh the next morning, in the foothills across the *kavir*, the petrol tanks, which had hardly a cupful left in them, were refilled. The pump-boy, who seemed as joyful to administer the petrol as were we to receive it, succeeded in spilling half a tin, squirted the liquid of another indiscriminately and with great glee into the midst of the spectators who had immediately collected, and lavishly covered David and himself with the contents of a third. Although the boy was only ten, he insisted on adding to the general excitement by puffing at a lighted cigarette as he worked.

A last long valley winding into the mountains brought us to the main road from Isfahan. In the little tea-house at Dhebid we refreshed ourselves thirstily, sitting cross-legged and comfortable on the earthen ledge, under the gaze of countless gaudy posters stuck to the mud walls: advertisements and lurid reproductions which included a dreadful rendering of Abraham about to slay Isaac, St. George and the dragon, Edward VII, toothpastes, and the perpetually smiling faces of innumerable Shahs. We might have rested there longer, had it not been for the attentions of a bucolic village policeman who had been sitting all the time opposite, pretending to drink tea and trying to summon up enough courage to ask for our passports. That he had such officious intentions was proved beyond doubt when, at a secret signal, we got up and dashed for the car, the policeman, suddenly galvanised into action, rushed out of the tea-house in pursuit, waving vigorously at our departing dust-cloud. I felt sorry for him, but there it was . . .

The tomb of Cyrus, a simple stone structure, stands out forlorn and white upon the dark plain of Pasargadae, 'camp of the Persians'. The body of the king whom the Persians called 'Father'; the Hellenes he conquered, 'master', and the Jews whom he liberated, 'anointed of the Lord', was interred here in 530 B.C. at a moment when his empire extended from the Mediterranean to India. Alexander came to view the embalmed corpse of the Great King and ordered the tomb to be repaired and full honour done to his illustrious predecessor. For the vision of world empire which ennobled Alexander's mission was first realised by this the greatest of the Achaemenians two centuries earlier. The wise principle by which the conquered nations ruled themselves under the sovereignty of the Great King, keeping their religions and their own customs intact, was the one followed by Alexander. But while Cyrus had a successor in Darius, who re-welded the empire under a new centralised government, Alexander had no one.

The tomb has long been empty, its treasure dispersed. When I climbed the rough-hewn steps to the little dark chamber at the top I found part of a Koran lying in one corner, a few loose pages scattered about the floor. Sticks between the joints of the stone blocks bore native offerings, torn shreds of clothing, locks of hair, as if some slumbering power still remained in the heart of these ancient stones.

From the palace ruins of Pasargadae, where the winged genius carved upon a tall plinth still presides over the moor, the road descends to the plain of Persepolis by a gorge winding steeply between high escarpments torn and twisted into a chaos of pinnacles and tiered embattlements. Herds of sheep and goats that had been grazing near Pasargadae swept down with us through the pass. We travelled at walking pace, hemmed in by a heaving sea of fleece and horns driven forward with bells and dogs and the cries of shepherds. The lowered sun pierced the crags and lit the pyramid of dust advancing overhead with bars of gold that turned to crimson with the sunset, grey in the shadow of the cliffs, until finally we broke free from the stumbling herds as they spread out into the twilit plain.

We came to a halt in a great silence under the cliff tombs of Naksh-i-Rustam. There was no one about. High on the rock face the Achaemenian kings had hewn their gigantic sepulchres, smoothing away the surface for a hundred feet below so that no man should disturb their bodies, or the treasure buried with them. Every tomb has long since been rifled of its contents. A ladder—a section of a railway line—rested against the cliff below the tomb of Darius the Great. The three other tombs are said to belong to Xerxes, Artaxerxes and Darius III. From the first platform a second ladder leads to the narrow ledge where is the entrance to the vault. Four half-columns decorate the exterior, soaring to the final platform that bridges the tomb where two rows of thirty figures, one above the other, tributary kings from every corner of the empire, stand yoked beneath the statue of the Great King himself, the winged sun disc of Ahuramazda hovering over all. I climbed the railway lines and sat in the dusk with legs dangling from the ledge with the sinister dark doorway of the tomb at my back. The stone was still warm from the sun and the whole cliff face seemed to retain a glow of colour, as if the sunlight had embedded itself too deeply to escape. Below me the plain was spread out, scarred with blue and grey. Coming to Naksh-i-Rustam I had seen the black tents of nomads scattered about the plain; now the tents were hardly visible, only the camp fires starting one by one flickered to life as the sky was drained of light, matching the first stars overhead. The swallows that had been circling and diving before me vanished, their place taken by bats that hurled themselves from the vault interiors out into the fading light. The crickets struck up their interminable chorus.

It was a fine place to stop the night; though somewhat eerie. We parked the car about fifty yards from the cliff and built a fire, a particularly large one, with a great reserve of firewood, as much as could be gathered of roots and twigs round about. There seemed very little to say, but we were especially glad of each other's company. It was decided, in the presence of the illustrious dead, and in their honour, to hold a feast; and so a priceless tin of English tongue and one of pears were brought out and ceremoniously cut open. The remains of a bottle of *arak* we drank in a forced attempt to be cheerful in this sombre place whose atmosphere of strange brooding, made of silence and shadows and the black outlines of those funereal cliffs, had been intensified by a pale moon rising over the hills. I began to recall how, according to the legends which every Persian knows, places of the dead are held to be most unsuitable for the living, especially at night; and to choose of one's own free will to sleep here of all places would be considered madness. Tombs, particularly those broken into and desecrated, are the haunts of the worst *djinns*, implacable spirits older than the hills who emerge to stalk the earth at night. This was Persia, and Persians should know. We piled more sticks on the fire. On the other hand we were not Persians; surely foreigners would be exempt from all such unwelcome attentions; we held British passports, and were ready to produce them if necessary for the scrutiny of any discriminating genie. But then again; a change of diet . . .

At this moment I distinctly heard a stone dislodged somewhere quite near, in the darkness under the mountain. We sat paralysed, with glasses motionless within an inch of our lips. There was another movement, over to the right. Voices. Three ragged figures converged on us and stood a little way from the fire. I relaxed; at least these were human; and no very dreadful humans either, even though one bore a long pole over his shoulder. They looked very poor and very uncertain, and stood blinking shyly in the firelight. Their faces were swathed in dark cloths, and the man with the pole wore a turban. He tried to smile, and we wished him good evening, pointing to the vacant space round the fire. They shook their heads; they were looking at the empty tins. Gladly we passed them over. All three retired with slight bows into the darkness clutching their booty. I could hear them conferring in whispers; planning a real assault perhaps? We decided to try an old trick which had always succeeded in dispelling visitors not altogether welcome. We began to take off our clothes and go to bed. It worked. The men moved off, calling gruffly over their shoulders, '*Khoda hafiz!*' God be with you! We answered with relief.

It is extraordinary, the effect this undressing has on all Persians. Whether it comes from a desperate shame at the sight of the naked body, or, as one would prefer to hope, from a highly developed sense of decency or good manners, it is difficult to say. But the result is invariable; begin to remove your shirt, make it clear that your trousers will follow, and even the most stubborn, most inquisitive spectator will fall back, turn his head and go. It is true that Persians, especially the country people, never at any time, whatever the temperature, go without every part of their body well covered. Protection from the sun is probably the main motive. Yet I remember occasions when in the most desolate spots we have come upon a Persian bathing in a stream, and always he will be wearing, though under water, something round his middle; and on sight of us he will either duck well down in the water or scuttle into the nearest bushes. It was an appropriate setting, under the graves of Darius and Xerxes, to recall the story—a rather unfair, Greek one—that originated during the Graeco-Persian wars; how, when Greek and Persian prisoners were paraded naked and for sale in the slave market of some neutral town, it was said that the Greeks were ashamed because they were prisoners, the Persians because they were naked.

In the early morning we were overrun by a herd of goats. I was woken by their bells jingling in my ear. My trousers had disappeared. As frantic as any naked Persian I ran searching among the goats. I discovered them stretched taut between the clenched teeth of two brown she-goats angrily pressing for the division of the prize. If they had been in the jaws of the majestic long-haired white ram that stood on a hillock near by, jerking his sharp horns irritably, and glaring at me suspiciously out of his wicked small eyes, I think I would have yielded them quietly, only too glad to follow the custom of the country and wear pyjamas for a day.

We waited for photographs, for the sun to touch the tombs, slanting in pale gold upon the yellow rock. The Sassanians, not to be outdone by their royal predecessors, have also left their signatures at Naksh-i-Rustam. Seven bas-reliefs almost at ground level have been carved beneath the four Achaemenian tombs. Colossal figures, chiselled with a heavy hand; muscular kings with thick beards and high pointed helmets, with broad trousers decorated at the edges with what look like the buckskin fringes of American cow-punchers; prancing spear in hand upon their battle-chargers, under the benevolent surveyance of Ahuramazda, never too far away. One tablet reveals the giant image of Shapur I mounted upon a militant cart-horse receiving the homage of a diminutive figure in a toga kneeling at the monarch's feet; the Roman emperor Valerian, defeated and made prisoner in the Syrian campaign of A.D. 260.

Near the tombs there stands a most unusual building, a Zoroastrian fire-temple, a sort of squat tower so simply and cleanly constructed that I felt it might have been designed yesterday. On the hillside not far away I came upon two fire-altars, cut out of the rock. A path ran below the altars, and along it came a donkey with a young woman riding upon it, a man walking close beside her, his arm protectively round her waist. The woman's hair fell down in ringlets on either side of her face, and she wore round her head the green headcloth I had often noticed in this part of the country. Round her shoulders was draped a blue shawl spotted with white. Her eyes were deeply blacked and there were heavy gold rings on her ears and on her wrists. As soon as she saw me she pulled down the end of the headcloth and held it across her face until she had passed. They looked as if they had just been married.

As we drove the few miles to the ruins of Persepolis, I saw that the plain was different; the black tents were gone, the cloaked women with their pots and carpets, the men and the jingling herds and the night-shirted boys—the nomads were already on their way. A low yellow cloud of dust floating far ahead under the blue hills marked their passage. Patches of scorched earth, half obliterated, were all that could remind me of the constellation of last night's fires glittering below me. A few small cairns; a scrap of clothing, bright red, caught on a thorn bush; the plain was empty, swept clean. It was somehow important, and very clear, that I should have the first view of the platform of Persepolis jutting out from the bare hills and crowned with its tall sticks of broken columns, in company with that cloud of dust moving beyond it. The tribe had encamped here for the night; they had passed on, leaving nothing. A nomad's posterity is limited to the living, his children and grandchildren, his flocks and horses; he needs no memorial, no monument but the sun and the mountains which never change. For Darius and Xerxes it had been otherwise: a few columns were still standing.

I climbed the broad flights of stone stairway where the mounted guards of the Great King had ridden twelve abreast. The winged bulls of the gate of Xerxes stare sightlessly across the plain; there is nothing behind them. Everywhere there are carvings. Lions tear the flanks of unicorns, the ten thousand Immortals march spear in hand, the King gives judgement, makes sacrifice, is carried high upon the shoulders of his slaves, the conquered kings of Asia. On the great staircases of the terrace an unending procession of tribute-bearers mount to pay homage to their lord; chariots and camels, horses . . . The men step with a slow dignity, the men of the subject nations, one by one, carrying the wine and jewels and rare animals, gifts for their master; only, at the top, there is no one there. I rested in the shadow of one of the remaining tall columns. The dust-cloud of the nomads was still visible, retreating down the valley. Two boys had got left behind, staying to recapture a runaway goat. They were wrestling with its horns and managed to slip a rope about its neck. Under the corner of the terrace they stopped; they were staring at the rows of strange figures sculptured on the stone. One of them bent to pick up a stone and threw it, derisively, at the carvings. 'Go away!' I shouted.

From Persepolis to Shiraz it is only one hour's drive. The top of the pass that gives a first view of the city, spread out in the plain below, bears a name awarded to it by common consent: the Gate of *Allah ho Akbar*, 'God is Great!'—The murmured phrase that is supposed to come involuntarily to the weary traveller's lips as he catches a first glimpse of this longed for paradise. We stopped the car and looked. A dust-storm was blowing up far below around the cypress gardens of the city. The wind was driving dust between the minarets, half obscuring the domes, dulling the gleam of tiles that were already harsh and metallic in the fierce sunlight. The domes vanished and reappeared, floating for a moment above the yellow haze.

Allah ho Akbar! But I had faint misgivings. Neither of us had any money. Our last *rials* had been blown on an extravagant but enjoyable lunch in the modern government-run hotel that blots the landscape close under the terrace of Persepolis. The menu, in French, had promised at least two courses of European food; the temptation had been too great. It is not that Persian food is altogether intolerable; but it lacks variety. Stew and rice, stew and hard flat bread, eggs, sometimes a chicken, usually very old, when it can be afforded, excellent sour cream—these are the staple dishes of the tea-houses and wayside eating-rooms and they are enough to sustain and satisfy any but the most discriminating traveller. But after long periods of this sort of fare the European tends to be filled with a deep nostalgia for some half-forgotten flavour that seems to reach out to him across Asia from the grills and pressure-cookers of his far-off home kitchens; and certainly, at the Hotel Persepolis, his whim (at great cost) may be indulged.

Allah ho Akbar! But it was hot and dusty in the streets of Shiraz. Dust blew in our eyes and settled upon our faces, finely and irresistibly penetrating noses and ears. We must find a hotel; the hotels were full. We had no money; the banks were closed. A kindly clock-maker who kept despairingly brushing the sand off our shoulders, saying, 'So extraordinary, so extraordinary!' took pity on our distress and routed out an irritable money-changer who cursorily examined our travellers' cheques and pronounced them worthless. The clock-maker directed us to more hotels, cheap doss-houses, crowded and dirty, where the proprietors glared at us suspiciously, and shook their heads. Everyone was irritable (except the clock-maker) and blamed the weather. We became more ill-tempered than anyone else, and blamed Shiraz.

I suppose I am a bad traveller, or I would not have allowed these trivial details to colour my impressions of such a renowned and ancient city.

> 'Sweet is Shiraz and its incomparable site—
> O God, preserve it from decline!'

City of roses, nightingales, poets! I had only one desire: a cold bath. I am ashamed now of this shabby betrayal of my own earnest ideals. It is at moments like these that one's real self, stripped of its veneer of pseudo-culture, is revealed. My only consolation lies in the knowledge that so many greater souls, from Hafiz to the present day, have sung the glories of Shiraz, that my own omission will pass unnoticed.

At last, reluctantly, we forced ourselves to be reconciled with the extravagant tariff of the 'luxury' Hotel Saadi. There was nowhere else to go. Before sunset the sky cleared, and with it my depression. I sat on the balcony before my room breathing the cool scented air that rose from freshly watered paths and flower-beds. With new enthusiasm we ordered a bottle of wine. We tasted it, mixed it with water; ordered soda, and mixed it with that. Finally we left it, sadly. Surely—a bad bottle. The waiter who took it away remarked that the dust-storm was coming back. He pointed to the yellow haze that was driving down again from the hills. The cypresses rattled their dry leaves like bones. Indeed, as Ibrahim had said: roses were out of season in Shiraz just now.

3

Deserts

❀

I am not sure how the conversation in the tea-house got round to deserts. But I remember that Hassan had run out of cigarettes and with a grimace had accepted one of mine. He took a special pleasure in demonstrating his aversion for my English cigarettes, and never failed to make this plain to the friends of his who dropped in of an evening to the tea-house and sat round smoking my tobacco with the pride and enjoyment of connoisseurs. Hassan was in a bad mood, morose. His father-in-law—in whose house he lived—was being awkward again, and his own wife was siding against him. It was about Hassan's work, or rather about his not working. Ibrahim kept telling him that he should send his daughters to the new girls' school here in Isfahan, and Hassan kept replying that on the Oil Company's pension it would be impossible. Besides, there were other bills mounting up ... There was a sort of regular pause at the end of each of these exchanges, as an unspoken thought crossed everyone's mind. The thought was clear in Ibrahim's face, and in mine, and in any of Hassan's friends who were present. It was also clear to Hassan. He should get a job. But no one was impolite enough to put forward this desperate solution. After all we could see that Hassan was spending more and more of his time in the sanctuary of the tea-house; it was his last and only refuge. To hound him here of all places with such unpalatable notions would be unfair and cruel. On this occasion Ibrahim, who was sitting opposite me, his cane across his knees holding the tea-glass delicately between long, pale fingers just level with the point of his beard, pursed his lips meaningfully. I thought for a moment he was about to assault his friend with that forbidden topic. He drew a deep breath, hesitated, and finally changed his mind. He turned to me and spoke in a pained voice, with half an eye on Hassan, who had sensed the danger and was suddenly deep in conversation with his neighbour. The trouble with Persia to-day, said Ibrahim, was the miserably low level of literacy in the country. He waited for the words to find their mark. It was well known that Hassan could read little more than the headlines of the newspapers and could write his own name only with the greatest difficulty. But Hassan was immovable and flinched not at all. He was laughing sinisterly with the little fellow whom I had seen in the tea-house that first evening—the downtrodden-looking man for whom I had felt such sympathy when he was bargaining over his only lorry with the black-whiskered giant. In spite of my fears, and as Hassan had forecast at the time, he got a very good price and, according to all accounts, had swindled the ogre terribly. The lorry, when finally handed over to its new owner, had failed to start, and in spite of the attentions of the best mechanics in Isfahan was still immobile. It appeared that some important and very expensive parts of the engine had been found unaccountably missing. Hassan's friend looked as if he had invested part of his lately acquired capital in some new clothes; he sat resplendent in a glossy black-striped shirt fastened at the neck with a silver collar-stud. I supposed that the collar, and eventually the tie, would be following in instalments.

Ibrahim must have felt that my attention was wandering, for he tapped me on the knee and continued in a slightly louder voice, fixing me imperatively with his large black eyes. It wasn't as if the government were not doing their best, he was saying; the difficulty lay in the shortage of teachers—not just amateurs (there were too many of them) but qualified, *good* teachers . . . Ibrahim stopped and I suddenly realised what was expected of me. 'You mean,' I interposed quickly, 'like you.' Ibrahim smiled modestly, shrugging his shoulders very gently, and spread his hands . . .

Talking with a Persian

What we Westerners miss with our wooden gestureless speech!
We talk like soldiers giving each other orders, arms strictly to
the side, with only mouths working in our tense, controlled bodies.
To show emotion, to express oneself with anything else but
the tongue—so undignified, embarrassing, so naïve. Words, too
many of them, rolling out often only to obscure our true meaning;
words that take over the meaning, cut it down, or twist it to suit
themselves; words that build their own barriers against real
understanding. How great the significance of a silence, a certain
lift of the shoulders, the faintest motion of the hands! I was not
used to looking for these things; talking with any Persian, with
Ibrahim for instance, was a new experience. Something of the
dance, of mime, is brought in with the talking. In Persia the
whole of a man talks, not just his mouth. All of the body comes
into play; words become of auxiliary importance, the mere
vehicles of expression, their significance pointed with the subtlest
shades of the speaker's movement; gaining immeasurably thereby
in clarity and depth. Even when walking with Ibrahim I had come
to watch with a new interest and understanding the angle of his
head, the crook of his elbow, even the way he walked. Now that
he sat opposite me in repose there was all the more to look for,
to draw in company with his words into my mind. The gesture
of his just then, in response to my rather obvious—but welcome—
compliment; a wordless eloquence. The pause, lift of the shoulder,
the open, turning fingers: 'Well my dear fellow,' it seemed to
say, 'you are intelligent, you can see what I am, it seems, as
clearly as I see myself. Of course, I cannot agree with you in
so many words, but we understand each other . . .'

And then the modest smile, deflected glance with the gracefully
bowed head; a flicker of eyes under the arched brows returning
to my face with, 'Of course I can see what you're thinking: I'm
easily flattered; but then, you understand me, what harm in a
little compliment?' Finally the eyes wandering upwards, the hands'
faint flutter; casting about for a suitable phrase, the exact moment,
to continue . . .

'For example,' said Ibrahim, 'in the school where I am the

teacher. . .' Perhaps I was not as interested in education as I should have been, for there the topic rested. And it must have been about then that we began to talk about deserts.

I don't expect many people to share this obscure fascination which at that time I felt for deserts. Near Tabriz I had gazed out upon one of these limitless wastes; and again, on the road south from Tehran to Qum, we had skirted the central desert tract of Persia, that vast dead expanse extending for 800 miles to the south-east. This 'great desert depression, the most arid in the world,' has been divided by cartographers into two spheres; in the north, the Dasht-i-Kavir, in the south, the Dasht-i-Lut. 'The former is a series of mud and salt flats where nothing grows or lives. In some places life is possible round the hollows where the soil is less saline and there there are true oases.' And then, to continue the paragraph in Dr. Ghirshman's *Iran*, and this is the part which, I must confess, excited my imagination most, 'The Lut, on the contrary, is a completely dry basin, and the rare explorers who have had the courage to cross this inhospitable waste say that the great deserts of Central Asia, such as the Gobi, seem fertile regions in comparison. . .' Admittedly, on further enquiry, I found that this desert of deserts was not quite as virgin as one might suppose. During the war it was proved that well-equipped motor convoys could make the crossing, if they were careful to follow the ancient routes worn by the caravans of centuries, and to-day the tracks are still used by the occasional camel-train plodding north-east from Kerman on the 'short cut' (500 miles) to Meshed.

Hassan and Ibrahim, whose willing advice and criticism, dissolved in so many glasses of tea, had done much to shape our plans, suggested that on leaving Shiraz we should make for Kerman, and then Meshed in the north-eastern corner of Persia, near the junction of the Russian and Afghan frontiers. The route from Shiraz to Kerman presented little difficulty; although we had been sternly advised to follow the main road round by Yezd again, we had already decided secretly to go direct, by Niriz and Saidabad. The tentative project of crossing the Lut, however, met with complete disapproval. Hassan considered the scheme not worth discussing. As far as he knew there was only one way from Kerman to Meshed—east to Zahedan and then north on the main mountain road that runs along the desert's edge, parallel with the borders of Afghanistan. When I continued, rather feebly, to explain that I knew nothing about deserts and therefore wanted to find out, that there might be something of interest in a desert, Hassan cut me short with a long and searching glance before withdrawing from the conversation altogether, turning away to brood over his *kalian*. Ibrahim was scarcely more encouraging, and refused to take me seriously.

'What is there to see in a desert?' His eyebrows arched with amusement. 'No mosques, no tea-houses, no people ...' He searched about for an appropriate definition; 'Just nothing—*nothing*!'

But it was exactly this nothingness that interested me. Nothing? What was it, how did it feel? There must be something besides this strange negation, something positive. The doubt and the question, however absurd, remained and had to be answered.

It was easy to find a more adequate reason for planning this embarkation across the Lut. Nearly a fifth of Persia is barren desert. To travel in Persia and fail to sample a desert would be inexcusable. It was not the first time that the scheme had met with opposition. Friends in Tehran had tried to discourage us with blood-freezing descriptions of the hidden salt quicksands, had cited numerous cases of men, camels, even trucks being sucked down into their horrible depths, recounted stories of whole caravans setting out never to arrive, vanishing mysteriously, without trace. And if we broke down? Did we know how long a man can live without water, in a desert?

There were also hints implied in these dreadful warnings of non-terrestrial hazards, vague references to forces at work in those desolate regions that were neither human nor natural; malevolent spirits, *djinns*, ghosts ... Even Ibrahim had mentioned the *djinns*—until he had seen my interest aroused—and then had laughed it all off; of course *he* didn't believe these superstitions. It is a sad comment on human nature that all these objections, these kindly warnings, should have an effect so different from what had been intended. Deserts began to take on an unreal significance in our eyes; the crossing of the Lut loomed large as a momentous and inevitable episode in our journey.

So it was that at Shiraz we visited the petrol station and bought 100 gallons of petrol. The greater part was in 4-gallon cans which we packed, to the great interest of the petrol-station staff, in the back of the Land-Rover. As usual there was some difficulty about the price, and it was nearly half an hour before the manager was convinced that we were quite familiar with the true price of Iranian petrol, and for that reason were determined against paying at any higher arbitrary rate. His last and pathetic attempt to gain an extra commission—amounting to a considerable sum on a sale of that magnitude—consisted in taking us to view his petrol station from a short distance in order, perhaps, that our hearts might be melted at so inspiring a sight. The building had been repainted. 'So beautiful,' he said. But we remained firm.

Looking back on this transaction I have often wondered why we had to burden ourselves with so many of these frightful tins. Although it was only 200 miles to Kerman, the route was not clearly marked on the map, and there might be difficulties. At the same time our supply could easily have been bought at Kerman, when it was needed for the crossing of the Lut. The real reason was that we feared, and quite correctly as it turned out, that there were problems involved in the transportation of large numbers of these frail tins across rough country, and it would be well to experiment before the real need arose.

A kind and helpful Persian directed us out of Shiraz. It was almost dark when we left, following closely behind his car as he led the way through the labyrinth of back streets out towards the east. When we were clearly on the road, he stopped and we shook hands gratefully. 'A good journey, and *Khoda hafiz*!' The fact that, as we discovered the next day, he had put us on to the wrong road in no way lessened the warmth with which we regarded him. That he had gone so far out of his way to try and help was enough.

The truth was that both of us were feeling a little chastened after the experiences of the last week. That incident at Yezd, for example. Not that either of us referred to it much, except in terms of farcical comedy. However hard I tried to brush it from my mind I had to admit that it had left a most unpleasant impression. After all, it is not everyone who is driven out of a city with stones and execrations, and however deeply one broods on such subjects as 'ignorant stupidity', 'superstition', 'fanatical intolerance', 'officiousness', one is left still with a sense of dissatisfaction, a nebulous something that remains unsaid.

Of course we were right! What else could we have done? I have always been especially successful at explaining away things not quite to my liking. A neat logical process, clear reasoning applied from a position of calm detachment. This can achieve much, but not everything is equally easy; and unless I am very careful a small suspicion, wedged in here and there when I am off my guard, brings me right back again to this intangible feeling of ill-ease. I suppose I must make the feeble confession that it worries me when I am disliked. The attitude of 'rugged individualism', 'Take me as I am, or not at all: I don't care (much)' is all very well, and I suppose it satisfies one's aggressive instincts. It is an outlook permissible enough in your own country where you can assume an equality in your own right; though I begin to think it is an attitude more defensive than aggressive, and, except in the strongest of us, a pose rather than a deep conviction. Abroad, particularly in a country as distant and foreign in every respect as Persia, this attitude becomes less and less defensible, even useless; it defeats the entire purpose, if there is a purpose, of the journey.

I believe I understand why those citizens of Yezd objected so strongly to our photographing their mosque. I understand even better the feelings of the crowd grumbling with hostility packed round the car. Even the incendiary with the blow-lamp, should he have succeeded in carrying out his intentions of making a bonfire of the car, well, at least he had his reasons, however dubious they might appear to his victims. Yet I should like to feel that when from the burnt wreckage our charred corpses were at last dragged forth, at least through a few of those who had taken part there might have passed, if only momentarily, a pang of regret. But all this is irrelevant; equally beside the point the question of who was 'in the right'. (This right and wrong—black and white so neatly defined; orientals have always been more diffident in their pronouncement on such absolutes.) What remains is that the incident of Yezd was a demonstration of a profound misunderstanding, a symbolic clash, you might say, between two continents. For the traveller there is only one conclusion; unless he is prepared to take the consequences he must accept what he finds; or stay at home.

To those who find here confirmation of the belief that 'East is East and West is West and never the twain shall meet', I can only say that I consider the Stoning of Yezd a warning, a pointer rather than an irrevocable verdict; and I recall with pleasure the innumerable instances of hospitality and kindness met with elsewhere in Persia, in the towns or villages, or on the roads; meetings and conversations with Persians in which I discovered that the differences were less and the understanding easier and closer than I had thought possible. To the criticism, 'Anyone can meet and talk together, but what about *depth*, how real is this so-called understanding?' it is difficult to reply with certainty. I have found increasingly with a great many of my own country-men that this alleged communion of sympathy and understanding, whose existence one would automatically assume, simply does not exist. I have on occasions found myself as much at sea, equally at cross-purposes, in a London pub or restaurant as in a tea-house in Isfahan; which leads me to believe that these differences between human beings, in their more important aspect, are largely a question of personality, and not of race or creed.

Eleven miles out of Shiraz the headlights picked out a lorry, and four men waving their arms in distress. They were out of petrol and had been waiting in the middle of that desolate plain for more than four hours. As petrol was the one commodity with which we were well stocked, their difficulties were over. By the mouth of one brave man—he must have been the driver—two gallons were siphoned between the two tanks. The others stood shivering in thin coats, watching the operation, at first it seemed with indifference, then gradually brightening as the vision of warm beds in Shiraz floated realistically before their eyes. I think they had given up hope, and had resigned themselves to a night in the open. I was surprised, considering the short distance, that one of them had not walked off for relief. They would all have been in Shiraz by now, and with the lorry.

Perhaps cold had something to do with it. The October nights, though chilly, were hardly cold by European standards, but here they were, huddling round the front of the car, warming their hands on the headlights, their breath hissing between clenched teeth. There was an almost comic expression of misery on their drawn faces. But Persians, especially in the south, hate the cold as something basically alien and hostile to everything in their temperament; a force hardly worth fighting against, only to be endured. And in this I can sympathise wholeheartedly. If one is leading a physically active life then I suppose a certain amount of cold can be useful. 'How *bracing*!' people are apt to say brightly, though it is a phrase I seldom find occasion to use. For those who are not accustomed to low temperatures or who have been intended by nature to live under the tall rays of the sun, there is no enemy more dreadful than the cold. Not only does it paralyse the body, burning up every energy in the exhausting struggle to keep warm, but it also seizes-up, stupefies the mind. It becomes impossible to relax, to think—or in the full meaning of the word—to live.

It is interesting to notice in countries like Persia and Turkey, where there is a long and blazing summer followed by a winter short but equally extreme, how life is pivoted and centred upon the hot months of the year, while the cold are ignored. I have been in southern Persia in February, towards the end of the winter, and have been amazed at the lack of preparations for this short but hideous season. Few additional clothes, no fireplaces, inefficient stoves—and the people in agony, but quite apathetic, their faces showing a sort of dumb surprise at this monstrous and incredible turn of events; and in Turkey, on the shores of Lake Van, I have seen children blue with cold, barefoot and in cotton petticoats, scampering in the snow.

Poverty will explain much, but not everything. I believe that this is largely a kind of mental lapse, a blind spot that afflicts those who live in certain geographical spheres. Just as, I am told, in northern Siberia, where the winter is long but the summer extremely hot, people have been found dead of heat stroke simply because it has not occurred to them to remove more than three layers of their winter furs (still leaving two), so conversely it is the same with Persia and the rest.

Anyone will tell you Persia is a hot country, and for the Persian this is a double truth, almost a slogan. His life and mind is directed entirely towards the long burning summer months; houses, food, dress, habits—everything is designed for coolness, shade from the sun. The onslaught of winter is a shock that finds him utterly unprepared. Incapacitated by the cold, discouraged from constructive action, as anyone might be, by driving rain and snow, knife-like blasts of wind across the plateau, he is unable even to think clearly. By the return of summer the memory of winter is sloughed off like a half-forgotten nightmare. And who can convince himself then of the bitter reality of ice and snow when the temperature is over 100° in the shade and the dust-devils curl in the plain, when stones are too hot to touch?

The driver spat out a mouthful of petrol. With some misgiving I watched him light a cigarette to take the taste away, half expecting flames to shoot out from between his teeth. Everyone shook hands in turn, and then they crowded into the cab. Even before the engine had been wound up and started, one of them began to sing.

Rifles and Tea-cups

I woke with the early sunlight warm on my face. We had slept in the middle of a vast lemon-coloured plain as empty as the smooth blue sky, but for a pair of eagles hovering high above the sun. Two little boys arrived as if from nowhere and watched us intently from a cautious distance. The youngest, who must have been about four years old, was almost completely hidden inside a grey patched nightshirt that came down to his bare toes. They held each other's hands tightly, almost fearfully as if for protection, and when I waved they stepped back involuntarily, about to run. I fed them on peppermints and they stood quite silent and motionless, their bulging mouths slowly working, gazing at me out of large brown unblinking eyes. When we began to dress, the boys turned and walked off slowly, still hand in hand, to the polite distance of a hundred yards. It was time to go. The shadows of the two eagles passed like clouds over the yellow grass.

The white road wound between bare hills, climbed a pass, dropped wriggling to the next bare level, straightened out to vanish in the direction of the next blue haze of hills, like a hesitant snake now certain of its destination. Crenellated and loop-holed brown towers, Beau Geste block-houses under the limp Persian flag commanded the hill-tops. Police posts. Once we passed quite near one, overlooking the road.

Four blue-coated policemen sat cross-legged on a bench outside, sipping tea from white china cups that flashed in the sunlight. Their rifles leaned up against the wall behind. Four pairs of eyes, trained over the tea-cups, followed us round as we accelerated out of sight. Why these bristling outposts mounting the hills, surrounded by desperately armed police? We shot past a sentry-box where I glimpsed an officer slumped cosily asleep. But he wasn't. As we rattled by the figure sprang to life. I looked back, craning my head out of the window, and withdrew it immediately. He was dancing in the middle of the road, half obscured by the dust, brandishing his rifle. Mercifully a shoulder of rock cut off further possible contact. Could he have meant *us*? I brooded on the dangers of jolting armed men too suddenly from their dreams.

The province of Fars has never had a very law-abiding

reputation: too few towns separated by too many barren mountains. Of course if a foreigner should ask an official in Tehran about the existence of bandits in Persia he will be met at first with an expression of incredulous surprise. In Iran, *bandits*? Pressed more firmly, he might learn, as a sort of airy confession, that 'isolated' incidents have occurred in the past. Beyond this, information is hard to get. I suppose it is patriotic to deny the existence of desperadoes roaming one's country's hills, however remote; and it may display an admirable sense of civic morality to be so ashamed of these black sheep and play down their achievements. Everyone knows that there are outlaws in certain mountainous districts; that they are becoming scarcer year by year is also true. Those incidents that do occur, however, are hushed up and hidden away, particularly from foreigners. I believe it is all part and parcel of that indefinable sense of national inferiority which I feel exists in relation to the tribal problem. If nomads are out of date, bandits are even more so. A progressive Persian government who secretly shudders at the thought of the twice-yearly migrations, must regard the activities of brigands within the national confines with even greater horror. Bearing in mind the income, mostly in the name of progress and civilisation, that it receives from abroad, the government must feel it politic to stow away out of sight the ugly evidence of anything that would suggest its efforts to keep up with western standards were unsuccessful. (Though I cannot see that banditry in remote districts is any more shameful than gangsterism in the heart of cities.)

The real nightmare for the government is the fear that foreigners might come to be harmed. There is the unpleasant case of the four Americans robbed and murdered in south-east Persia in the spring of 1957. It is easy to visualize the storm bursting out around the Peacock Throne, the indignant and weighty protest delivered by the offended ambassador. . . That this should happen to Americans, of all people!. . . . The telegrams of ire that descended upon the unhappy governor in whose province the outrage was committed, the galvanizing of every force to expunge for ever those responsible for the atrocity. . . And so, with the aid of troops, the bandits are eventually caught and executed. Vengeance is done.

A terrible lesson for their kind! Kill your fellow countrymen (though be reasonable; not too many at a time), *but beware of touching a foreigner.* Fortunately foreigners are very rarely molested; so rarely as to be altogether remarkable, considering how wealthy they must always look. And as this is true for almost every country I can think of, I can only conclude that the lesson and the principle have been well learned. From the peaks of Pindus to the valleys of the Taurus, from Makran to the canyons of the Hindu Kush—how often has the young bandit risen eagerly from his ambush, his finger joyfully caressing the worn tooth of an obsolete trigger, only to be restrained by the sad and sober hand of his experienced sire: 'Not this one, my son!' while you or I have passed on below, brightly and unaware, admiring the splendid scenery?

Descending into a valley, the car turned a sharp corner and nearly collided with a posse of rifle-strung policemen, their blue coats white with dust, wearily wheeling their bicycles up the hill.

About midday we stopped at a solitary tea-house, a windowless cube of clay hardly distinguishable from the mountain-side. I stepped gratefully into the cool interior, scattering chickens at the threshold. The broad ledges around the walls were whitewashed and covered with matting, and we sat for some time motionless and unthinking, drowsily watching the flies dart back and forth across the glaring yellow parallelogram of the open doorway. In the back room a girl was dropping onions on the floor; an old woman tended a black cauldron as big as a giant's bowler hat that steamed and spat over the brick stove. Tea would suffice for the moment; the contents of that pot were no secret. I had looked; a chicken. There was all the time in the world to wait, and eat it.

Our host tucked in his shirt in our honour and set out four little stools before us: after rummaging in a wooden box he produced with unconcealed pride the largest spoon I have ever seen, and a vicious two-pronged fork. These he laid reverently on the stools. There was one other occupant of the room, hardly visible so deeply was he wrapped in the corner shadows; only the tell-tale bubble of the *kalian* set between his knees betrayed the old man. A rustle of rats above the smoke-blackened rafters; no one spoke—except the old woman and her remarks were for the chicken's ears alone. The meal that followed might have been quite perfect had it not been for the appearance of a boy who poked his head in at the door, beckoning us outside. He pointed to a dark stain spreading in the dust beneath the back of the car. Some of the petrol cans were already leaking.

I had read of the salt lakes of the south, but never could imagine them successfully. My first sight of one later that afternoon, through a gap in the hills, was unforgettable. It seemed that we had been magically transported to the edge of the polar seas. A dozen miles of level whiteness, smooth and brilliant as ice, stretched across the valley to the far blue hills. At every step upon the hard glaring surface the thin crust broke, my feet sinking into the black mud underneath. In the evening we descended to the edge of another and even greater inland salt sea, more beautiful in the sunset. A central sheet of water, smooth as glass in the windless valley, mirrored the pink-and-purple slopes of the eastern mountains.

It was almost dark when we entered Niriz to buy eggs and cigarettes. Inevitably a policeman attached himself to us as we made quick purchases at the bazaar gate. In spite of remonstrances to the effect that we were neither spies nor foreign agents, but only the most harmless of tourists, our passports were stubbornly demanded. When actually faced with them the policeman found himself unable to read the European characters, and so together we drove in despair to the police station. We were left in the charge of a young officer while a messenger was sent to fetch the captain.

An *otaq* was offered; we must stay the night. It was too much. I regret to say that we practised a gross deception on our intended hosts. On the pretext of a fault in the engine, David started the motor. The officer, a pleasant enough young man, searched his pockets for a box of matches to light his cigarette. Sensing the opportunity I also pretended to be out of matches. With a trust-ing smile the young officer disappeared indoors. Perhaps we were his first prisoners. I fear that the childlike faith displayed on this occasion will never be repeated. Probably in that one moment of his career a whole life outlook was refashioned; illusions of human dignity and truth for ever exposed; an embittered official was to remain. And we, to our shame, must be held the sole agents of this degradation. As soon as he had stepped indoors we drove off smartly into the darkness; cunningly avoiding the Kerman road, we followed an indistinct track high into the hills.

The place eventually chosen to stop in and sleep was not of the sort to encourage remorse. Close by a grove of giant olive trees a fast-flowing stream rushed bubbling over pebbles. Moonlight flashed on the water, and the olive trees shook out their leaves in cascades of silver in the faint breaths of cool air fleeing down the valley. Cicadas sang a litany to this natural perfection, marred only by an all-pervasive odour of spilt petrol that rose like an avenging angel from the broken cans, impregnating for ever each corner of the vehicle, all our possessions, setting a seal for all time upon cups and cutlery, clothes, books, bedding and food.

The following afternoon found us with only a few hours driving for that day. The morning had been spent in re-arranging the petrol, scrubbing the inside of the car and lying luxuriously in the running water. Our sole visitor, a woman on a donkey, quickened her pace as she passed, hiding her face in horror under a black shawl. Near sunset we debouched from a valley, over-taking the long shadows of hills upon the golden plain. Resting on a hillock above the track we surveyed the plateau. We were hungry; there was no food left; and it had been thought unwise in the circumstances to venture again into Niriz. Over to the east blue spirals of smoke ascended from the close-packed roofs of a little mud-walled village. The map gave it a name: Quatru. We set off bouncing along the dusty path through a sea of long grass.

Deserts

The ground was in shadow, only the tips of the tall blades shone gold in the failing sun.

We parked not far from the village walls and walked towards the gateway, where a few men stood or sat about smoking and talking. The children stopped their capering in the dust and stood up to observe us with serious eyes as we passed, nodding their heads in a chorus of 'Salaam; Salaam'. The men before the plain brick arch rose to greet us, and one of them stepped forward. *Salaam aleikum!* We broached the subject of eggs, and in a moment a boy had been sent running off into the narrow lanes to buy twenty, if they could be found. The man who had first spoken to us seemed to be a person of some importance in the village; he looked not more than thirty-five. He had dark, deep-set eyes shadowed beneath the brim of a sort of brown forage cap. We stood about for a little time answering the few slow questions relating to our destination and nationality, and then the man with the forage cap bent to whisper something to the boy at his side who dashed into a nearby doorway.

Five minutes later he invited us to have *tchai* with him, and with many gestures of deferential humility led the way to his house. A barred wooden door opened upon a little courtyard surrounding a pool that still reflected the last vermilion streaks of sunset. A young plane tree grew in the corner, a few chickens quarrelled over a heap of grain by its roots. We walked along a verandah a step above the yard. In an open room on the left three women sat in a row working over a large loom. They glanced up quickly as we passed, and the youngest tightened the shawl about her face. Our host ushered us into what must have been the main living-room. At the open door he stepped easily out of his slippers, and we followed his example, awkwardly kneeling to untie the laces of our cumbersome shoes. It was a small room with no windows. A low hearth in the centre of the opposite wall faced the doorway. A kettle was heating on the charcoal ashes, and in the recess above it were two flowered china teapots. Two carpets filled the floor space on either side of the hearth, a strip of matting in the middle; there was no other furniture. We were directed to the places of honour, one on each side of the fire, the host squatted down on the carpet beside me, his son, a chubby youth of about seventeen, by David.

I knew there was a considerable protocol in the giving and receiving of hospitality in Persia. Unfortunately our ignorance of the language made it impossible to enter fully into the ritual of phrases and polite responses. We could only sit and look grateful, smile and mutter inaudibly phrase-book cliches like *mota-shekeram*, and *khaili-khub*—'Thank you very much' and 'very good'. Persians do not usually pay strangers the compliment of inviting them into their homes. Usually their houses are 'too poor for your kind attention', the host is 'unworthy of your condescension'. It is partly the polite code of Persian manners, but there is real feeling behind it. The privacy of a home, a few rooms about a yard, is guarded closely; the normal meeting-place is the tea-house. I so very much wanted this evening to go well, and perhaps erase or make up for the memory of Yezd. I need not have worried.

There was silence as the kettle heated on the hearth. Fresh coals were brought in by the boy and gently blown upon until they glowed with a smokeless red heat. The father produced from his pocket a bottle labelled 'Waterman's Ink' from which he carefully measured tea, by way of his palm, into the teapot.

The news that two strangers were being entertained in the village must have travelled quickly, for several voices could be heard in argument at the courtyard door, with a woman's—one of those, I guessed, working at the loom—raised high in protest. Eventually two men, followed almost immediately by another, tramped along the verandah and rather sheepishly poked their heads in through the doorway. They were welcomed a little impatiently, and places pointed for them on the carpet; but I felt that in spite of the mild annoyance our host considered himself bound to display at this mass intrusion, he was not altogether averse to showing off his peculiar guests to his friends. We exchanged solemn greetings with the newcomers, who sat down diffidently, shoulder to shoulder on the rug.

The tea was ready. Two little glasses and saucers on a brass tray were handed in through the door, and a bowl of freshly cut sugar lumps was brought out from a corner. There were no spoons. I was glad that at least I had learnt the trick of popping the sugar straight into my mouth and sipping the tea through, and so avoiding the embarrassment of being unable to reach the sugar once it was at the bottom of the glass.

With some concern I observed the entry of another visitor, a burly police sergeant, who filled the doorway with his massive shoulders and broad smile. I was glad to see him leave his gun belt with his shoes at the door. It became clear as he sank puffing and gurgling on the carpet that he was here in a personal, non-official capacity; and surely it would be a gross abuse of hospitality to arrest his friend's guests at the hearth which he was himself sharing. I was reassured by the genial if somewhat glassy smile that seemed a constant fixture on his well-fed countenance. He must have found the tight-fitting collar of his blue uniform too uncomfortable in this warm weather; he had had the courage and presence of mind to rid himself of the nuisance by simply cutting it off!

The glasses were filled and handed ceremoniously one to each of us. Three rounds were pressed upon me in quick succession; and as there were only two glasses I realised that unless we insisted on a refusal no one else would have a chance to drink. The sergeant was served next, the others followed in turn, finally the son and our host, who was crouched over the glowing coals busily replenishing the glasses, deftly washing out each one with a little scalding water from the kettle, swilling it round and pouring it away into a large brass bowl.

The hot tea was breaking down everyone's reserve and we were flooded with questions often easier to understand than to answer; but our Persian was improving, and the elaborate pantomime employed to clarify each sentence added to the conversation the entertainment of an amateur circus. 'Do you like Persia? Who is more beautiful, Queen Soraya or Queen Elizabeth? Didn't you find that Persians are much nicer than Turks? What are you doing in Persia, anyway? Don't go to Kerman, they'll rob you there'—and from the policeman a quick rider—'If it weren't for me they'd rob you here!' (Hoots of laughter; the joke seemed much appreciated.) The teapot was refilled and filled again, the glasses flew round; the party was turning out a success. From time to time dark faces filled the doorway, eager to join in, only to be waved imperiously away; there were no seats left; a full house. David and the son exchanged names by means of a phonetic script on a piece of paper: Mansura Habibi. His father's name was Achmet.

It was very dark in the room, lit only by the heat of coals blown red in the hearth. I looked round the circle of faces, eyes gleaming from shadowed sockets, the features clear and deep in the bold contrast of light and shadow; the bulky sergeant, balding and bright-eyed, his red face shining with sweat and good nature; his neighbour in red-striped pyjamas and a tattered ski-ing cap, twitching the little moustache under his thin pointed nose; the son, Mansura, chubby-faced and eager, in a long blue patterned coat and dirty skull-cap set on the back of his close-cropped head; the gentleman with the brown trilby balanced on his shock of black hair, whose hands would never stay still; and his friend, with a hint of Mongol in his cornered eyes and flat nose, who burst into loud laughter whenever anyone spoke. . . The glow of cigarette ends; fourteen bare, horny feet crossed upon the deep blue and crimson of the carpet. I was amazed at the transformation; so dull and unintelligent had their faces seemed at first, and now so full of life, with rapid expressions overtaking each other as they talked and laughed and listened, as if we had all become quite drunk on warmth and pleasure and tea.

It was time to bring in the lamp. Achmet called out for it, and a brand new pressure-lantern was brought in by a bent and wrinkled old woman and was placed amid a murmur of admiration in the centre of the room. Achmet set to with the pumping of it and in a moment and with an alarming hiss the room was ablaze with light. Mansura pointed out to David the mark on the chromium plate: *Made in Canada*. 'Where is Canada?'

For the first time I noticed a pile of blankets in the corner, which the old woman was gently shaking. There was a silence as a little boy about five years old crawled out and was set down tenderly within his father's arm. He blinked his red dull eyes in the strong light and began to sob almost soundlessly, his little body convulsed every few seconds by a terrible hoarse coughing. His father looked at us helplessly. He had been like this for a fortnight, and was getting worse. Had he seen a doctor? Achmet glanced at me with surprise. I went out to the car and returned with a tin of Ovaltine tablets. 'Two every day,' I said. The tin was examined respectfully as it was passed round the circle. Achmet promised to take the boy to see the doctor in Niriz as soon as he could. I wonder if he ever went.

We had several times risen to leave, each time only to be pressed back in our seats. We had been drinking tea now for three hours. But supper was being prepared, only wait a little! Faint but impelling cooking odours were already floating in from the courtyard, and as if these delightful smells were signals throughout the village for everyone to return to his own house, the visitors got up one by one to make their polite bows and farewells, slip on their shoes and leave. The sergeant, perhaps because he had no family of his own in Quatru, stayed with us.

Achmet started the tea round again, and refused another English cigarette; he said they made his head go round. Instead he brought out his opium pipe. Then from another of the strange receptacles which he seemed to keep about his person, this time a 'Brooklax' tin, he carefully took out something dark brown, about the size and shape of a coffee bean, which he cut in half with a razor blade.

Although opium can be taken in a number of ways and is sometimes mixed with tobacco, the usual method in Persia is through a special pipe. It consists very simply of a wooden stem, often—like the one I bought later in Istanbul—carved, and bound with silver or copper, leading to a spherical bowl sometimes made of polished black clay. There is only one opening in the pipe besides the mouthpiece; a small pin-hole in the side of the bowl. I had never smoked opium and so was glad to accept when the pipe was offered to us. When he had finished, David handed me the

Opium and a Photograph

pipe without a word. As before, Achmet worked a needle through the hole to clear it and placed half a bean on top while Mansura touched the opium with a live coal pincered in a pair of tongs. At the touch of fire the black substance dissolved, bubbling like burnt treacle. I inhaled cautiously: thick sweet smoke, heavy and smooth; like smoking toffee. A decidedly pleasant taste. In less than two minutes the bean was finished. We looked at each other carefully and waited for a possible reaction. Nothing . . .

Achmet confessed sadly that he was a confirmed addict; his son agreed—and it was very expensive. Although Achmet seemed quite sorry about it all it was clear he had no intention of stopping, or even trying to stop. The fact that he could not do without the drug he accepted philosophically. It was the will of God; too late to change now. Besides, he had learnt to look on the bright side of the matter. Everything had its compensations, and obviously he enjoyed his opium immensely. As to the deterioration of his health—would it not be asking too much of life to insist on the pleasures of opium *and* on good health? Achmet had made his choice, many years before.

The question of ill-effects from opium smoking was of great interest to both father and son. Mansura went to a wooden box in the corner and returned with a creased photograph of his father taken five or six years ago. The contrast which was immediately apparent was not only one of dress and grooming. The celluloid reproduction presented a young Achmet in a new suit and silk tie, his thick glossy hair precisely parted. The Achmet before us stooped inside a brown woollen coat and torn soiled shirt, and his hair was lank and unbrushed. Advertisers for modern dandruff lotions would have paid enormous sums to possess the contrasting negatives. But this was of incidental interest; the real point of comparison lay in the face. The photograph gave an impression of vigour and sensitivity, a full face and shining eyes. Now the eyes were sunken and dull, the mouth not so firm, the whole face was very much thinner. Six years had certainly left their mark.

I have never really understood why that photograph was produced for our inspection. Was it that, having seen us take our first opium with such evident enjoyment, they wished to discourage us from further experiments by means of this dreadful warning? It was somehow unconvincing. Or were they both uncertain themselves and wished us to corroborate, or preferably deny, the possibility of opium working such havoc?

This also seemed unlikely, for the habit of opium smoking is a common one both in villages and towns throughout Persia— so much so that it has become a national problem. In 1955 it was calculated that 2,800,000 Persians were addicts. The following year the government passed a bill prohibiting the cultivation and sale of opium and over a thousand opium dens were closed down in Tehran alone. It will be a long time before such an ingrained habit is destroyed, though the practice is hardly a century old. Originally it was intended for the European market, and has always been a government monopoly; but the poor soil of most of Persia is peculiarly suited to the cultivation of the poppies, and the crop requires little attention. Opium offers an escape from the tedious routine of poor people's lives, and is often a valuable anaesthetic, used to dull the pains of illness and old age where medical attention is rare. The police sergeant patted Achmet sympathetically on the back. Supper was ready.

A white plastic cloth was spread on the carpet and layers of bread placed at each corner. Mansura appeared bearing a huge round copper tray heaped with rice which he laid down in the centre, and bowls of steaming roast meat and onions were arranged by its side. He withdrew to sit by the door as the four of us gathered around. Eating is a serious business, and no one spoke. When all was finished we stepped on to the verandah where Mansura poured water over our hands and returned to more tea in our original positions by the hearth. It was getting late and everyone was very drowsy. In spite of protestations from our host who offered us the room to sleep in, we insisted on leaving. Achmet led the way with a lamp to unbolt the door of the courtyard. The whole village was blacked out, asleep. I saw them as we drove away, the pair of them by the village walls, the sad-eyed Achmet with one hand raised in farewell, swinging the lantern, the bulky sergeant grinning sleepily over his shoulder. He could hardly keep his eyes open. We drove on silently in the brilliant moonlight, and stopped upon an expanse of hard, cracked mud; and slept, disappointingly enough, without a dream.

It was another two days before we reached Kerman. The track deteriorated until in places it was impossible to travel much above walking pace. Various unspeakable faults began to develop in the car, essential mechanical accessories, such as the silencer, fell off, to be retrieved and tied on again with rope and wire. There was no shade. We collected brushwood to cook a meal and sat gasping among burning dunes too hot to touch with bare feet, sifting through our fingers the grains of glass and crystal that sparkled from the sand. There was a diversion in the cautious pursuit of a long black-and-yellow snake that fled among the stones; earlier that morning a strange animal had leapt across the path. It looked to me like a cross between an alsatian and a hippopotamus, but David, oddly enough, thought it might be a Persian fox. I was fascinated by the crimson bushes, juicy and full of liquid, that flourished in this arid wilderness; to part the soft buds and gaze upon the jade-green depths within produced in me a sensation of hypnotic cool. By afternoon the half-ruined villages on the outskirts of Sirjan came into view upon the plain.

Saidabad the town was called when Tamerlane's army pitched tent about the walls, and a rich and important centre it must have been to deserve a siege lasting two years. We crossed the level plain where the horn-helmeted cavalry of the King of Samarkand had circled and waited with such deadly patience. The siege and holocaust of destruction at its fall were the end of Saidabad. The plain was littered with ruins, towers and walls reduced by centuries of rain to shapeless mounds of mud. The innovation of tarmac and flowered pool, so successful at Nain, had failed at Sirjan; the tradition of decay was too strong. The pond was yellow with mud, the desiccated plants around it wilted brown and dead in the dry earth. Parched trees, their leaves lifeless and caked with dust lined the broad half-deserted streets; even the frail buildings which could only have been lately erected seemed already on the point of collapse.

This unpleasant impression of the town was perhaps aggravated by a period of several hours duration in which we were forced to wait in the courtyard of the police station, suffering a monotonous inquisition on the subject of our passports. A young captain, with a moustache and bulging cheeks, remarkable for possessing some knowledge of events outside his own country, as well as for his unusually scruffy uniform, stood over us in a malicious attempt to prove we didn't know who we were.

'Which way you come into Persia?'

'By Turkey.'

'Aha! Then why you have no Turkey visas?'

'But the British don't need visas for Turkey, and anyway, what has that got to do——'

'*Everybody* need Turkey visas; me, him, and *you too!*'

It seemed it was just another wicked example of British imperialism. A number of other policemen lounging in buttonless shabby tunics and down-at-heel boots, gathered round sympathetically to pass the time with us as a clerk copied out the details of our age, parentage, place of birth and birthmarks in a laborious but beautiful long-hand. Further official demands for details of our past life were invented I regret to say on the spur of the moment. David claimed to be a cabinet minister in disguise, and I proudly traced my descent from a fourteenth-century Pope, speaking with nostalgia of my teak palace in the Outer Hebrides. With our patience long exhausted, we attempted a menacing and outraged attitude of imperious anger which might well have carried the day had not the impression been ruined by helpless laughter in which our good-natured persecutors were delighted to join. We left Sirjan not long before sundown, climbing into hills blushing under the small red eye of the sun. In the east the full moon was already shining, a huge disc of silver set in a wine-red cummerbund.

❀

Next morning we entered the city of Kerman, a brown mass
of buildings dwarfed at the bottom of a towering 12,000-feet-
high range of barren mountains, the only barrier separating us
from the Lut. I had written to England weeks before from Isfahan
for a set of War Office maps that would include the Dasht-i-Lut,
as our own dear Bartholomew was very vague on this area. But
at the post office there were letters, but no maps. Leaving the car
at a garage, where mechanics armed with hammers and blow-
lamps set about the repairs with ferocious energy, we set off in
search of Persian maps. A small but enthusiastic group of schoolboys followed and led us through the bazaar on this hopeless
quest, besieging us with questions as we walked.

'Sir, our teacher say we must speak to Englishmen to improve
our knowledge. You are Englishmen, sir?'

'Yes, we are.'

'Well, then, how you pronounce "egg"?'

'Egg.'

'Egg?'

'Egg is quite correct.'

'Ah, thank you, sir! Our teacher say——'

Perhaps Ibrahim was right about Persian school-teachers after
all. In return for our valuable services in the field of English
pronunciation, we managed to extract a little information on the
subject of the Lut. Besides, 'No, sir, my father say Dasht-i-Lut
bad place—you cannot go,' we learned that a village called Shahdad, on the other side of the Kerman range, was the usual point
of departure for caravans bound across the desert for Meshed.
How to reach Shahdad, however, was another matter; no one
we asked had ever been there. Somehow we would have to cross
the mountains, or go round them, which would take several days.

Two maps were bought, on a larger scale than Bartholomew,
but even less informative. We gave up in despair and instead invested in several beautiful clay water-jars with slender tapering
necks, which were packed with improvised stoppers in the back
of the Land-Rover. We left at night with a wind thick with
flying dust howling through the city, rattling the white leaves

of plane trees in the streets where men and women hurried by bent under their shawls with scarves and pieces of cloth pressed to their faces, spirals of dust and paper whirling at their feet. Out of Kerman a succession of fantastic crags reared above the road, their terrifying shapes distorted in the swirling dust-clouds that fitfully obscured the moon. Wind and dust dropped suddenly as if they had never been, leaving a mysterious stillness. Across the sand the mountains glimmered white as snow, as if challenging with a high disdain the puny violator of their slopes.

That challenge we took up at dawn. No less than three attempts were made to penetrate the range, each one ending as before at the head of some cul-de-sac between converging cliffs scalable only by mules or goats. At midday I dropped the largest of the water-pots at the edge of a stream, shattering the lovely thing into a hundred ugly fragments. A final attempt brought us some-how into the rear of a military zone where the desert was scarred with tank-tracks and littered with cartridge cases. Returning to the main road we drove out between high barbed-wire gates where two sentries smartly presented arms as we passed through. Keeping the mountains on our left we continued on with a deepening despair south-east towards Bam.

Seventy miles from Kerman a track branched left, disappearing into the mountains. With a new excitement we followed it, steadily climbing until the track breasted a pass and entered upon a long upland valley enclosed on each side by sheer rock walls grotesquely spiked and corrugated. By a miracle we had pene-trated into the centre of the range. As the early twilight shut down over the valley we descended into a gloomy canyon, travelling on the sandy bed of a dried-up river, whose steep eroded banks leaned overhead. An eerie place of weird sand-towers, crevices and caves as sinister as blind eye-sockets; an unearthly scenery spelling terror as much as beauty, where tales of demons must be believed as easily as they are told.

In the distance a high ridge barred the valley, dominated by two small forts; below, the clustered cottages of a village. If Bartholomew were right, this must be Guk. The presence of the forts seemed to imply a pass of some sort; at least there was some hope now of getting through. With binoculars I could see, faintly discernible on the ridge, the zig-zag of a track.

During the night we were disturbed by an unaccountable noise of a motor-engine, stopping and starting, not too far away. With the morning the mystery was solved. Reinforced with eggs and coffee we came almost immediately upon a scene of disaster. A bus, the weekly one from Guk, stood bogged down in mud at the edge of a stream. They had been trying to extricate it, inter-mittently, all night. An enormous load of red carpets, nearly doubling the height of the bus, was roped upon the roof. It seemed hardly credible that in the circumstances no one had con-sidered removing such a crippling weight. The passengers, men, women and several children, sat around shouting encouragement, the driver sat in his cab bringing forth periodical bursts from the engine, while his mechanic was dutifully digging a hole in the mud into which the back wheels were sinking every minute a little farther.

At the first attempt at pulling out the bus with the Land-Rover the ropes broke, and the passengers sitting by the stream let out a chorus of groans. David and I consulted together briefly. It was clear that in this instance, unless the bus were to remain in the mud for ever, it would be necessary to impose, for a short time only, the hideous principles for which our native land was notorious: discipline and the team spirit. I pray we shall be for-given. After all, it would only be for a moment, and the dismal lesson would soon be forgotten. Perhaps the dangerous memory of it would be treasured among these unsuspecting villagers, to be recalled with delight at some future date and put to some useful purpose, on a rare occasion when it might be valuable. We in-structed the driver: he was to let out the clutch, not just at any time, but when I gave the word. I persuaded the male passengers to rise reluctantly from their comfortable seats and placed them, shoulders to the bus, at strategic positions at the back and at the sides. *Not* before I give the word!

'Yek, doh, seh . . . *Yah!*' The two engines roared, the pushers gasped with the effort. With a squelch and a slither like some antediluvian monster rising for the first time from the primordial marsh, the bus heaved itself up on to dry land. The passengers were surprised and overjoyed, and expressed their gratitude with presents of grapes and shining red pomegranates.

The streets of Guk were running with water; the *quanats* had been opened. Little girls sat in the rushing water holding their petticoats high over their heads and chortling with glee, to be dragged splashing and resisting from our path. We stopped at the last shop above the village.

'Where are you going?'

Proudly: 'To Meshed, by the Dasht-i-Lut!'

'There are no *kahve-kaneh* in the Lut, no biscuits——'

We bought a packet of biscuits. Over the col the track wound gradually, descending through the mountains. We exchanged greetings with a party of *quanat* workers standing over their wheel. Soon the path disappeared into a torrent that had outlived the summer drought, bubbling and gushing through a steep gorge whose toppling cliffs scarred by landslides were separated at times by no more than fifty feet. We took turns in walking knee-deep and trouserless in the water before the car, poking with sticks to try the depth of pools and the hidden course of rapids. The wheels seldom showed above the water, and sometimes the car seemed to move forward like a ship, amphibiously. As the gorge opened out, palm trees waved feathered heads above the cliffs; a hot wind fanned our faces. A man was bathing in the stream, and at the sight of us grabbed his pantaloons and bolted, shirt tails flying, for the bank. Cruelly I raced him to the path and caught him. "Which way to Shahdad?" He pointed and fled, leaving his turban on a rock at my feet.

The hills fell back. For the first time we looked down upon the Lut. The view was similar in a way to that first sight, winding down the Khyber, of the plains of India; but while there the distant plains are dotted with trees and patched with cultivation, here there was nothing but an infinity of white waste bound for the far haze of horizon, where sky and desert merged without a sign. Salute to the Lut! I am certain that no desert has ever been greeted with such enthusiasm. We stood on the bonnet of the car, waved binoculars and shouted. Any Persian, or for that matter anyone else, who might have observed our wild caperings would have thought us mad.

At desert level a number of villages appeared scattered at the mountains' feet, each one surrounded by a forest of palm trees, welcome splashes of dark green in the arid landscape. A boy rode in delight upon our front bumper, directing us through close mud-walled streets where the car could barely pass. We drove hooting, the boy waving and singing, into the tunnelled chaos of the bazaar where shopkeepers cursed and ran to retrieve the tottering pyramids of ironware, pottery, rolls of cloth and cases that obstructed the way. In places it was so dark it was difficult to see; faces jostled and pressed back and peered in at us through the windows as we made our slow and interrupted progress under the crowded vaults. We came to rest finally in the open sunlight of a small market-place that was also the caravanserai, where many camels lay chewing thoughtfully in the shade of the palms.

We had strayed into another Persia, a Persia of the past, a past which though 'out of date' still survived, fulfilling more nearly the romantic dreams of childhood. The faces were darker here, the skin more burnt; turbans were the rule rather than the exception, and spectacular turbans at that; yellow-and-white bulbous domes, gigantic, onion-like; loose shirts and voluminous baggy trousers; brown feet bare or filling curled slippers big as canoes. Surrounded by a group of people who watched our every movement with an interest as intense as it was returned, we walked back into the bazaar to make the final purchases of eggs and bread and green water-melons.

Everyone was anxious to help, even the policeman. A young man, one of the very few dressed with any approximation to a Western style, in pin-stripe jacket buttoned over broad cotton trousers and polished black shoes, came forward and made all easy with his willing interpretation of our needs. He had a grave gentle face and spoke English with a passionate concentration,

slowly but well, in a beautiful way that only orientals can sometimes acquire.

'First,' he said, 'you must go to Naibandan. You will find bread
and water on the way. These men', and he pointed to the camel-
drivers who were already bestirring themselves in preparation for
the coming night's journey, 'these men you will see, and they
will help you find the road. They, too, go to Meshed.' There
were some pilgrims, he added, travelling with the caravan. To
travel on foot to the holy city has always been for Shias the most
glorious of pilgrimages, though nowadays a bus is held quite good
enough. Even the great Shah Abbas walked all the way to Meshed
from Isfahan, no doubt to earn himself in paradise the palaces and
pomp he already possessed on earth.

It was getting dark; the sun had dropped behind the peaks.
From somewhere a muezzin wailed the call for evening prayer,
and the camel men laid down their sacks and boxes and knelt
towards the mountains blackly outlined against the luminous
bright arc of sky. Fires burning within the circle of prostrate
camels were stamped out, the cooking-pots and carpets packed
away. With a dreadful slow rumbling in their throats the camels
were prodded to their feet, rising ponderously, one by one, sniff-
ing the cool evening breeze, and with sinuous necks outstretched,
bellowed in an agony of hopeless protest. I pressed myself back
against the warm metal of the car as the camels stepped softly past,
brushing by me so closely that their bitter odour stung my nos-
trils, while their turbaned riders in ragged silhouette swayed
silently above me, passing in procession under the black-tufted
palms. That night we slept on the edge of the Lut, wondering at
the silence, for the first time unbroken by the hum of even a single
cicada.

Dasht-i-Lut: *dasht* means 'plain' or 'desert', and *Lut*—well,
travellers and geographers have guessed that the word was the
same as 'Lot', and therefore giving the setting for the dramatic

metabolism of Lot's wife, who looked back, and was turned immediately into a pillar of salt. Much as I would have enjoyed developing this myth, a certain Englishman who became a great authority on Persia, and its historian, discovered on one of his peregrinations in the area at the turn of the century that the word *lut* was in use among a certain tribe who existed on the edge of this desert, and in their dialect the word meant nothing more spectacular than 'bare' or 'naked'. So 'the naked plain' it will have to be, though on that first morning, as we progressed slowly across the rough salt flats, I could not help looking perhaps more closely than was necessary at the extraordinary protuberances, pillars and towers of sand, caked with salt, that rose haphazardly from the surface of the plain. Was she a tall woman, or was she short?

The desert had become like some vast steppe, studded with black rocks, powdered with the first snows of winter, though the hot wind blowing steadily from the north was enough to destroy any such illusion. The Kerman range to the west and south was dropping out of sight, the pale-red and purple ribs of the mountains fading into the trembling horizon. Sawn-off palm trunks marked the crossing of a salt stream trickling over a glittering crust as brittle as glass. The desert changed quite suddenly, the salt finished, and we plunged into a wilderness of soft yellow sand and baked mud flats overhung by strange outcrops of rock and sand, cast as if by some prehistoric eruption into weird tapering turrets and crags, terraces and caves; grotesque shapes, rearing over the path, that at a distance would assume the carved likeness of hideous monsters and half-human faces. So convincing did these images appear that often I would go scrambling towards them, intensely excited that perhaps I should discover in them the hand of some long-extinct race of men, only to find even as I approached and laid my hand upon their rough brazen surfaces that the lines of regular inscription, the sculptures and statues that had seemed so certain from far away had vanished utterly as if they had never existed. Returning to the car I had only to look back to see that the figures had resumed their attitudes—the giant warrior with his fantastic helmet, the cut letters almost legible under his raised sword, and the lion's head, lop-eared and gaping mouthed, that regarded me now, I felt, with a trace of a sneer.

Persians, especially the humbler sort, whose lives for generations have been spent in constant struggle with the desert, have no doubt as to the true significance of these places. They are the cities of the *djinns*, the evil places, sinister abode of demons and lost spirits. Too many stories are told of the disappearance of entire caravans, there are too many incidents in their own experience of men returning mad with horror from wandering lost in these desolate regions, for them to attribute any but the workings of a supernatural demonic power. Of course there is thirst and exposure to account for these disasters; the quicksands and storms and general nature of the Lut, its vastness and lack of permanent landmarks, the malignant power of the midday sun which turns desert and sky into a single scorching crater. But the Persian who lives with the desert will reply that these are only the natural dangers; it is in these helpful conditions that the devils can do their work most successfully.

Nasnas, palis, ghuls, ifrits, these are the evil spirits, the armies of the *djinns* that Mohammed in the desert outside Mecca was forced to recognise and claimed in vain to have subdued. Survivals from a pre-Islamic faith, they are the servants of Ahriman, the power of darkness, pledged in eternal warfare with the angels of Ahuramazda for possession of men's souls. Beware of the *nasnas* who adopts the guise of a toothless old man, and who will greet you feebly by the river's edge and beg a lift across on your shoulders; those legs of his that look so frail will twine about your neck to strangle and drown you. The *ghul*, whom you may never see until it is too late, will call to you in the voice of a friend or relative, calling for help in some lonely place; and when you have been lured there will assume again his own monstrous shape, tearing you to pieces with his teeth. Be careful how you sleep in the desert, or the *palis*, the foot-licker, will get you. He will creep up on you as you lie, and like a vampire will fasten upon the soles of your feet, sucking your blood to the last drop. There is the story of the two muleteers of Isfahan who tricked the *palis* by lying down feet to feet, so that when the monster approached, however much he circled about, he could not discover the pair of extended soles so necessary to provide his supper; and so was compelled to retire, stalking off in considerable gloom.

It is true that neither of us were unfortunate enough to encounter any of these murderous demons on our passage through the Lut, a fact especially remarkable perhaps as we had not even taken the elementary precaution of equipping ourselves with an armoury of protective talismans, charms and amulets that sell so briskly in the stalls of every caravanserai on the edge of the desert. But there are circumstances in our case which must be taken into account. The noise of a motor-engine must have been enough to upset the most strong-minded of *djinns*, accustomed as they must be in those silent regions to sounds no louder than the tolling of a caravan bell and the thump of camels' feet plodding in the dust. No *nasnas* waited pathetically for us at the edge of the salt-stream. Perhaps he guessed that we should only have told him to seat himself on the bonnet of the car as we crossed.

We heard no voices of either friends or parents calling to us from behind some dusty pinnacle; but any intelligent *ghul* would have realised how unconvincing their cries for help would seem to us in the middle of the Lut. And at night, by tacit agreement, we slept inside the car with feet thoroughly wrapped, though possibly as much to avoid the cold as to escape the rasping tongue of any prowling *palis*.

The wind had failed. Heat fell on the desert like the slow rhythmic beating of a great bird's wings, soft feathers stifling every breath. The pale expanses of sand ended as abruptly as they had begun; skirting a tall escarpment, the track rose to a level where a succession of long low ridges of dark gravel rolled to the empty horizon. The pace quickened. There was nothing living, no blade of burnt grass, stalk of camel-thorn. Every few miles the path was marked by a heap of bleached bones, horrible relics of a camel left to rot where it had fallen. Until the sight of these crumbling skeletons became familiar we would stop to examine them, fingering the gleaming bones polished so white and smooth by the sand and sun. The maps had long ago ceased to be of any assistance. Occasionally, more for form's sake than for any practical reason, we would take out the compass, sagely to note that the sun still kept its proper course. But really there was no alternative; only that faint white track pointing north and north-east, ribboned across the gloomy sands, to be followed wherever it might lead.

The night came suddenly, and cold. When the moon rose, flooding the black sands with silver, I walked away exactly as I had promised myself in the tea-house at Isfahan, and stood alone in the enormous silence, listening intently. Slowly and gravely I turned, keeping my eye on the curved unbroken line where sky and desert joined, turned until I had come full circle. I waited. Nothing? For a moment, looking up, I felt as if poised between the twin circles of earth and heaven. Planets, stars, constellations wheeled in an ever-gathering motion, gyrating in a tumultuous whirl of light until I could hear the thunder of their passage through the sky, like drums beating at the walls of my brain. In a desert a man feels very small. Most Persian scenery has this effect, but in a desert there can be no illusions. There are no mountains which he can pretend hide other people; what there is to be seen, he can see, the world is bare, empty. Except for the sun, or the stars, he is quite alone. Deserts are known to produce madmen or prophets, and I don't know which is the more dangerous. The madman has been beaten by the enormity of it all; but the prophet has survived; for I think the trouble lies in his being in a desert too long, for then the smallness-feeling may wear off, and instead he begins to feel very big indeed. We were not long enough in the Lut to experience more than the first part.

By afternoon of the following day we found we had travelled two hundred miles from Shahdad. It was odd, and a little disturbing, that not one of the oasis-villages marked so confidently on the maps had appeared. Although none of the maps agreed on their exact positions, I felt we had a right to presume that the track would pass through at least one of these villages. Tabasin, Bala Hauz, Dilaram—where were they? A solitary mountain far to the west rose above the skyline and dropped out of sight as we continued. We guessed it was the 9,800-feet peak over Naibandan. Clearly we had taken a slightly different route.

"You will find bread and water on the way. These men . . ." Once we paused to wait while a long train of about forty camels came up the path, bells sounding as they passed with slow swing of neck and knee. We exchanged cigarettes with the drivers, and asked them where we were going. Their replies were unintelligible, but on the mention of water they waved confidently into the empty distances. We went on.

The landscape was relieved by the appearance of hills, hills that seemed to hover in mid-air. Wide lakes of calm water lay at their feet, perfectly reflecting the yellow cliffs upon their smooth shining surfaces. As we advanced the hills receded, taking their fine lakes with them. Tall trees dotted the distance. As we approached, covering the interminable miles between, they shrunk until when passed they were found to be bushes no more than a foot high. A pair of gazelle bounded across the track. We followed their swift progress until they were no more than dark specks flying in the desert. Are gazelle deceived by mirages, I wondered?

A bunch of brown peaks rose up in the north; after some hesitation the track made directly for them. For want of a name— and certainly none of the maps even considered the possibility of mountains in this neighbourhood—we named them, solemnly, the Gaunt-and-Carroll Mts. and set about collecting rough turquoise lumps from a dry stream-bed under the hills.

There was a hut visible on the hillside, and there we startled an unkempt little man who was keeping watch over a dozen camels resting about the well-head. Bitter warm water smelling strongly of camel-urine oozed among patches of blessedly green grass. '*Ab-garm*,' the little man said, 'Hot water.' He pointed up the valley lined with tamarisks; 'Khusf, Birjand.' We had found ourselves again. Farther up the track we were welcomed by five or six raggedly-clothed troglodytes, all men, who ushered us into their rock dwellings and gave us tea. They lived in the caves for eight months in the year, mining for lead. They showed me their pick-axes and a lump of dark-veined rock that one of them produced from a sack.

We sat on evil-smelling rugs and blankets, brushing the flies off our faces, and sipped a tainted brew so plainly made from bad water that I resigned myself to the prospect of severe illness. So kind and hospitable were they, and served us with such a delicious melon, that I felt it would be a crime quite unforgivable not to drink their tea, and praise it too, even to the death. Seeing the cameras they begged to be photographed, and lined up stiffly to attention outside their caves, faces grimly composed as if they stood before a firing squad. They said goodbye with the old oriental salute—head gracefully inclined, right hand passing from the heart to lips and forehead. I turned for a last glimpse of them forlornly leaning upon their picks, for a last sight also of the Lut, before both men and desert were shut from view behind the hills. For some time we continued without a word, each intently waiting to receive from within himself the first signals of internal revolution; signals, miraculously enough, which were never made. Not far from Khusf is Birjand, where we touched the main road again. Two days later we arrived in Meshed where our interest was turned from the Lut to that antithesis of the Persian desert; the Persian carpet. For we had come to Meshed to buy carpets.

4

The Art of Bargaining:
Carpets and Bazaars

❋

The traveller returning home from his eastern wanderings with saddle-bags stuffed with curios and ornaments, pipes, carpets, silver, loot of the great bazaars from Istanbul to Benares, may greet the shops and markets of his own country with mixed feelings. At first he may be relieved at the extraordinary rapidity which once again marks every purchase, the abrupt sequence of events in which he sees what he wants, enquires the price, pays and emerges parcel in hand; all in a matter of a minute or so. When everyone, including himself, is in such a hurry, what a blessing to do these unimportant things so quickly and effortlessly! At the same time, after he has been in and out of fifty shops, exchanged curt monosyllables with fifty faceless and mechanical salesmen, he may begin to find returning to him a faint nostalgia, memories of pleasant hours spent over tea and cigarettes and small talk in shaded bazaar vaults of hot cities far away. Perhaps he will throw down the weighted parcels and string bags with disgust. He has had the money, he has paid; he has got everything he wanted. What more could he want?

Persians look at these things very differently. With them, buying and selling is an art; not an unpleasant and meaningless chore to be got through as quickly as possible, but a valuable and integral part of their life and civilisation, of their manners. To spend more than five minutes buying potatoes is indeed ridiculous, but no longer than one spends queueing in a London store. But when one's heart's desire is a piece of silver, an antique sword, or a carpet, then the quick in-and-out method is exposed as something callous and soulless, an affront to the object of acquisition and an insult to the shopkeeper, who may love the thing he sells as much as you.

In the tea-house at Isfahan I had amused both Hassan and Ibrahim with doleful tales of how at first I had been cheated wholesale by their countrymen. 'Give a Persian something to sell,' I said, 'and he will turn into a rogue.'

'Either we are rogues, or you are a fool,' countered Ibrahim gently, and left it there as if the issue were still in doubt. He drew attention to my constant visitations to Jacob in his antique shop on the other side of the Charbagh and laughingly foretold the most expensive disaster of my career, if I were not very careful.

The whole question of bargaining in Persia would not have arisen, or would not have become so important, had there not been a miscalculation on the amount of currency necessary for our journeys. Everything, food and petrol included, was so much cheaper than expected that each of us found he had a certain amount of money to spare, with the result that our baggage became gradually swollen with irrelevant but delightful oddments, pieces of this and that, from every bazaar in Persia.

In Isfahan I had developed a passion for jade; nothing spectacular, only old coins inscribed with Arabic or Kufic medallions, bits of jewellery—never more than a few shillings apiece, but each one attractive and significant in itself. Handling the rich cool pieces of stone excited my imagination to trace their passage on the old caravan routes from China. At first I had felt the business of bargaining, haggling over prices, to be thoroughly distasteful: to argue about small sums of money, I felt, was degrading. Then, in self-defence, as I came to realise how much in the long run my refusal to bargain was costing me, I began to take more interest in it all. It was evident, as I watched the complicated rigmaroles drawn out in shops and bazaars, that much skill was involved, and a natural working knowledge of psychology, in the successful completion of any of these transactions. With practice, my confidence grew. I was determined that those bitter experiences recounted in all their painful detail to the appreciative audiences in the tea-house would never be repeated. I would beat the Persians at their own game.

Jacob was a Persian Jew, a young man, neat and well dressed, who kept his shop trim and clean, ready for the American tourists on whom he lived. It was not the tourist season and so I became the whole object of his kindly attentions. In the afternoons I would drop in for the tea that was always ready, entering often as a woman, heavily veiled, scuttled out. Jacob would be putting away a piece of gold, a bracelet or an ear-ring, for it is an old custom among the poorer people in Persia for money saved to be turned into jewellery and worn by the womenfolk; and when a pressing need arose Jacob was always ready to transmute anything offered into ready cash. Sometimes I would find his aged father sitting by the door, a marvellous old man, the faithful replica of a Biblical patriarch, complete with cap, long gown and drooping white beard. But he was there only occasionally. Jacob had taken over the business, which must have profited by the plausible English he spoke and his excellent manners. Jacob and I would talk and examine together the innumerable pieces of enamel work for which Isfahan is famous, the wood inlays, Indian brass and Persian cloth, old coins, boxes and jade, and I would pick out the piece I wanted and, pretending only a passing interest, enquire the price.

'Ah, that,' Jacob might say with a warm smile, as if with my unerring good taste I had as usual unearthed the jewel of his collection. 'To you that will be only 500 rials.'

'Five hundred! A pity. I thought you were going to say fifty.'

'Oh, Mister Carroll, how can you make joke with me? We are friends? I tell you, because you are such good customer I make a reduction, for a friend. Look, 400 rials, it is yours.'

'Jacob! You know perfectly well I couldn't pay 400 for something like that. Look at it. Even if you'd said 200 I couldn't do it . . .'

And then, without a word and only a pained incredulous smile, he would put the jade away, and for the next few minutes we would chat of other things. It was an important moment, a supreme test of self-control. To have continued to show interest or concern would have been a mistake. Only hard-earned experience had taught me that the jade had not disappeared for ever. Finally I would rise to thank him for a pleasant afternoon and at the door, perhaps, he would call out: 'But the beautiful jade, you have forgotten——'

'Jade? Oh yes'—helplessly—'but the price.'

'Sir, quickly I *give* to you—my last price, 360 rials!'

A pause, as I put my head round the door: 'The most I can raise you, 240!'

A wistful agonised lift of his hands, sadly: 'No, sir, you will ruin me.'

Equally sadly, I wave goodbye. Time is on my side now. We had made progress, already the gap was narrowing. I would call again tomorrow, and I would not be the first to mention the jade. Time, and another factor, the appearance on the scene of Joseph.

I was sitting alone over my breakfast in the tea-house, warming my shoulders in the sunlight that streamed in through the dusty windows. The place was almost empty when he came in, a tall gangling figure with thin hair awry and a shabby suit that hung on him like a scarecrow. He made straight for me and bent low to my ear as if to impart some dreadful secret. 'Jade, sir—I have something to show; you want to see. Please in my shop, sir . . .' He gave me directions and, refusing tea, left as precipitately as he had entered. He seemed thoroughly ill at ease.

I responded to the invitation that afternoon and at the same time solved the mystery of his knowing me, and his strange approach. His shop was further up the Charbagh, towards the river. Although I had often walked up there, somehow I had never taken the shuttered door and cobwebbed windows of Joseph's establishment for the treasure-house it turned out to be. It seemed that for days he had been standing outside peering anxiously down the street as he watched my progress up towards him under the plane trees, noticing with despair how each time the hoped-for visit was prevented by the situation of Jacob's shop which engulfed me for so many long hours.

All was well now, the balance was put right. Joseph's shop merited more than a cursory inspection. Rows of dusty shelves and cupboards reached to the tattered ceiling, each one crammed with pottery and candlesticks and glass and curious ancient weapons. David, who had a well-indulged weakness for antique pots, spent whole hours with Joseph, sorting out the bowls with their soft glazed colours, rough beautiful designs, leaves and flowers, and sometimes animals, green deer leaping upon fields of dull blue and yellow ochre. Joseph brought out each new wonder with an air of loving triumph, placing with trembling hands the frail curved vessels that glowed in the sunlight upon the cracked glass counter, muttering praise in Persian and occasionally dropping mysterious syllables, 'Kufic', 'Safavid', 'Sassanian', greeted regularly by David's snort of knowing disbelief and glance of affected disparagement.

For two days this happy state of affairs continued. A third shop, where any desirable objects were obscured by piles of teapots, picture-frames and broken samovars, had entered the lists, the proprietors, two elderly Persians, brothers, played cards all day by the door, *kalians* bubbling at their elbows. There I had fallen in love with an ancient sword, sheathed in rough green blood-stained leather, and a pair of turquoise-inlaid book-ends. So far none of these things in any of the three shops had been paid for. We had wisely decided that it would be cheaper to buy in bulk, all or nothing. It was a powerful bargaining lever. As yet the subject of prices had been scarcely touched, each party had delicately made his own suggestion, to be smilingly brushed aside by the other. Jacob had set aside my jade and coins, our inlaid cigarette-boxes, in a special little drawer. Joseph had cleared a whole counter for David's pots, at night they were discreetly hidden by a cloth, and the two jovial brothers kept my cache in a little stack behind the door.

The Art of Bargaining: Carpets and Bazaars

But the day of reckoning was drawing inevitably closer. As the piles grew daily, so did the tension mount. The excitement seemed to have spread beyond the close confines of the antique shops. Even Ali, grinning as always as he saluted us at the hotel gate, made allusions to our prospective purchases. Ibrahim had seen the light in my eye and came with me once to inspect some of the pieces and find out what was going on, lecturing me afterwards on the vanity of earthly things. And in the tea-house I caught sly glances in my direction, interrupted smiling conversations which ceased immediately I appeared. I fancied that bets were being laid as to the amount by which we were going to be swindled.

Clearly the whole affair had grown out of all proportion; it was beginning to assume the status of an international test case, the reputation of Englishmen in Persia was at stake. 'Either we are rogues, or you are fools . . .' David and I took counsel for the forthcoming campaign.

The third evening marked the introduction of a new element in the long-drawn-out proceedings. Already it was plain that something was bound to happen soon. The attitude of indifference which everyone was at pains to affect was beginning to wear a little thin. Price-figures were bandied about with a new earnestness, with a sense of strain, an imperceptible sharpening of the conversational tone. In this highly charged atmosphere the first explosion was fired in the brothers' shop. With dramatic solemnity we were issued with the most serious warnings. Beware of those men, Joseph and Jacob! They were Jews, and of the worst sort! Our stern rebukes for this barbarous anti-semitism only increased their fervour. Joseph and Jacob were angrily denounced in the most bitter terms; the biggest rogues in Isfahan, ask anyone! The little group of bystanders who always gathered at their open door were duly asked and gave an amused consent. Everyone, except perhaps the two brothers, was enjoying himself hugely.

Heartened by the undoubted rift that was appearing in the ranks of our adversaries, we passed on to Jacob. It was as if the tidings of war had preceded us by some mysterious bazaar-telegraph. As soon as we were inside, Jacob closed the door. In a moment he had started. He dismissed the two brothers in a few terse phrases. It was unlikely that we had found anything of interest in that 'junk house'. Besides, we were intelligent and experienced, we must by now have fathomed their deceit, their sharp practice was a byword in Isfahan.

His real concern—and here he lowered his voice confidentially, almost guiltily—was Joseph. Because we were his friends, he must speak out. He could tell us a few things about Joseph, and proceeded to do so. It appeared that our friend Joseph had outdistanced every rival in the art of swindling, in his own sphere he was unique. Practically everything in his shop was a fake (glancing at me), coins especially. As for the 'antique' pottery—Jacob gave a short almost hysterical laugh and laid a protective hand on David's shoulder—did we know how Joseph had got them? He spent his mornings prowling round the rubbish heaps in the poorer quarters of the town, picking up the cracked discarded bowls and jars—he even kept a stock of the better pieces 'maturing' in the sun and rain, out in his back yard . . .

Half an hour later we were leaning across the counter in Joseph's den. In an innocent, frank manner, David taxed him with these incredible rumours. 'I have even heard (laugh) that you go round the rubbish heaps.' A spasm of rage contorted Joseph's features. He must have guessed the source of that slander. I winced as the dreadful catalogue of our friend Jacob's crimes was recounted to our astounded ears. Inlaid boxes, indeed! It was all paint—very cleverly done—but paint. And the 'jade'—we were experts, it must be obvious to us—nothing more than soap stone . . . Back in the hotel we fixed the date for the conclusion of all the deals for the following evening, steeling our wits for the inevitable, final conflict.

That memorable evening it seemed that every shop in the Charbagh stayed open an extra two hours. At eleven o'clock, when normally the great avenue was as silent and deserted as a graveyard, the lights were still blazing and people still moved laughing and talking up and down under the lamplit leaves. On our unsteady but triumphant progress from shop to shop, laden with packages and parcels, we were accompanied by a small but eager band of men and boys, as excited as we were, who at every opportunity offered unasked-for advice and opinions, attempted to mediate, or inflame the already highly flavoured and resounding disputes in which the whole avenue became involved. The spectacle of foreigners taking on their fellow countrymen on their own terms, using their wits and bargaining powers rather than simply the weight of their money, must have appealed to the Persian sense of humour, and certainly they must have enjoyed the expressions of shocked amazement on the faces of our opponents, provoked by our hardened and calculating approach.

The memories of that evening have been reduced to a single blur, like a rapid display of fireworks that blaze and vanish in the night sky. The scenes were re-enacted with variations in each separate battlefield. I remember the arguments that started pleasantly enough, the gestures, magnificent theatrical flourishes, impassioned rhetoric; faces under the bright shop lights, the simulated expressions of anguish, innocence, anger; our staged walk-outs, timed to a hair's-breadth of accuracy, the suspense before the entreaties to return. I can see the two brothers, *kalians* knocked over in the excitement, haranguing the spectators in discordant unison, too fiercely brandishing my green sword in demonstration of its deadly powers; Jacob, a world of honesty in his outstretched arms, imploring me to burn down his shop if we could prove he lied, offering his jade to the test of axe or knife; and Joseph, wounded to the heart by David's adamant refusal to pay more than a third of his price, putting all the pots away in a fury—and, when we had marched to the door, bringing them all out again.

Street lamps and the moon lit our exhausted but triumphant passage loaded with booty, back to the hotel. No one will ever know who was the real victor in that barter battle. A Persian, no doubt, would have done better, but I believe that in the circumstances we had acquitted ourselves honourably and I am convinced that the pugnacious tenacity with which the passing of every *rial* was contested, must have given those delightful antique merchants food for serious thought. Perhaps in future they will eye the brisk foreigner caught in their net with a little extra wariness. We were content, and still are, though even now in England when I visit David I cannot refrain when handling one of the shining bowls that grace his shelves from a sly reference to its 'Kufic' origin; nor will he, returning the visit, hesitate to compliment me on my fine collection of 'soapstone', or examine without a smile of heavy sarcasm the alleged bloodstain on my green Persian sword.

Hassan throughout this episode had stubbornly refused to take any interest. He should have had some sympathy for my search for jade because like many Persians he kept a piece in his pocket at the end of a cord, and in the tea-house I had often seen him take it out to finger the cool substance for a moment. I think he felt that any connection with something so artificial and shady as the 'antique' trade, designed, he considered, purely for tourists, would be lowering to his dignity. I fancy also that he saw himself at a disadvantage in any transaction opposed to the sophistication and smooth talk of a man like Jacob. In the bazaars, however, he was in his element, and gladly offered to buy a *kalian*, with all its accessories—bowl, stem and a supply of the specially ground tobacco which I was certain was unobtainable in England.

The entrance to the great bazaar of Isfahan is through the tall arch on the north side of the Maidan. The galleries above where once the musicians of Shah Abbas played so noisily are now occupied by a daylight choir of soft-voiced pigeons. The tiled recesses flanking the archway are reserved for an army of beggars who lounge in the sun sheltering from the gentle rain of pigeon-droppings. The beggars, if they can see that far, look down the whole length of the Maidan to the blue dome of the Masjid-i-Shah, before whose portal others of their comrades lie in wait. I suppose that the maimed and blind who sit there place their hopes on the generosity of the devout passing in and out of the mosque; the others, before the bazaar gate, rely for their alms on the workings of less high motives. Merchants and shoppers emerging after the conclusion of some successful deal are likely to drop a few coins into the cupped hands that beckon outside; even those who enter with high hopes of enriching themselves are tempted to ensure the support of the Almighty by a timely, previous offering. I noticed that there were many more beggars in front of the bazaar arch than before the mosque . . . but in all fairness it must be said that the positions in front of the mosque enjoy considerably less sun.

Stepping from the quiet sunlit spaces of the Maidan we were immediately engulfed in a subterranean world of darkness and noise. My eyes soon became accustomed to the dim twilight, the glare of electric bulbs above each stall, the beams of dusty sunlight that pierced the vaulted tunnels and fell like searchlights in pools of brilliant gold upon the uneven earth floor, catching the heads of men and donkeys for a moment as they passed, haloed in a brief unearthly radiance. The parts of my *kalian* were on sale separately, bowl, stem, wooden mount; all in different sections of the bazaar. We passed by the clothing stalls where gaudy ties and suits and shirts were strung up for view, the glass section, ironmongery, woodwork, basketry, a confusing thickly populated city of shops where the merchants sat enthroned in their dens above the narrow passageways loudly calling on the passers-by to stop and look and buy.

Hassan had donned his dirtiest skull-cap for the occasion, and our progress was interrupted by the salutes and exchanges from his many acquaintances. My presence was obviously not facilitating business. As Hassan complained, I looked too rich. Protestations to the contrary, my torn shirt and patched trousers, were of no avail; I just looked rich. Anyone who is not a Persian must be. So I left him discussing the flaws in a large glass *kalian* jar and made my way towards the coppersmiths' market, plotting a course through the rabbit-warren of tunnels towards the resounding clamour of their hammering.

I had come here before, early in the morning when the bazaar was unlit and almost empty, to find these craftsmen industriously at their tasks, labouring by the light of flares in the gloomy caves of their workshops. The shaven-headed little boy was still lying on his back pumping the bellows with his bare feet, his grandfather gingerly applying tongs to the bars of white-hot metal. Others who recognized me waved greetings and I stood and watched them, the sweat glittering on their arms and foreheads, beating out copper sheets, soldering brass and lead, and heating over their fires in little spoons and dishes molten metal that gleamed and ran like quicksilver. Mostly they were making samovars and kettles and cooking pots, repairing breakages, while the owners sat by them waiting patiently, refilling their tea-glasses from the trays of boys who passed up and down from the nearby bazaar tea-houses.

The word 'bazaar' or *bazar*, in common use all over the East, is by origin a Persian word, and in English it has always sounded to me peculiarly appropriate, combining half-consciously in my mind 'buzz' and 'bizarre'. In Persia the 'buzz' is all too evident; sometimes in the great bazaars of Tabriz or Isfahan one has to shout to be heard. The 'bizarre' element, however, I have often found to be entirely lacking, at least in the overwhelming majority of the goods on sale, which are usually the worst and cheapest that Western factories can produce.

Nevertheless the thronged interior of a covered bazaar offers an amazing contrast with the placid world outside, as if every Persian who strolls gently along the somnolent warm streets of his native town on entering the bazaar throws off the mask immediately to transform himself into a demon of vociferous energy. At the same time it seems that the main bazaars of Persia are gradually decreasing in size and importance, their trade moving to the modern shops opening along the new avenues and streets. Certainly at Isfahan there is nothing more depressing than to escape from the bustle and animation of the central hub and wander down these deserted avenues like a ghost returned, or, in a little town like Nain on the edge of the desert, to pass through a bazaar deserted,

The Art of Bargaining: Carpets and Bazaars

the walls and ceilings almost falling from disrepair, while the few merchants in the midst of their meagre stocks sit hopelessly and half asleep.

Tabriz, in the north-west, has still the most flourishing bazaar of the country, and the largest; there is an estimated twelve miles of these brick-vaulted tunnels crossing and recrossing each other like the intricate pattern of a maze. It was here that my first introduction to a Persian bazaar took place. We were trying on fur hats in preparation for the coming winter when Ali first made his appearance, ducking his head in and out of the discussion with little squeaks and despairing mutters. He was nothing more than a stubble-chinned old bazaar coolie who still carried the load-pads on his back and walked bent double as if he still shouldered an immense burden, and it was his intention to make our every purchase look ridiculous and ill-advised, the prices we paid seem exorbitant and the hats themselves unfitting and of poor quality, with the implication that if only we would act on Ali's advice we would be immediately led to the best and cheapest in Tabriz.

In this he was remarkably successful; our confidence, never at any time very great, was fast evaporating. Yet pride forbade the acceptance of services so brazenly thrust upon us, and we brushed him off each time, and eventually, in our irritation, ignored him utterly. It was only when we found ourselves finally lost and had almost given up hope of ever extricating ourselves from the labyrinth of tunnels that we were at last forced to turn to him for help, finding him standing patiently and expectantly at our elbow. From then on we belonged to Ali. Every morning he would meet us at the entrance and conduct our search for whatever was required, shuffling along triumphantly in the lead with the two of us following humbly but confidently at his heels. Not only was he our trusted guardian in the bazaars—and our peculiar trio became quite well known in every sector—but it was from Ali that I took my first lessons in the art of bargaining.

❈

A Tribal Rug

'If you've seen one bazaar you've seen the lot,' has sometimes been said to me. But if you are looking for something then every bazaar is new and interesting, and in Persia—and this goes without saying—we were looking for carpets. Tabriz, our first big city in Persia, was a little disappointing in this respect. The carpets were there, with design and colour enough to dazzle the eye and palpitate the heart. But at that time we knew very little, our experience of bargaining was still primitive, and the prices seemed too high—lower, of course, than anything in Europe, but if we were to acquire more than a couple each on the short funds available, then we should have to be very careful.

As we travelled south through Kurdistan we adopted a theory that it would be best to seek out the carpets in the places of their origin, in the villages where they were made, and so cut out the middle-man commissions which would have accrued by the time they were assembled in the big bazaars. After we had made enquiries, had sat longingly over expensive rugs at Kermanshah, Hamadan, Tehran and Isfahan and made abortive sallies into the countryside between, the problem began to be seen in a different light.

It became increasingly clear that it was impossible for us, foreigners without proper knowledge or contacts, to find the carpets we wanted in their original locale. Most of them are made in the tribal tents, by the women, in the winter; the rest are brought in every season on the backs of donkeys and horses to the cities and find their way into the stocks of the carpet merchants in the bazaars. At Shiraz David acquired a *gilim*, a large rough-woven tribal rug patterned with flowers, pale red, green and yellow, and nearly bought a beautiful prayer rug. But two days is not long enough to buy a good carpet at a fair price. At the same time our tastes were developing, and narrowing. The close-knotted elegance, the pastel ivory shades of Kerman appealed to neither of us. My own taste had already been formed by the Turkoman and Bokhara rugs I had been brought up with in India. I wanted something dark and rich. I loved the ox-blood pink and lilac blues, and more than these the deep velvet reds, soft plum and almost purple-black, a royal feast of sombre shades to soothe and satisfy my eyes.

'Those are the Baluchi kind; you must go to Khorassan for them, to Meshed.' We must go to Meshed and so the journey from Kerman north across the Lut had a double, a deeper purpose. In Meshed, shrine of carpet-lovers as well as pilgrims, we promised ourselves the final release from the long frustrations, the agonies of self-control which had attended our carpet-questing for so long.

The journey across the Lut desert was over, and we had reached Khorassan, land of the rising sun, as the Arabs had called it in the days when to them it was just that, the country farthest to the east that they knew of, before their armies overran it and passed to Afghanistan, and India beyond. A land of broad valleys edged with violet hills, with scattered villages where cultivation is easier and men were crouching in the fields of golden grain, swinging their scythes as we drove leisurely by. Blue is the colour of Khorassan. I had never seen such gay and colourful dresses, the women with petticoats spangled with reds and blacks under blue shawls, the men in blue waistcoats and long blue coats set off by white cotton trousers and flat turbans, white as was every donkey, decorated with blue beads, that they rode.

It was getting noticeably colder; we had come a long way north. In the mornings we seldom rose without receiving some visitor, a shepherd in long lemon-coloured fur-lined coat with his sheep surging about us, and once an old man twisting wool from a distaff in his hand. Fine wool, wool for our carpets.

Not far from Birjand, where we joined the main road travelling north to Meshed, we passed through a village where the entire population was gathered dressed in their brightest clothes around a funeral bier set in the market-place. The men and women sat round it sorrowfully, twenty deep, the grey-bearded elders in a solemn row next to the corpse laid out under a white sheet. A line of mourners passed regularly by the foot of the bier, stooping to kiss the shroud before resuming their places.

It seemed a good omen, almost an expected one, to drive through the villages on the outskirts of Meshed and see the brilliant array of rugs and silks and carpets suspended from every balcony and window in the main streets and squares.

On enquiry we found out that the carpets and flags were intended not to welcome us but to celebrate the Shah's birthday.

It was the beginning of autumn and the leaves of the chenars lining the road were already turned to reds and yellows as if cherries and lemons were sprouting together from the branches. The brown plain was bright with a piercing sunlight that gave a breathless clarity to the air. Against the clear blue sky flashed the golden domes and minarets of Meshed. We passed and nearly ran over two turbaned Persians, one of whom was teaching the other to ride a bicycle. The beginner's white flapping trousers kept catching in the spokes and his companion ran alongside shouting intructions and trying to keep a grip on the wobbling handlebars. I looked back in time to see them fall together in a puff of dust into the ditch. A further spectacle, heralding I felt a stay of some moment in the pilgrim city, was a moustachioed peasant shepherding a flock of six donkeys, each one bearing what I first thought were upright sacks of vegetables, and which turned out to be women, mute and muffled in their shawls.

In Meshed, so long accustomed to the fervour of pilgrims gathered here from every corner of the Shi'ite world to kiss the tomb of the martyred Imam Reza, the celebrations of the Shah's birthday were conducted with an especial frenzy. Flags and streamers were strung across the streets, carpets and sashes hung from open windows, and every taxi (all English cars) flew the green, white and red of the national colours. The tea-houses were usually full, and we had difficulty in finding places. Everyone was dressed in his shiniest clothes and sat happily drinking tea from out of extra-sized tumblers. Lorry loads of howling shorn-headed fanatics, waving their arms and brandishing banners, swept by in the streets outside.

The Art of Bargaining: Carpets and Bazaars

I could not help being impressed by this demonstration of loyalty to the Shah. I had heard, particularly in Isfahan, too many hints of discontent with the present regime, and I wondered how much of to-day had been staged and how much was a spontaneous outburst of affection for the royal family. Or was it mainly because it was a public holiday? At any rate, the radios blaring from every tea-house and fruit-drink shop in the city gave evidence of powerful external impulses. They were broadcasting the joyful functions in Tehran. Commentators beside themselves with passion bawled and sobbed over the loudspeakers; cheers, speeches, drums. I felt the radio in the tea-shop might burst itself apart with the noise. The oriental rhythms that are the Persians' normal musical diet had been replaced to-day by the crashing orchestras of an unidentified Beethoven symphony. The men in the tea-house sat solemn and bemused at the unaccustomed strains, loyally sipping their tea.

'There are two things for which Meshed is famous; carpets and *chelo-kebab*,' said Amin the young schoolmaster, who seemed to have scented out our hiding-place as soon as we arrived, and came to call on us at the hotel where we were settled in two pleasant rooms overlooking the garden. '*Chelo-kebab?*—You must taste and see!' We agreed to meet that evening and Amin promised to introduce us to the best restaurant in Meshed, if not in the whole of Persia.

Fortified by the promise of this future delight we went in search of a *hammam*, a bath. Persians have always set a high value on bathing: it is part of their deeply rooted appreciation of water and all its life-giving properties; and besides applying it to their crops and internally to themselves, often feel that some of the precious liquid can be spared to pour over their own bodies. They love to wash—and would do it more often, could they afford it. As long ago as 1628 Thomas Herbert had remarked on the profusion of public baths in Isfahan: 'Hummums in this city be many and beautiful; some are four-square, but most be globous ... the inside of these hot-houses are divided into many cells and concamerations, some being for delight, others for sweating in,

116

Courtyard of the *Madraseh* in Isfahan.

Autumn Migration: Tribe on the move near Kermanshah.

Kurds: A ploughman; and woman and child.

Naksh-i-Rustam; Shapur I receiving the homage of the captured Roman Emperor Valerian.
Tomb of Xerxes.

Persepolis: Bas-relief.

Persepolis: the Great King holds court.
Tribute-bearers from all the Empire.

An independent camel in the mountains south of Yezd.
Hand-loom in a Baluch village.

The bus we rescued near Guk.
Down the rapids on the way to Charbahar.

We shall leave to-morrow, *Insha'allah*.

Young and old in Baluchistan.

A street in Kerman.
Across the Elburz.

A *Mullah* at Isfahan.

all for use; for, the truth is, bathing with these people is ... no less familiar than eating and drinking.'

But *hammams* are more or less the same in any town in Persia. They advertise themselves by displaying chequered cotton towels outside the door, and this means also that they are open. We left our shoes and took the pieces of soap provided and descended into the central hall. The room was divided by painted wooden partitions into cubicles and couches and surrounded by an upstairs gallery leading off to private sleeping-rooms.

Shed of my clothes and wrapped in a piece of purple-striped cloth, I stumbled in wooden slippers down into the steaming heart of the place where muscular and sweating attendants, naked to the waist, laid violent hands on me, thrust me into pools and out, slapping, soaping, pummelling, and at length held me protesting but helpless under a selection of hot and cold showers. It seemed the fashion to make a lot of noise in the bathing-rooms; rest and relaxation came afterwards; when downstairs, business only. There was a large warm pool in the main room where a number of the citizens of Meshed were disporting themselves, splashing and ducking each other in its murky depths.

I was a sympathetic witness to a scene in which a little boy, brought in for the monthly wash-down by his father, refused to be tempted under the final cold shower. Coaxing and arguments were of no avail; he was adamant. Eventually two of the attendants were summoned and lifted him bodily, shouting and screaming, to the shower where he was able to repay his persecutors by dousing them liberally with the icy water. On the hot stone slabs round about, older and fatter men sat gasping and heaving, hoping to escape for a moment the relentless vigilance of the bath men, before being hustled off for the next treatment. However beneficial it had been I was glad when it was all over, and I was able to stagger exhausted, but many shades lighter, upstairs to the waiting couches, to lie dozing and at peace with tea and a soothing *kalian* by my side.

At the appointed hour, with mouths watering, we accompanied

Amin to the restaurant. Cherished visions of a plush restaurant of European style were quickly dispelled. It was little different from any other better-class city eating-place, though perhaps cleaner and patronized by a more prosperous looking clientele, shaved and in business suits. We waited expectantly for the *chelo-kebab*, and when it arrived composed our faces to the expressions of delight for which Amin was happily waiting. The main ingredient, as with almost every Persian dish, was rice; excellently prepared as it always is in Perisa, and decorated with saffron. Two steaks of indifferent meat came with it, and the yolk of a raw egg was broken over the whole. Tomatoes and spices were added, followed by bottles of *dugh*, a kind of sour milk which every Persian regards as an essential part of at least one meal a day. Good, but so similar to my diet of the past two months that I could not compliment and congratulate our kind host as sincerely as I would have wished. So much for *chelo-kebab;* now for the carpets——?

For the week we stayed in Meshed Amin was our constant companion. He was a thoroughly likeable person, tall and pleasant-faced, with the fine sensitive features that are typical of so many Persians. He possessed those qualities, rarely combined, of charm and sincerity. As David was destined to teach, and was naturally interested in Persian education, he was invited by Amin to the city, school where we were introduced to some of the staff and where David gave a masterly address to the pupils of Amin's English class. Ever after we were greeted with profound respect by schoolboys who passed us in the street. Amin wanted to go to England and read English Literature at a university, and talked enthusiastically of his hopes and plans, asking our advice. In the afternoons, joined by other friends of his, we would go out to visit the Firdausi memorial (a pseudo-Persepolitan place redeemed only by its fine garden), the Kusangi rocks and other parks and pleasure gardens outside the city, beautiful in the bright autumn colours.

As for carpets, Amin was the very man. He had a great friend, by name Ghani, who was once a carpet dealer, and knew everything there was to be known about carpets. Because we were friends of Amin's, and Ghani was his friend, Ghani would be sure to help. So we went one afternoon in search of him down a maze of narrow streets and knocked long and loudly at a wooden door set in a windowless clay wall. While we waited I read the inscription scribbled in chalk upon the door: 'We are such stuf as dreams are made and our little life is rounded with slep.' It seemed only natural that Ghani should be asleep, but when he at last came out rubbing his eyes and Amin told him of our quest he made a great effort to wake up and agreed to take us to the bazaar at once.

Ghani was a little man with a short moustache and cropped hair, a pair of bright beady eyes above a comic mouth. Altogether he had the look of a benevolent dormouse. Amin had to go and teach and so the three of us set off at the determined pace set by Ghani. He was anxious to learn English and knew only a few irrelevant household phrases that Amin had taught him, so the conversation, with everyone attempting the other's language, became impossible, and we were forced to resort to sign language, which of all forms of communication can be the clearest and most expressive.

At the entrance to the bazaar Ghani paused to give us a final briefing. On no account were we to say a word or give a sign, whatever the carpet produced for our inspection. For the next two hours we passed from stall to stall, reeling from an endless display of rich colourful weaves from every province of Asia: Karabagh, Bijar, Sereband, Afshari, Turkoman, Baluch, Herati, Muslavan, Bakhtiari, Yomud, Bokhara, as well as the representatives of the Persian cities we already knew, unrolled and thrown down at our feet by the score, until with senses glutted and overflowing we rested for a little, while Ghani consumed by way of a straw the pepsi-cola we had pressed on him. So far no one had said a word and no price had been asked or given; we had just looked, and the dealers had spoken to us, all the time watching Ghani warily; and afterwards, when we were out of earshot, we would tell Ghani the ones we especially craved, and he would store them in his memory.

The Art of Bargaining: Carpets and Bazaars

Ghani led the way to a comparatively deserted corner of the bazaar and, crossing an ill-lit courtyard heaped with apples and empty packing cases, rapped upon a low-arched door. After some time I heard the rattle of bolts being drawn and a little aged crab-like man in white pyjamas and a red-wool nightcap, welcomed us inside. At the door of an inner hall we followed Ghani's example and took off our shoes. I have never seen so many carpets together in one place. They hung from the walls, were stacked in rolls and piles in the corners of those two rooms and the floors were layered with them, five or six deep. A boy brought in tea, and for the next hour the three of us knelt and rubbed, stroked, scratched and minutely examined the specimens that the old man kept rolling out, until at last I gave up and was content to sit back and gaze, while Ghani with his professional eye and sure fingers judged each one of the array.

After supper both Ghani and Amin called round, and we talked prices and played an odd but enjoyable game something like 'Up Jenkins', called 'Poosh', or perhaps 'Khoosf'. It entailed the taking of sides across a table with palms turned down in front of each other; the object of the game was to discover by means of a ritual question-and-answer the whereabouts of a coin hiding under someone's fingers. It was really a matter of psychology, and Ghani won every time.

I had already been a witness to another demonstration of this admirable man's powers, and one which quite revolutionised my conception of bargaining. At the edge of the bazaar, opposite the mosque of Goharshad, where unbelievers are forbidden to enter, I had noticed a little shop with a small piece of green jade visible under the counter. Ghani asked how much it was worth to me and I told him, hesitantly, 300 rials. He marched in, and we listened and watched from the door. The shopkeeper was asking 700; clearly he had seen us outside. Ghani was offering only 150.

This time, I reflected sadly, he had overstepped himself. The dealer's voice took on a note of anger, hysteria. Ghani fished out 150 rials and laid the money on the counter, the shopkeeper shook his head scornfully. For a few moments Ghani talked angrily and then slapped down a further hundred, seized the jade and stamped furiously out of the shop. Aghast at this piece of daring we followed him into the street, the cries of the outraged shopkeeper ringing in our ears, where Ghani passed over the jade with a triumphant grin.

I discovered that Ghani knew nothing about jade; but that was of no importance; his action had been intuitive, an instinctive summing up, fruit of years of bargaining experience, from which he had calculated the lowest sum that shopkeeper would take for that object; a conclusion reached by a lightning assimilation of clues; the dealer's voice, his tone, the finest shade of responses to his own probing. No one can deny it was an impressive piece of bargaining; but not of the kind I would recommend to any foreigner, or for that matter to anyone not of Ghani's experience. I tried it myself once, months later in the spring, in a town called Zahedan. I wanted biscuits for a journey and, faced with the extortionate price insisted upon by the sneering shopkeeper, I determined to put the Ghani technique into action. I leaned across the counter and fixed the man with a piercing gaze, put down the usual sum for those biscuits, picked them up and stormed towards the door, only to find my exit barred by the shopkeeper's two stalwart grim-lipped sons. Hours later, eating those most expensive biscuits, I consoled myself with the thought that at the critical moment, confronted with those muscular doormen, my common-sense had not deserted me. I had judged the atmosphere, even as Ghani would have done, accurately.

During those days when Ghani was our guide and master in the Meshed bazaars, I learnt a little more about carpets. I learnt at least to look as if I knew something about them; to glance appreciatively at the design and workmanship of the upper side but never to omit the quick professional turnover of one of the corners, the knowing touch of the underside, calculating the number of knots to the square inch, by which all carpets are judged. I had often been disappointed to find so many carpets in Persia unexpectedly coarse in their design, dyed brightly and garishly with raw crude colours. This is a modern trend; the importation of quick aniline dyes which the government has tried in vain to prohibit, to take the place of the vegetable dyes which are difficult to mix and to apply, but which never fade or run. The contrast between the new and the old colours is striking; as clear and as disastrous as the difference between the old minia-ture paintings of India as well as Persia with their soft stone-powdered shades, and the new harsh paints with which their modern imitations are applied.

It is the same with the designs. The greatest buyers of Persian carpets are the Germans and Americans. The taste of the buyers has become all-important; more and more carpets are produced not as the Persians would have them but as the drawing-room dwellers of New York and Berlin think they should be. In the factories on the outskirts of Meshed women and children sit in line under the looms, picking and knotting the coloured wools and silks from overhead, deft fingers moving faster than the eye can see, while the overseer in a sing-song drone calls out the colours and the knots.

A good carpet takes months, sometimes a year to make; there are carpets which are the work of a lifetime. The women in the tribal tents make them in this way, unhurriedly and with care. But, as the standard of living in Asia rises, the anomaly of selling the fruit of months' work for only a few pounds will become painfully more evident. Automatic looms, the machines, will be taking over; and then, if I can ever spare the money again, I might as well go to Wilton for my carpet. At least I shall save the fare to Kashan.

Ghani used to point out irregularities in the carpets; how one side was broader than the other, how the pattern sometimes failed or was changed half way. It is difficult to maintain an exact equality over a long period of time, but Persians believe it is also unlucky, almost blasphemous, to make a carpet too symmetrical. I loved to look at some of the Turkoman rugs, to see how some-times the colours altered, soft reds and brown fading into each other in thick bands, two or three times across a single carpet.

These were the differing dyes, Ghani told us, as the nomads moved from one pasturage to another.

A Persian carpet, said Ghani, improves with wear; I would compare it with a musical instrument, which finds its best tone only with playing. A good carpet should lie in the sun; it is only then that its colours will ripen to their full glory; and they cannot fade. If you have no river, like at Isfahan, to wash it in, then take a brush, said Ghani, and scrub it. The greatest harm which you can do to a carpet, which is also to insult it, is not to use it.

Once, over a prayer rug that David had set his heart on, there was an interesting scene in which a point of origin could not be proved, even by Ghani. There followed an acrimonious discussion which ended with Ghani satisfied; the dealer had sworn 'by Abbas', and though our friend had by necessity a somewhat cynical view of human nature, the oath 'by Abbas' was good enough for him. I have not been able to discover the origin of this oath, nor the identity of the Abbas so compellingly invoked.

In the evenings we waited with Amin in our rooms for Ghani to arrive. There would be the sound of steps up the stairs, a pause at the door, and Ghani would burst in, bowed under the weight of the rolled carpets on his shoulder, and fling them triumphantly on the floor for our excited inspection. He judged each of our tastes marvellously and the prices were lower than our most sanguine predictions.

Often Amin would bring his friends, young lawyers and a doctor, to while away the evening with us over tea, talking or playing the 'Poosh' game. They complained to us sadly of the inequality of wealth and opportunity in Persia, of the 'Hundred Families' in whose laps untold riches would never cease to accumulate; of the corruption and nepotism; of the big estates and grasping indifferent landlords; how it seemed that the oil revenues had changed hands indeed, but only to be concentrated in the bank accounts of unscrupulous aristocrats and officials. Persia was as far from seeing the benefits as ever. Our encouraging replies, quoting the text-book assertions of the Shah's distribution of estates, the building of schools, hospitals, foreign investment and American aid, were met with a sort of sad unshakeable scepticism. But I felt that neither Amin nor his friends were revolutionaries; they were dreamers; they waited and hoped.

Amin was deeply religious. He believed, contrary to the opinions of most young Persians, that the salvation of the country lay not so much in its industrialisation as in a return to a simple and practical way of life implicit in the basic precepts of Islam. I shall not forget the expression on his face as he spoke of his own beliefs, trying to explain to us what his religion meant to him. 'When the muezzin calls,' he said once, 'that is the time that my heart beats.' When at last we had to leave, richer by the possession of several carpets, Amin presented us each with some of the beads, amber and white, which Persians love to handle, and we replied with a copy of E. M. Forster's *Abinger Harvest*. Not to be outdone, Amin went away and returned with two copies of Omar Khayyám's *Rubaiyat* (the poet is buried at Nishapur, not far from Meshed), inscribed in his neat handwriting: 'In memory of the happy times and friendship we have had together in Meshed, and with our friend Ghani, the carpet expert.'

5

Tehran and the Caspian

❀

Almost everywhere I went in Persia people were wishing heartily that they were elsewhere. In Quatru Achmet pined visibly for his gay young days in Shiraz, the police sergeant regretted a previous and more glamorous appointment to a slightly larger village, while the boy Mansura dreamt only of the lights of Tehran. Students in Kerman, bank clerks in Zahedan, army captains in the depôts of Baluchistan—whether their ambition was to go abroad, or be rich, 'get on' or simply to be civilised and in the centre of things—they all wanted to go, or go back, to Tehran. To the ordinary Persian (who doesn't live there) Tehran is the ultimate city paradise, the source of all government and all preferment. It is partly a question of size; for if the nine largest cities in the country were put together their combined population would still not exceed the population of the capital, which has trebled in the last thirty years and has now reached the figure of one and a half million. Tehran is also the warehouse, so to speak, of everything Western—and therefore 'superior', whether cars or ideas, machinery or clothes, the dumping-place of new stock which has not yet had time to be diffused throughout the rest of the country. The Dick Whittington story should be rewritten with a modern Haji Baba as its hero, and the substitution of Tehran for London. The story, or the dream of it, is at the back of most Persians' minds.

Even in Isfahan was felt the dazzle of the capital, though I was surprised to find that the most fervent admirers of Tehran had never been there. Ibrahim was exceptional in that his love for Isfahan was based not so much on what it is to-day, but on what it was. For him Isfahan would always remain the true capital of Persia, the perpetual seat of the Shah-Emperor even if the throne-room in the Ali Kapu, high over the Maidan, was occupied by no more than a ghost. But he was the first to admit that Isfahan was now a provincial backwater possessing only the shadow of its former prosperity and fame; yet he enjoyed describing to me the Tehran of his younger days, an immense teeming shanty-town remarkable only for the poverty and viciousness of its slums. Hassan also had no wish to visit the capital, but then he was pre-occupied with drawing his pension and sipping it away in the tea-house. But when I announced one morning that we had received an invitation to stay for some time in Tehran, he could not help but congratulate me, while others in the tea-house went through the usual pantomime of expressing pleasure or admiration—thumb and forefinger circled together, a soft whistle—Tehran indeed was the only place.

It is a long day's drive from Isfahan to Tehran, and we started at dawn, stopping to look back on the brown roof-tops, minarets, poplars, domes of the city spread out in the plain rimmed with its uneven shield of sunlit mountains, before the upland valley closed about the road and we drove between the red-and-brown ramparts of the Bakhtiari hills, on the road north to Qum.

There is a Persian saying, 'Qum exports beggars and imports corpses', which refers to the pilgrim traffic on which the prosperity of the town is founded. Here lie the remains of the Lady Fatima, who died there it is said in A.D. 816, flying from her persecutors in Baghdad. She was the saintly sister of the Imam Reza, whose tomb in Meshed renders that place an identical service, for Qum is one of the sacred cities of Persia, second only to Meshed. Nowhere are there so many beggars relying on the piety of pilgrims for their keep, and as Benares is to the Hindus, Qum is to the Shia Moslems, regarded by them as a very suitable place to die, or at least to be buried; hence the corpses. Shah

Abbas, as well as many other kings and a host of princes, have their tombs at Qum.

In spite of the haze I saw from a long way off the golden dome of the holy Lady's tomb, flashing like a heliograph in the sun. We drove through the town, snatching only a quick guilty glance at the sanctuary portal as we passed, bearing in mind the fate of an American not many years before who displayed too much interest in the Lady Fatima and her mausoleum, and was consequently torn to pieces by an angry mob. Across the Anarba river we paused to photograph the dome and slender blue-tiled minarets reflected in the stagnant snake of water where women in red shawls crouched over their washing.

A black mushroom-cloud north of the city warned me that we were approaching the great oil gusher that had been unloosed some months before and was not yet under control, still shooting a column of flame hundreds of feet into the sky. The army had moved in and the area was cordoned off, the road diverted. We fell into line behind lumbering oil-tankers, lorries and other vehicles ploughing through the black oil-soaked sand, and passed the wrecks of many which had overturned and crashed in the quagmire. On every side pools of the crude oil gleamed darkly in the sand, a line of guards standing watch with fixed bayonets upon the dunes. Until the arrival of these ferocious watchmen the citizens of Qum had swarmed out on donkeys and camels, horses and trucks to scoop up the oil in cans and cooking-pots as it lay inches deep upon the ground.

There is a special pleasure, for Englishmen at least, in driving through the high-walled gates of the British Embassy in Tehran. A blue-uniformed porter swings the doors open, saluting him as he passes through. At rest within, parked amid the smooth green lawns and giant trees, he will become aware of a strange peace, as if the dust and turmoil of an oriental city, left only an instant before, had never existed; as if he had been transported back to

England to the grounds of some exclusive country club. The buildings are white and cool, discreetly remote; gardeners are silently at work over the flower beds; rivers of impeccable gravel wind to destinations obscured by well-groomed shrubberies. If he is quiet and listens for a moment there will perhaps be borne upon the warm air the sound of cricket bat and ball, the thump of a tennis racket; if lucky his rhododendron vigil maybe rewarded by the sight of one or two athletic young men, pale or slightly reddened, striding in flannels or bathing trunks towards the swimming-pool. The apparition of a First Secretary elegantly attired, biting his pipe, feet ruminatively crunching the gravel as he broods upon the latest blunder of the home government, will necessarily be a rare one; a glimpse of the ambassador is too much to hope for—unless, look! Gates are swung back, orderlies salute, present arms, a cavalcade of black shining cars sweeps in—surely that was him, the weary figure half visible for a second behind the polished glass of an imperial Rolls? But where were the salvos, the trumpets? 'Oh, nothing official, he's been having tea with the Shah.' High on the flagstaff the Union Jack floats gently in the breeze, bored but imperturbable.

There is a fiction relating to the British Embassy in Tehran which the majority of Persians insist on regarding as fact. In spite of protestations to the contrary from the Embassy personnel themselves, it is generally believed in Tehran that the Embassy exercises an extraordinary back-room influence over the policies of the Persian government. 'If you really want to know what's going to happen next, get to know someone in the British Embassy . . .' I would have thought that the events of the past few years might have destroyed this cherished illusion, but the myth still holds.

Our host in Tehran was a friend of David's, Martin Berthoud, at that time Third Secretary. Since our last flying visit the previous autumn Martin had changed flats, but his servant Asgar was with him as before, ready as always to apply the balm of his culinary skill to our jaded palates. During our stay, which owing to an unforeseen disaster was longer than we had intended, we were given the run of the flat, a delightful place not far from the Embassy, with its own paved garden surrounded by high walls, a verandah on one side and a large blue-tiled pool in the middle.

We had arrived at an opportune moment. Asgar was getting married, and we were cordially invited to the wedding feast. For the few days before the great event not even Martin could get much talk out of him. Never at any time very forthcoming, Asgar was unusually silent and seemed to wear most often a look of pensive vacancy. His responses to our rather pointed questions at table were confined to inaudible mutterings and sheepish grins as he served the vegetables. His best man at the wedding was to be Ali, servant of another diplomat friend of Martin's who would also be there, and as the day approached Ali called continually on the bridegroom and the two of them would step outside to discuss last-minute arrangements.

On the appointed afternoon the three of us left in Martin's car and drove out to a crowded suburb in the north-east of Tehran. At the end of a lane we were met and directed between high mud walls until we came to a wicket gate leading into a courtyard. Although we were early—the assembly hour had been given as four o'clock—a number of uninvited people from adjoining tenements were crowding about the decorated doorway, and inside the courtyard it looked as if most of the guests had arrived. A patched awning had been slung across the yard, supported by a pole in the middle, and a raised carpeted platform was erected in the centre. Along each wall were set chairs and benches and little tables covered with gaily covered cakes and sweets; our arrival seemed to be the signal to start on these refreshments. We were led to places of honour across the yard and sat with backs to the wall facing the entrance on rickety chairs spaced between young lemon trees.

There must have been at least eighty people in the courtyard, with more coming in every moment. Steps in the centre of each side wall led up to two rooms on each side, with low windows overlooking the scene. One of the rooms was gleefully pointed out to me as the bridal suite, where the couple must spend their first night together. I wondered vaguely and a little anxiously whether or not I had read something about these Persian marriage rites. I hoped sincerely that Asgar and his bride would be allowed to fulfil their own personal side of the contract in private and in their own good time. 'Ushers' were handing round tea and cakes. I glanced at Asgar who stood between Martin and Ali, receiving, it seemed, last-minute words of encouragement. He was a well-built man about twenty-four, and just then he was squaring his shoulders in a courageous attempt to look confident. His thick black hair was heavily oiled and combed, and the lips beneath his short moustache were set in unsmiling determination.

I turned to look at the women who sat all together on benches in one corner, fluttering and preening themselves in their gayest shawls and scarves; stout elderly matrons with big-eyed children, freshly washed and polished, straining on their knees, nervous young wives dividing their anxious attention between their squalling babies and their husbands on the other side, and the unmarried girls, giggling and whispering in coy huddles, with more than half an eye for the young men across the yard. Tehran women pride themselves on being comparatively emancipated. Certainly there was hardly a veil to be seen; the younger women were in short cotton dresses, and some of them, in painful deference to Western fashion, had frizzed their hair with cheap perms. The men also were dressed in their smartest, mostly in blue pin-stripe set off with flashy silk ties, the light gleaming from the toes of their pointed shoes. The majority were talking together, laughing and making jokes, half showing themselves off to each other and to the women folk; they were not yet fully at ease. In the corner by the platform, a few feet from where I was sitting, four members of an amateur orchestra were setting up and tuning their instruments, zither, drums, clarinet and accordion. Children had climbed the walls outside the courtyard and poking their heads under the canopy were peering excitedly down upon the scene.

Ali, the best man, sensing that things should be starting soon, came over to the band and begged them to begin. There was a brazen twanging from the zither, a patter of drums and the clarinet and accordion launched into an American quickstep which was born and had died in the place of its origin many years before. I began to wonder if I should have come at all. I glanced at David. He had lately been afflicted with that internal malaise commonly known as 'Tehran Tummy'; he was gazing distractedly at the cake in his hand; the pale green of its icing was reflected all too faithfully in his face.

It was time to fetch the bride. Martin was to chauffeur the pair back from the bride's house, leading as many cars as could be mustered. It is the custom in Tehran on this return journey to drive slowly through the streets with one's hand pressed firmly on the horn; no one complains, I was assured, about the noise of wedding processions. Of course, the marriage ceremony itself, or rather the betrothal, had been concluded many years before. This evening was a more social occasion, to celebrate the final contract and the first night of their new life together.

The departure of Asgar seemed to raise everyone's spirits, the feeling of constraint disappeared. It was getting dark and coloured lights around the windows and doorways were lit, the electric bulbs shaded with red-and-green paper turned on. Despite their initial and perhaps ostentatious enthusiasm for American jazz, the musicians were getting bored with a type of music that none of them really liked (though they felt they should), and when a young man stepped onto the platform amid the applause and cat-calls of his friends there was an abrupt and relieved change of rhythm. He danced alone with his dark suit tightly buttoned, clicking his heels and swaying to the monotonous rapid sentences of the drum. Another jumped up to join him and together they paced out a shy duet to the jeers and laughter of the spectators. From then on the platform was never empty, a professional female dancer hired for the occasion and a troupe of comedians following each other's turns in quick succession. Two men, one very obviously dressed as a woman, acted a slapstick pantomime of married life whose witty repartee was unfortunately lost on me, though the long act was greeted with huge delight by the audience.

The noise of talk and clapping was not enough to drown the approaching clamour of the bride's procession and as Asgar and his wife came in together, she in white with long veil and roses in her hair, he upright and inscrutable, everybody pressed forward with their congratulations. Seated in front of the wedding cake the bride raised her veil for a moment and we were able to admire her blushing face, while Martin, poised over his flashlight camera, begged Asgar—in vain—to try and look a little more natural.

The immediate excitement over, the party was able to settle down and enjoy itself. The courtyard was very warm and crowded now, the doors blocked with people and every window filled with eager faces. A crackling microphone was rigged up and three or four men took turns before it, singing Persian songs alternately sad and gay. I learnt from those near me that all except one of the singers were Afghans, friends of the bride's parents. Soft drinks followed the tea and as the evening drew on the tempo of the dancers and the gaiety of the guests rose together. After some time Asgar and his bride retired to their room at the side of the court and throughout the evening friends and relations swarmed in the passage outside and on the steps waiting their turn to see the couple and wish them happiness.

As there was at least some religious connection with the occasion, we had decided after sad debate to bring no liquor of our own, and we knew there would be none at the wedding. Fortunately I was able to forget any cravings in this direction as my interest in the dancing increased. When I had first seen ordinary villagers in the bodegas of southern Spain get to their feet and execute solo and impromptu dances to the guitar accompaniment, I had thought that it was partly a mock imitation of a woman dancing. After I had seen more Spanish dancing, and had witnessed the passionate exhibitions of Greeks in their tavernas and once of a number of soldiers returning by night on the deck of a tramp steamer to their homes in Crete, I realised what a ridiculous mistake I had made. The men were dancing and expressing themselves as they were here in Persia, in their own right; and I saw that their gestures were in no way feminine, in fact, when properly done, had a peculiarly controlled masculine flavour. It was also clear that as much as these dancers enjoyed an audience their main impulse was a personal and private one; as soon as the rhythm had taken hold of their limbs and brain they danced as if they were themselves the only rhythm, self-hypnotised, absorbed and utterly alone, and I noticed that when one of these young Persians achieved this state of near-trance, even the gate-crashers by the door stopped their chattering and everyone watched and held their breath, as if not daring to break the spell.

There was something else too which had been holding at least half my attention for the last hour. A girl had been standing among the women in the far corner and occasionally darted up the steps to join her friends at the windows. I had never seen a girl in Persia quite so lovely. She was in a loose knee-length dress and wore her hair naturally in brown waves to just above her shoulder, and her face was oval, with high cheekbones, and large green almond eyes. As the dancing became more spirited I noticed her growing excitement as she tapped her foot and tossed her head to the music. She knew she was the object of several men's glances, but I was congratulating myself on having received at least one of her shy charming smiles, when I turned to David and Martin beside me and discovered to my annoyance that both of them had been watching her for some time. Those delightful smiles had been skilfully diffused. I forced Martin to find out more about her; obviously she wanted to dance; well then, let her. Messages and information were passed discreetly back and forth along the line of guests, mostly Asgar's friends whom we knew quite well by this time, and eventually we learnt that she was the younger sister of the drummer, a sailor on leave, that she was seventeen, that she did indeed want to dance, but her brother objected to her displaying herself in public. It was some time before her brother's scruples could be overcome, but on his final though reluctant consent I was rewarded by her demure and grateful glance—or was it for Martin? or David?

The floor was cleared, the girl came on. She had tied a scarf round her waist and stood barefoot by the awning pole in the centre of the platform, waiting for the music to begin. At first she was self-conscious and danced to the drum and zither with a light girlish step, swinging her skirt, with outstretched arms and fingers in graceful motion above her head. And then the beat changed, and she stood quivering and taut, her eyes closed, waiting for the rhythm to fill her; and as it came her neck curved, her hips and shoulders moved almost imperceptibly beneath her thin dress, and she began to step, quickly, then slowly, with a deadly poise, an infinite control. A moment ago she had been the very image of simplicity and innocence, and now, this . . .

As I watched I began to feel that rare tingling of the spine, as if a hand were clutching at the back of my neck. She had twined her arms about the pole and danced as if it were her lover, with head thrown back, lips parted, passionately receiving his kisses and embraces, until the mood changed and she came apart and her body began to sway like corn in summer, and then like a snake risen and hovering above its coils. With back arched, breasts pointed, she danced, writhing, like a woman with all the world's mystery told beneath her lowered eyelids, in her slow smile. The rhythm quickened, drum and zither, and no one in that courtyard moved or spoke, until the pace became too much and the zither fell out, and now it was only her brother, the sailor, tense and expressionless, palms and fingers flashing over his drum, and the girl, dancing with a contorted violence that was unbearable; until even the drummer faltered, stopped, and she collapsed flushed and exhausted on the platform, acknowledging with tears of triumph the long burst of applause.

We left shortly afterwards, after joining twenty of the most honoured guests for supper on the floor of the next room where steaming dishes and mountains of rice were arranged upon a white sheet. We wished Asgar a good night. We had been at the wedding for seven hours. The girl's name was *Mahnaz*, which means, 'like the moon'.

Politics on Skis

Tehran, I decided, was just as it should be, modern and full of shiny American cars. Museums and public buildings of that sort have been constructed of granite and marble as if Darius was still the Great King. Xerxes had come back to earth, dressed in parti-coloured shoes and a double-breasted suit, and in heaven he had found out about concrete and plate glass. On the whole I liked Tehran. I realised I was one of those weak-minded persons whose impressions of people and places depend largely upon their own state of comfort or discomfort of the moment. It was the second time that Martin's hospitality had supplied the springboard for our Persian journeys. Armchairs, books, good food, privacy, these are the luxuries that I like to be reminded of on occasions, and which made Tehran a pleasant place for a short stay. In a few days, when we and the car were serviced, we would move on, cross the Elburz Mountains and descend upon the Caspian shore.

I liked the light in Tehran. The light is wonderful anywhere in Persia, but here it was spring, and streets, people and houses were seen with a scintillating clarity. In the mornings, when it was still very cold, I would step outside and sniff the clean bright air; buildings threw shadows as cool and blue as ice. At the end of every northward-sloping street were the Elburz, rearing close over the city, the snow-covered cone of Mount Demavend, 18,600 feet, glittering under a pale blue sky. To be a successful diplomat in Tehran one must be able to ski. The sport is patronised by the resident royalty; it is even said that few vital state decisions are made, threats delivered, promises given, anywhere else but in the ascending or descending ski-lifts. Martin and David would dis-appear with the other Embassy people into the white mountains, and on their return David would try and arouse my envy by telling me how he had tripped up the Grand Vizier, fallen over the Shah and had remained embedded for hours in a snowdrift with a dusky Princess. No skier myself, I was content to remain sitting by the blue-tiled pool listening to the tap dripping in the water, the hum of traffic far away, warming myself in the sunshine that grew stronger every day.

March 21st is *No-Ruz*, the spring Festival, and the first day of

the Persian New Year. It is a cheerful festival, and the Persians
send each other cards and greenery and flower-pots, and for days
before they set off fireworks and light bonfires in the streets of
every town and village in the country. They say they are burning
away all the old year's rubbish, its sorrows and troubles. There
is no nonsense about the time of the New Year's inception—our
midnight, the first stroke of twelve (or the last?), must seem very
amateurish to them. The Shah's astronomers go into solemn con-
clave not long before and calculate the exact moment, which
varies of course from place to place in Persia, and is different
every year. This year in Tehran it was 12.34 a.m. and forty
seconds. Thirteen days are given over to public holiday, and on
the thirteenth it is the rule for everyone to pack a picnic lunch and
go out into the country; to stay in the towns is considered bad
luck. So on that day the towns are deserted—except for a detachment of police and a large number of burglars, who regard this
day as their most lucky. Last year in Tehran they were not so
fortunate; thirty-nine were caught before sunset.

We planned to be out of the city by *No-Ruz*, and celebrate the
happy day among the rice fields of the Caspian. Everything was
made ready for our departure on the 15th. With great difficulty,
and only by the help and intervention of Martin and his Persian
friends, we obtained the necessary permits to include on our Caspian tour the village of Astara, in the furthermost north-west,
where lies the Russian frontier. That morning the car was backed
up the lane to the door of the flat, and we set about transporting
the numerous trunks and cases that had accumulated in the last
seven months of travelling. It was only when the front door was
finally locked and we were seated in the car that one box was
discovered missing. It happened to be the one that held not only
our library, notebooks, maps and papers, but also passports, visas,
permits and the carnet. By the afternoon, when the whole flat
and car had been ransacked, the conclusion was reached that the
box had been left for a moment on the front doorstep and someone had walked by and picked it up . . .

The police were summoned, and arrived with an extraordinary

promptitude. Blue-coated constables, armed to the teeth, escorted a chubby but impressive detective who assured us that all would be well, the box would be recovered within hours; he was in charge. We were driven in a fast car to the central police station where every conceivable detail that might expedite the recapture of the stolen property—mothers' maiden names, our ages, places of birth—were meticulously noted down. The theft, after all, was a serious one. Not only were we foreigners, (paying) guests of the nation, but it was generally agreed that the doorstep of Martin's flat came within the bounds, laid down by international convention, of so-called diplomatic immunity; though the occurrence of that morning might have proved that it had been immune to nobody and nothing. The flat was leased to the Embassy; the doorstep, therefore, was the property of the British Government. By a rapid and irresistible process of logic it became clear that the robbery was a matter of international concern; an affront to the dignity (such as remained) of Great Britain, to the Queen herself.

That evening Persian friends of Martin's came round to encourage and commiserate with us. The Tehran police, they said, were amazingly efficient. They kept dossiers, including addresses, of every thief in town, knew exactly what was each one's speciality, and would, probably that very evening, make a lightning and successful sweep. One told me how he shared a flat with a friend and returned one evening to find their entire wardrobe stolen. Within six hours every article of clothing had been recovered—except, of course, one or two items which the inspector fancied for himself and which were, undoubtedly, his fair commission. It was especially fortunate, they added, that diplomatic pressure was being exerted on our behalf; there might even be no need to bribe anyone.

Days passed. The chubby detective called less and less often. He looked harassed. Once he said he had a clue, but refused to divulge its nature. I could see where the difficulty lay; the theft could hardly have been planned, and therefore could not be tied down to any of the reputable gangs. On the 19th Martin left with a Persian friend to spend *No-Ruz* in Ahwaz. He left the flat in our keeping, presented us with whisky, wine and cigarettes to tide us through any further delay, and sent a last menacing telephone message to the Chief of Police. Somehow, absurdly and incomprehensibly, I managed to break up Martin's lavatory, with most unpleasant results. While the plumbers were busy we went out into the streets where shops were overflowing with flowers and branches of white blossom in bud, and bought six bowls of gold fish, on sale on stalls at every street corner.

Goldfish bring you luck at *No-Ruz*, and I wished to atone for my ungrateful destruction. We filled the bottom of the bowls with the brightly coloured stones gathered from the Dasht-i-Lut; the goldfish looked happy. And then we thought of the pool; they needed space. So we drained it and polished the lovely pale blue tiles until they shone with a splendour truly Persian, and launched the goldfish into their new home. At the four corners we placed the curved clay water-jars that had been bought at Kerman. All that was needed now was an almond tree, and Asgar could buy a yellow turban and a long blue coat, and could sit on a carpet under the almond blossom, pretending to read poetry. But at that time Asgar was on his honeymoon.

So far the police had been busily achieving nothing. We decided to do some sleuthing on our own. From the haul in that box the only saleable objects were the books. If the thief were unwise and unprofessional, as he seemed to be, he would have sold them immediately, almost certainly to a secondhand bookshop which sold European books. We would separate and scour every bookshop in Tehran. That there were several we already knew. Only that morning we had been browsing in a bookshop a few streets from the flat. There had been a wide selection of English books. Walking round the shelves I had seen a copy of *The Woodlanders*, and, pointing it out to David, had said, 'If we don't get the books back at least you can get another copy of that.' 'Yes,' he said, 'and there's another *Road to Oxiana* for you.' It was a good shop, certainly.

So we would search the bookshops ... And then, suddenly, the thought occurred to each of us simultaneously. As one man we sprang to our feet and raced for that bookshop. At the door we paused, composing our excited faces and adopting an air of casual unconcern. With trembling fingers David took down *The Woodlanders*. On the flyleaf was written, in his own handwriting, his name. I opened the *Road to Oxiana*; inside were my initials and the stamp of a Cambridge bookseller. In ten minutes we had found over a dozen of our own books all freshly priced; and ridiculously cheap some of them were. But where were the maps and passports?

I made a neat pile of the books while David slipped out to telephone Hussein, Martin's Persian teacher, who had been asked to look after us. Within half an hour the lane and the bookshop were swarming with determined policemen. The detective appeared, rubbing his hands triumphantly. The unfortunate bookseller, who it occurred to me might well have bought the books in all innocence, was arrested and bundled, terrified and protesting, into one of the waiting cars. We drove to the police station.

In the Inspector's office we were shown to chairs by the wall. There were several people in the room, a few police on guard. All eyes were on the Inspector and a thin raggedly dressed youth who stood trembling before the desk. The boy seemed transfixed with terror. I watched, not quite realising what was happening, while the Inspector, a short paunchy man whose little eyes were half hidden between rolls of fat, got up, opened a drawer and took out a buckled leather strap, and advanced testing it on his thigh towards the boy. He said something, very quietly, and the boy as if mesmerised slowly held out his hand. The strap and buckle, poised for a moment over the officer's shoulder, descended with a crack upon the boy's wrist.

I don't remember exactly what happened then, only that we were both across that room in a flash. David had ripped the raised strap from the grinning Inspector's hands, and I was standing before the boy. I was so angry I could not utter a word. Later, when order had been restored and the boy who held his arm close to his chest had been removed whimpering from the room, when Hussein had done his best to smooth things over, and we were sitting down again, glowering in our chairs, I remember that I was still shaking.

The interview was as brief as possible. What happened to the boy after we left, I shudder to think. Hussein told me later that the police suspected him of taking our box, but he kept denying it. I refuse to regret our interference. The Persian police may have their own methods of dealing with criminals, but it was clear that beatings of that kind were unofficial, and quite 'off the record'. If corporal punishment has its uses, then it is only when properly and legally administered. What I hated at that moment and shall not forget, was the expression in the police officer's eyes, the secret lust of inflicting pain that gleamed in them despite himself, the quiver and jerk of his fat body as he viciously brought down the strap.

Later that evening we heard that our papers had been found. The bookseller had described the man who sold him the books and the police had broken into a certain garret, discovering the remains of our property under the bed. I had no wish to see the Inspector again, and David went round to collect the papers. Mysteriously enough the box was missing, so were the maps. It was only when David persisted in his demands for the latter that the Inspector reluctantly took them from a drawer and handed them over. The box remained 'missing'. The next morning, the first day of *No-Ruz*, we packed up again and dropping a slice of bread into the pool to sustain the goldfish, left Tehran for the Caspian.

West of Tehran a road branches north, winding up the steep valleys of the Elburz. We left the desert, brown and arid, warming in the spring sunshine, and followed upwards by the side of a rushing snow-water torrent, lined with willows and thin poplars; up, keeping pace with the afternoon sun that threw the valleys below into shadow, until it became very cold and the road was a black line twisting higher across huge snow-fields, disappearing into cloud. At the top we passed through a long tunnel piercing the final watershed, whose entrance was hung with icicles like the teeth of a portcullis, the walls buttressed with giant growths of ice; out and down through wisps of cloud, dropping into a deep almost subterranean gorge winding northwards down toward the sea.

We stopped under a dripping rock overhang to peer up at three ibex delicately picking their way over the cliffside. The country had changed completely; it was Persia, but unrecognisable. Thick wet woods, choked with fern and bearded with silver waterfalls, covered the mountains. The earth between rocks green with lichen was damp, black and rich. The contrast of a few hours back, the barren spaces cut with a sword-like clarity of light with this sudden moist luxury of vegetation, was overpowering. The hillsides steamed. Heavy mist fused with the dusk as we descended through hills starred white with blackthorn blossom.

Chalus, on the coast, was a further shock; tarmac lamplit streets shining in the rain, brightly painted two-storey houses, neon strips over the shops; and the prices were treble. We passed quickly through a descending scale of hotels before finally coming to rest in a heated argument with a slightly drunken landlord. Everyone seemed to have touched some alcohol—after all, it was *No-Ruz* —but I had noticed before that most Persians, who don't usually drink at all, with only a glass of beer inside them become very jolly indeed. So there was a long and fiery battle with the tipsy manager supported by his tipsy staff, while we made up for our shameful lack of liquor by dramatic gesticulation and a brilliant exposition in bad Persian of the defects of manager, staff and hotel. We walked out twice, but as it was raining, walked back in again. At last, with the price reduced by no more than half we fell on our hard-won beds utterly exhausted. Staff and land-lord, however, were vastly stimulated by the encounter and continued to argue with each other far into the night.

A very familiar atmosphere it seemed in the overcast misty morning. I felt that I should go walking along the sea front eating an ice cream. But there were no ice creams and instead of a front only distant dark sands. So we drove off west, wondering at this so un-Persian scenery. Wooded hills, their tops in cloud, stuck out over the shore, a flat belt of fields and cottages and trees, green turf and white blossom. Sometimes it was like driving along a lane in Sussex, except for the glimpses of the Caspian breaking on the beach and the long black boats drawn up on the sand. Certainly it was Europe, with the gay painted little towns every few miles, down by the sea or sticking out over the trees on the hills; the Persian Riviera, for the rich of Tehran; though not quite in season. Being *No Ruz*, everyone was about, walking or lounging, the children playing all over the road. The men were in their best suits and the women like butterflies in bright shawls of red and yellow. Between the towns lay rice fields half under water, bullock teams ploughing deep in mud. Thatched cottages sprouted everywhere, so heavily thatched one might think the logs and planks would collapse underneath; and some of them pointed like fir cones; and reflected with the white blossom in the fields under water.

Resht, Pahlevi; nothing much to see here—only a few tiny steamers moored in the river mouth. The weather was beginning to depress me; I might have been in England. We turned north, following the curve of the coast. Mountains closed down from the left; more rain; on through thick forests with open glades of brown bracken and wet green turf. Most of the bridges had collapsed in the recent floods, so we did some fording; and pulled a Persian in his Cadillac from the middle of one stream, to the tearful thanks of his wife and daughters shivering on the bank. Astara, at last, in the dark. It was the Russian frontier and so the army took us over, a cheerful colonel gave us tea and chocolates in his office while he signed our papers. He spoke French and told us he preferred Tehran to Astara, and hated the Russians.

Before breakfast next morning I sneaked down to the sea, avoiding the sentries; must get a good look at Russia. I made a long detour and came out on the bleak sea-marsh behind the barracks. Yes—there was the fence, high barbed wire stretching into the sea, Russia beyond. A cow was munching just on the other side; a Russian cow. I leaned through the fence and patted its nose. The gesture, I realised, had an international significance. Nations may shake their fists at one another, advance to the brink of war. But here were facts; an Englishman and a Russian cow; here there was real understanding. Just then a soldier approached. I smiled politely and cast about for a Russian 'mot'. A bugle blew—off he pelted. Smart chaps, these Russians. I followed the direction with my eyes; the soldiers were forming up under a flag. The Hammer and Sickle? *No!* The Persian flag! It was all a hideous mistake. Across the field, that other fence, *that* was the real frontier. I looked dismally down at the cow, Persian after all.

With the car packed up we calmed the group of police and soldiers anxious to get us off, and separated each in different directions to get this 'closer look'. In twenty minutes both of us were back. I had been arrested in the village by a blue-coated policeman, David by an M.P. . . . both in disgrace. But we need not have worried. The road took us for twenty miles along the bank of the frontier stream. A soldier was our escort. Not ten yards away were the Russian watchtowers and the double barbed-wire fencing that extends unbroken across the Caucasus to the shores of the Black Sea. Two Russians with rifles were sitting— perhaps hiding—in a tree. Once I saw a couple of Russians walking in a field wearing, of course, enormous boots.

The road followed along the edge of the frontier valley high into wooded hills. We changed escorts at several Persian posts, climbing higher along the muddy lane as we peered down and across into Soviet territory. There was no barbed wire on the Persian side; it would have been too expensive. A few pill-boxes, one or two 'hidden' gun emplacements; in the camouflaged outposts the soldiers sat about drinking tea. A young officer took us the last stage, before the road climbed south. We gave him cigarettes and a box of Turkish Delight, and looked for a last time down the long blue valley to the dark line of the Caspian sea. Over the pass.

At once we were back on familiar ground. The trees had

stopped short on the other side. The great Persian plateau, ranged with snow mountains, stretched brown and bare to the south. A wind that never stopped blew coldly in our faces. A string of camels, thick and shaggy in their winter coats, plodded across the plain. A village of low mud-bricked houses, slots for windows, straggled colourless under a brown hill. Persia again.

6

Diversion to
the Gulf of Oman

✱

The main road from India to Persia runs through the deserts of Baluchistan, to the south of the Afghan border. In India we had said to each other: 'When it's spring in Persia, the deserts flower. We must not be too late.' So, foolishly, we crossed the frontier in early February, and in the midst of a combined sand- and snowstorm, ran out of petrol a few miles from Zahedan.

To make one's entry into Persia on foot, carrying an empty petrol can and leaning against an icy wind, cannot be regarded as in any way auspicious; nor was Zahedan the place to wait comfortably for the spring. The roads to the west and north were impassable, washed away by floods, the worst for years; in a week, perhaps, they would be clear. One way out remained; the road south, 400 miles to Charbahar on the Gulf of Oman. An overwhelming desire came over me to get off the Iranian plateau, leave the cold and the wind, to be warm again. Huddling over the stove in a draughty room, with flurries of snow whitening the cracked window-panes, there came a vision: hot sands and a blazing sun, palm trees shadowing the blue breakers of an Arabian sea. . . .

Opinion in Zahedan was divided as to the advisability of our venturing into so little known a corner of Persia, the province of Makran, especially at this time of year; the innkeeper was strongly against our leaving Zahedan at all. From two bank clerks and a

garage mechanic we received some encouragement. A Land-
Rover could travel, with luck, as far as Khash, where there was
a military depôt. Beyond that the chances were small; difficult
hilly country, at least one desert, and finally a range of mountains called the Bashgird, which blocked access to the sea. A
single gorge, impossible for a car just now, they said, cut through
the mountains, dropping 5,000 feet to the coast and Charbahar.
But it was worth trying anything; besides, the bank manager had
whisked the latest gaudily tinted map of Persia from his desk,
and there, marked plainly enough, was a road from Charbahar
following along the Persian Gulf through Bandar-Abbas even
as far as Basra. By the time we reached the latter place, I thought,
in about three weeks, it would undoubtedly be spring, and the
Persian plateau would be bearable again. Further, the bank-
manager assured me that once at Charbahar it would be hot,
very hot. He fanned his face expressively.

There is a small cinema at Zahedan and, wishing to refresh
ourselves at the fount of Western culture, we went to see an
American cowboy film at that time the rage of the town. The
place was crowded and so we sat in the expensive seats upstairs
in a narrow gallery. I could lean over the balustrade and look
down on the densely packed heads in the hall below. Everyone
was talking, sucking sweets, cracking nuts and drinking pepsi-
cola through straws. I could see no women down below, but
there were three beside me, who clearly intended to be incognito,
and removed their veils only when the lights went out. The
lights came on again very shortly, and so did the veils; something
had gone wrong. With the fault rectified we started again. The
film was in English, and I was determined to enjoy myself. Unfortunately the film was stopped regularly every four minutes
while pages of the preceding dialogue in Persian were projected
on the screen. As most of the audience were unable to read, about
forty of the lucky ones took it upon themselves to help the others,
chanting out the words in dreary unison.

The whole performance, which normally might have taken
seventy minutes, lasted on account of these tedious interruptions

nearly two and a half hours. There were two official intervals during which the audience set to work again on the monkey nuts and pepsi-cola, and several other unofficial black-outs while the projector ground to a standstill. The manager of the cinema stood behind me throughout the film—except for frenzied dashes towards the projector when it failed—and kept whispering encouragement into my ear. He was very proud to have us honour his cinema. . . . Were the seats comfortable? Were we enjoying ourselves? Tomorrow there would be a new film, even better. Would we come again tomorrow as his guests? I assured him that his cinema was altogether exceptional but regretted our inability to come again; we were leaving Zahedan in the morning.

We arrived in Khash at dusk, after a hard day's drive across a barren land of rock and sand where dry, stunted bushes pricked up between patches of melted snow. Until we came upon the bus stuck in the middle of a river we saw only one other human being; a man, a bundle of rags and patches, leading a sad-faced donkey, searching among the rocks for firewood. It had been raining in the Kuh-i-Tafran, a 13,000-foot peak covered with snow, that fell gradually behind us in the north. Every stream had become a river. Sometimes cairns marked the fords, at other times we had to strike out blindly, praying for a safe crossing. Once, when the engine stopped in mid-stream, I had to get out and push, and fell straight into a hidden pool. When we found the bus, the passengers were in the process of disembarking, the men carrying the women and children on their backs to the dry land. Every bush was covered with clothing put out to dry in the sun, and there was a samovar already bubbling over a fire; hot tea for everybody.

A second bus from Zahedan had also arrived, but wisely enough had decided to turn back. The driver of the abandoned vehicle stood in the water beating the torrent with a stick; he alternated between moods of apathy, as if on the brink of tears, and fits of wild activity. But there was nothing we could do for him; the bus was too deep in the mud. Really, the driver was being philosophical. There were only two things that could happen: if the water rose any more, the bus would be swept away and buried in the mud; if it subsided, then in a week perhaps they could dig it free. A gaunt she-camel was standing on the opposite bank overlooking the disordered scene with an expression of heavy sarcasm. 'Now a camel,' she seemed to be saying, 'could do this on her head!'

A smart-looking Persian officer was standing in the main street of Khash, talking to a group of soldiers, and we asked him where we might stay the night. David mentioned in passing that he still clung to the rank of lieutenant in the British Territorial Army, whereat the captain was both charmed and delighted. He pointed out in excellent French that, while in the absence of any hotel in the village we could of course sleep on a bench in a tea-house, he and his brother officers would infinitely prefer us to be their guests, and invited us to proceed to the Officers' Club, just round the corner.

An impressive white gateway was guarded by a tiny Persian soldier bearing a huge rifle. As we halted at the entrance I could see evidence of indecisive struggle on the poor fellow's face: whether to demand our papers, call out the guard or simply shoot . . . However, the military appearance of the vehicle decided him, and perhaps he had caught sight of David's face, which was already assuming (to my horror) that sneer of cold command bred only in an Officers' Mess . . . I was becoming a little gloomy at the prospect of these martial surroundings, but consoled myself with the promise of a fire and a night in comfort. Besides, David was obviously enjoying himself. No doubt I was taken for his travelling batman.

We were ushered into the dining-room which resembled to a surprising extent the interior of a third-rate Brighton café. The floor was bare, the walls undecorated save for the ubiquitous tinted photograph of the smiling Shah; wooden tables were set the length of the room covered with plastic tablecloths, ashtrays of the same material advertising coca-cola, and neatly arranged cruets including mustard pots inscribed *Coleman*, but empty.

A soldier came in with a bundle of firewood which he applied to the stove, and we sat round it enjoying the new warmth, sipping glasses of sweet tea. A toast to the Persian army! It was not long before I became aware of a strange sensation on my head and hands. I looked up at the ceiling. The architect designing the Officers' Club, while adhering strictly to principles of ruthless simplicity in the construction of the building, had evidently discovered in the ceilings a field where he could experiment inexpensively with Art. While the paint was still wet, sand had been applied generously with a brush in graceful geometrical flourishes; but whenever the room became warm and the air dried, the sand was loosened and descended on the heads, clothes and food of those below.

Later, groups of young officers sat round the tables eating *chelo-kebab*. We were joined at supper by two English-speaking Persians engaged in the new government *Village Projects*. Here in Baluchistan the nomad problem was not so acute; most of the tribes had settled in mud or palm-leaf villages and were attempting to alleviate their boredom and make a living by cultivating the barren earth. Tehran had issued an edict to the effect that from now on the Baluch were to be educated, their diseases were to be cured and they were to be taught how to grow vegetables. A network of fast motor-roads was to spring up—and the province must prosper. Apart from the fact that the Baluch are firmly opposed on principle to any innovation, and are darkly suspicious of the slightest interference, the government has been unable to back its edict with enough money, and so the Baluch, to their considerable relief, will be allowed to remain illiterate, diseased and starving for many years to come.

The elder of the two Persians, a heavy, smooth-faced man, was surprised to hear that we were determined to reach Charbahar; the road in the gorge had been destroyed by landslides. He told us he had only just arrived from Charbahar, and had had to take a camel. He moved uncomfortably at the memory. Three days had passed before an army lorry had picked him up at the top. He looked depressed. I sensed that here was a typical example of the modern Persian intelligentsia, an idealist whose head was stuffed with technical knowledge and benevolent plans for a new Persia, but whose enthusiasm was beginning to cool in the face of the enormous difficulties, lack of local support, the stubbornness of his countrymen and the rigours of the countryside.

'No,' he shook his head firmly, 'it is best for you to return to Zahedan. And there are bandits in the gorge.'

Had he seen any? No, but what would they want with him, on a camel? He sighed. He was going back to Tehran, to 'make a report'. His eyes lit up at the thought. It might have been my imagination, but it occurred to me at that moment that our friend, once back among his superiors in the luxury of the capital, would suddenly forget his own hardships and the magnitude of his task: the report would glow with hope and confidence, and the bureaucrats of Tehran would congratulate each other and make more plans, forgetting the money again.

His companion was a pleasant young man of about twenty-four who had been only a week in Baluchistan, and whose enthusiasm was correspondingly high. He was tall and thin and, unusual for a Persian, had blond hair and blue eyes. He had been educated abroad. His intention was to visit a number of villages farther south and exhort the headmen to delegate their powers among the village elders. He would teach them self-government, and the elements of democracy. . . . We decided to call him Bertram. He was travelling south to Iranshah to-morrow, in a jeep with a driver, and he offered to lead the way. Unless the road was impossible we should arrive by evening; and if the police or the army did not forbid it and we still wished to reach Charbahar, then it would have to be on our own. Very tired now, we were shown to our rooms. The ceiling decorations were extended to every part of the building. I fell asleep to the gentle benediction of falling sand.

❀

We were already beginning to loose height, winding down through barren hills heaped with boulders under jagged peaks of eroded rock that cut fantastic shapes in the sky. The sun seemed to be stronger. At midday we came upon a lorry stranded in a river. While Bertram encouraged the occupants in the hopeless attempt to free the wheels, I boiled some eggs, in the absence of firewood using a cocoa-tin filled with sand and soaked with petrol.

We halted in the first Baluch village, a few mud cottages erected in a grove of palms and plane trees at the mouth of a valley. The headman greeted Bertram cautiously but politely. In a few moments a pair of brown, heavily bangled arms held out a tray of glasses and a teapot from the interior of a hut, immediately taken and offered to us by a boy. We stood about drinking tea in the warm sunlight admired by some friendly half-naked children. In an adjoining wattle enclosure shawled women were plaiting palm-leaf trays and baskets, giggling frantically as I photographed them. Undisturbed against the crumbling wall sat an old man with eyes closed, gently turning in his hands a blue-and-green glazed bowl of a *kalian*, pleasurably exhaling into the still air a thin blue stream of smoke.

The headman, a fierce-looking man with a large blue turban and black-and-white striped cloak, seemed anxious to prove to Bertram that his village was 'progressive', and proudly led the way to an old man lying in a trench laboriously operating a hand-loom. A goat, anchored by a chain to the wall behind him, stood by with a proprietory air. Bertram pretended he was both pleased and impressed, and with mutual bows and expressions of good-will we got into the cars again and drove off, followed at a distance by the children who, now we were leaving, exposed their true feelings towards us, implementing their howls of derision with pieces of earth and goat dung.

At Iranshah Bertram helped us buy last-minute provisions and collected the latest information about conditions in the gorge. It seemed that the road had indeed collapsed, and we should have to try and follow the river-bed. No vehicle had passed through for over a week. Bertram made a final attempt to persuade us to turn back. There was, it appeared, one genuine danger with which we were duly impressed. If, he told us, we should see a single cloud in the sky or notice the faintest hint of rain in the mountains we must immediately make for high ground, for if it did rain in those shale mountains the river would rise six feet within the hour. . . .

We left the kindly Bertram standing with a crowd of idlers in the street, waving sadly. We drove on, past the ramshackle cottages of Bampur, for an extra hour that night, skidding slowly across a desert of fine white sand, the headlights picking out the old wheel-marks ahead. A dead tree, half-buried in sand, marked a convenient camping place; we built a fire from its branches and sat round it shivering and wordless under the cold, starlit sky.

Bampur has been identified with the ancient Pura, the city and the province in Gedrosia where in 325 B.C. Alexander the Great rested his army after the disastrous desert march from the Indus. Until they came down to the coast and found water at Gwadar, about fifty-five miles east of Charbahar, the Greek army had been wandering for two months among the deserts and mountains of Makran, suffering so terribly from thirst and sunstroke, and the shifting sands across which they marched, that most of the mules and horses were lost, if not through weakness then through being killed for food by the soldiers, and the men who fell out exhausted from the march were left to die in the sand.

Arrian, in his history of Alexander the Great, says that Alexander chose this difficult route not only because he could leave supply dumps along the coast for Nearchus and the fleet, but 'because, apart from Semiramis on her retreat from India, no man, to his knowledge, had ever before succeeded in bringing an army safely through', and she with only twenty survivors. Cyrus, son of Cambyses, had come out with even less: seven. 'Alexander heard these old stories; they inspired him to go one better. . . ' At Bampur the lucky survivors of Alexander's army were allowed to recuperate. It must have been fertile in those days, though now the plain looked to me unexceptionally barren, draining away in the west into a great salt-marsh.

✳

In the light of the new day we left the sand and entered the foothills of the Bashgird Mountains whose bare peaks filled the southern horizon. The country was changing already. Dead palm trunks littered the rocks; even the desert bushes had died away. From a ridge we looked down upon a grove of palm trees; palm-leaf huts shaped like beehives, which could hardly have changed since Alexander's day, were grouped round a clearing: Ispakeh.

We sat on two empty petrol-cans outside one of the huts drinking tea, watched curiously by a circle of squatting villagers. Next to me sat a ragged policeman, cleaning his rifle. The conversation was carried on mostly to our exclusion, but I picked up the general trend of it. The policeman was referring to us alternatively as 'Americani' and 'Inglees'; England and America, he explained were different names for the same place: it was all part of a large island situated somewhere far to the north called Australia ... He drew a map in the dust for the benefit of the ignorant and admiring villagers. No information as to the road to Charbahar seemed forthcoming except for a wave in the direction of the mountains, and at my jocular allusion to bandits the policeman got up and went to collect our eggs, a few from each hut. We decided to use the cameras, if no one minded, and diffidently approached a colourful group of Baluch collected outside one of the palm huts.

I was kneeling down to photograph in front of a faded pink eiderdown stretched flat on the ground, when suddenly the eider-down moved, and a low moan issued from under it. Horrified, I looked more closely, and found that in a shallow pit dug into the sand, covered to his eyes with blankets, lay a man apparently in the last stages of some painful illness. His family and friends were gathered round him, the men smoking, the women at their sewing, trying to divert him with their talk. Two of the men rose to welcome me, and by a series of graphic gestures explained the nature of the sick man's complaint. He was suffering from an affliction of the bladder. For two days he had lain there declining all food, but with a terrible thirst. Any liquid he took went straight through him.

Everything that was possible had been done for him; they were simply waiting for him to recover, or to die; it was now in the hands of Allah the All-Merciful. But there was a silence in the group: all eyes were fixed upon us. I began to feel uncomfortable as it became unpleasantly clear what was expected of us. We were foreigners, and all foreigners have the reputation of being great doctors, *hakims*, versed in the higher skills of medicine which to these people border on magic. A number of villagers from nearby huts had come over and stood round us, waiting. A woman, probably the patient's wife, sat at his head and looked up at me with beseeching eyes. A large turquoise shone in her nose. David and I exchanged nervous glances.

David cleared his throat: 'Tea,' he said, in Persian.

'Milk,' I added desperately. 'Hot milk.'

These useful suggestions were greeted in stony silence. They were remedies too simple, altogether unworthy of two foreigners dropped as it were by God into their village in this hour of need. We consulted anxiously together, and David went off to unearth the medicine chest. An English doctor had presented him with a few large and very expensive yellow pills, shaped like bombs, with the advice: 'if all else fails, use these'. Unfortunately he could not for the life of him remember the exact complaint for which these pills were intended, but, he said, he had a strong suspicion that it was 'bladder'. If so, they might well be helpful; if not . . .

I explained that pills were on the way, and the news caused a general stir of relaxed confidence round the sick-bed. The woman with the turquoise bent down to pass on to the patient the information of his impending cure in an excited whisper. The patient groaned. David returned bearing an impressive little box, and the villagers stood back respectfully. We gave them two, one to be taken now, the other at sunset. Anxiously I watched them administer the first pill, swallowed with difficulty with the help of a bowl of filthy water. We shook hands all round. It was time, I felt, to be going, and quickly; to leave Ispakeh at once, take our eggs and go. There was a last view of the village before the hills engulfed us. The beehive huts were almost invisible among the palms. A splash of pink in the clearing marked our patient buried in sand, the watchers round the sick-bed.

The track had turned west, following the range along its base, searching for an opening in the barrier. By early afternoon we found ourselves at the head of the gorge, a cleft opening at our feet that wound deeper each mile as it cut into the heart of the mountains. At first the narrow road which had been built high along the hillside seemed possible, but as the gorge descended and the gravel cliffs drew in together, progress became increasingly difficult, edging past falls of rock and sand until finally a whole section of the mountain had collapsed leaving us staring over a precipice two hundred feet down to the foaming river bed. An hour's painful backing brought the car to the head of the landslide down which we made a hair-raising descent to the bottom.

Fortunately it seemed that the level of the water was falling. Stretches of sand were visible at intervals, and where the stream broadened and was shallow, flowing over pebbles, the going was easy, crossing and recrossing to avoid the pools hidden under still water. One of us waded ahead to plot the safest course.

As the afternoon wore on the character of the gorge changed. The sun's rays that had lit the cliff-sides and sent the water sparkling over green-and-russet stones were withdrawn for ever. The sun never penetrated to these depths. Great cliffs of dark rock, worn smooth in the ages of the river's channelling, leaned across to each other, obscuring all but a faraway ribbon of blue sky. The river had taken a new strength from these gloomy vaults, the water turned black, hissing and gurgling, and slid round the boulders with a new menace, to break in white walls of foam at the foot of the rapids. No longer was there a convenient margin of sand to follow: shining wet rock, loose boulders slippery as ice lined the river bed. The car was never out of the water.

In the thunder of the rapids it was impossible to talk, only to shout into each other's ears. Sometimes the river fell fifteen feet in a few yards: it was necessary to set the car at the slope of falling water and let it slide often out of control to the next level: moments, for the driver at least, of real fear. From these tumultous places the river would slide suddenly quiet and sinister between dark walls of rock, contrasts of eerie silence. During one of these pauses it was discovered that a rear wheel was grinding strangely; something in the axle (later found to be the bearing) had broken, and oil was seeping out from the hub. Nothing could be done at the moment; at all costs we must get out of the gorge by nightfall.

I could not help thinking anxiously of Bertram's warning about the danger of floods in the gorge. It was all very well to say, as soon as it rains make for higher ground—but a car cannot scale cliffs. Arrian relates a similar disaster that actually happened to Alexander when he was in this district: 'It so happened that the army bivouacked by a small stream, for the sake of the water it afforded, and about the second watch of the night it was suddenly swollen by rain. The actual rain was falling far away out of sight, but the stream nevertheless grew into such a torrent that it drowned most of the camp-followers' women and children and swept away the royal tent with everything it contained, and all the surviving animals, while the troops themselves barely managed to escape, saving nothing but their weapons . . .'

Round a corner in the gorge we came upon a terrible example. Some ten feet above us the body of a large eight-wheeled lorry lay up-ended, a hideous spectacle, smashed almost beyond recognition, wedged between massive boulders. How it could have been thrust so high above the present water-level, what power could have so pulverised it, did not bear thinking of. The metal body had been beaten as if by the hammers of giants, the axle ripped off, the engine torn from its casing. I looked up apprehensively at the sky: a pale cloudless blue, slowly fading as the evening set in.

The gorge came to an end, the cliffs falling back. We found

ourselves in a valley studded with wooded islands where the river wandered shallow and gentle again. We camped exhausted in a wood, driving away the day's memories in a blaze of firewood and what was left over from the bottle of *arak*.

The next day, the fourth from Zahedan, was the last. At every revolution of the injured wheel we were reminded that at any moment the car might break down irremediably. The cooling system failed; the engine boiled, and only now when every drop of water had been sucked from the wilderness we were crossing, it became an obsession with us, to reach the sea. At every ridge we paused to study the horizon in the hope of sighting a distant blue line of ocean. The track was so rough we could not travel much above walking pace. At sunset I climbed a hill and with binoculars scanned the southern skyline; in the fading purple light I could see the country flattening out, the hills at an end; it was just possible that that faint dark line was at last the sea. Hours later the road debouched upon smooth sand and all traces of it vanished.

A cool night wind blew in our faces: I could taste the salt. We travelled under gigantic cliffs cut out by a brilliant moon into huge shadows, the fantasia of a nightmare, cliffs which I felt would fall upon us. Stopping, we listened: surely? A faraway booming of surf. We came upon the track again and followed it up onto the cliffs. Standing at the brink I looked out under the stars upon a glittering expanse of the Arabian Sea. Far down to the left a cluster of lights sparkled at the edge of the bay: the lights of Charbahar.

In the morning we drove into Charbahar with half a dozen small boys clinging to the back of the car. It was smaller than I imagined. There was hardly a main street, hardly a street at all: only a little square surrounded by whitewashed houses opening onto a long beach where a few fishing boats lay stranded. Deep fine sand covered the square, littered with shells and fishbones. A few narrow lanes led off, lined for a short distance with cottages, before faltering into open paths along the shore. A number of dejected donkeys stood tied to the walls in the morning shade. We demanded tea, and sat uncomfortably round a wooden table, hastily erected, which we shared with a goat. Two cats lay under the table and a thin piebald puppy wagged its tail hopefully at my feet. The news of our arrival had begun to circulate, and a little crowd gathered round the table curiously.

These people were quite different from the Persians inland; many of them had almost black skins and seemed to come of African stock, with thick lips and broad noses. Later I learnt that these were mostly the descendants of slaves shipped over long ago from Oman and Muscat across the sea, in the days when Charbahar was a flourishing centre of the slave trade. A man, the picture of an eighteenth-century pirate, sat kicking his bare heels on the wall opposite, grinning at me diabolically between mouthfuls torn from a coconut. He wore loose dirty trousers and a knife stuck in his belt, a pink-and-black cloth was wound about his head, with one end hanging down the cheek, and in one of his ears there glittered a brass ring.

We were joined at the table by a young man who vaunted his superiority over the others in a double-breasted jacket which he had over his pyjama trousers. David ordered more tea while we waited for the inevitable questions. No, we were not Dutch, but English. Yes, from Zahedan. Why had we come to Charbahar? This was a question that was becoming increasingly difficult to answer. 'To get warm,' I replied. Our friend was uncertain whether to take this answer as a joke or an insult. We 'want to drive along the coast to Bandar-Abbas'. He smiled pityingly: 'There is no road for motor, only camel.'

This was absurd: the manager of the Bank Melli in Zahedan had shown us the latest maps—a road was quite clearly marked. 'Ah, there *will* be road! It is now planning!' He smiled triumphantly. He turned to the car where some children were drawing in the sand with the oil leaking from the axle. 'Your truck is sick?' 'Very sick; could you show us the garage?' He took this as another of our little jokes, and said nothing.

Governor in Pyjamas

The situation was becoming ridiculous. The axle trouble had occurred before, in Afghanistan the previous autumn. A twenty-ton press was needed to 'draw' the axle, equipment which only a large garage possessed. But surely this was Charbahar, a seaport? I turned to the beach, scanning the empty sands along the bay's gentle curve, the bare horizon of the sea beyond. A single dhow lay anchored out in the bay; a rowing boat was pulling towards the land. There was not even a quay.

A policeman shouldered his way to the table, hastily buttoning on his coat and slapping the dust out of his trousers. The uniform, I thought, must only be worn on occasions of importance. I was flattered, and offered him tea. He had come to take us to the Governor, and we left willingly enough: from the Governor at least we would learn the true facts.

We were shown into a large room with wooden chairs round the walls, a flat desk in the middle. A man in pyjamas sat behind the desk, writing. At our entry he jumped up, shook our hands hastily and with some embarrassment, and rushed out of the room. I was not quite sure if this was or was not the Governor. We were left alone for nearly an hour, helping ourselves to tea and bread, while we stared gloomily at the Shah's portrait on one side of the desk, the map of Persia on the other. The coast road to Bandar-Abbas was confidently marked in red. There was still hope. I would have preferred the interview to have taken place with the Governor in pyjamas to match our own disreputable appearance, but when he returned he was immaculate in a blue suit and suede shoes. With the help of an interpreter we discussed the situation. The Governor was charming, with a long sad face and beautiful hands with which he offered us the best cigarettes from Tehran. No, unfortunately, the road did not yet exist. Nor was there a garage in Charbahar. But perhaps the 'Hollanders' might help us. . . He would instruct one of his men to take us to them at once.

We were most curious to see these 'Hollanders', and drove past the village to a walled enclosure some way along the sand. It was quite true, they were Dutch: a Dutch engineering company, here to survey the coast, fully encamped with neat rows of tents, a kitchen, bread-ovens, servants. We were received with extraordinary kindness. A tent was put at our disposal and we were invited to stay as long as we liked. Any final confirmation that was needed as to the impossibility of the road we received from our hosts. They likewise had been taken in, and as a result were badly short of equipment. Most of it was still at Bandar-Abbas, with the rest of the group, though they had chartered a dhow which was expected with supplies any day.

That afternoon I indulged the vision dreamed up in the cold of Zahedan, walking for miles naked and unobserved along the sands, bathing in the warm blue water. I found a dead sea-turtle, stripped of its shell, some three feet across, lying decomposing in the sun. Once I was startled by nearly treading on a trunkless face that grinned up at me from the beach. The body was completely buried in the hot sand. Though he shouted a greeting I passed on quickly, with memories of the sick man of Ispakeh stirring uneasily in my mind. A cool breeze blew up at dusk. I watched a pair of long black fishing boats race in-shore, the dark-skinned half-naked fishermen leaping into the waves with shouts as they dragged their craft high up the beach.

At supper we met the rest of the group, about thirty of them, mostly young men. The bay was being methodically plumbed. The Persian government, I learnt, wished to develop the coast. Charbahar, it was hoped, would become a great sea-port. According to the Dutch it could never be more than a dream, as the amount of money necessary to convert this shallow bay into a harbour deep enough for big ships was so great that even a wealthy and industrialised country would hesitate at the undertaking. But there was a hint of politics in the background. Afghanistan craved an outlet to the sea, a port through which she could trade independently of Pakistan, whose refusal to hand over a large slice of Pakistan territory was still the cause of serious friction. The Afghan scheme was simply to run an autobahn from Kandahar down to Charbahar, if not through Pakistan territory then via Zahedan, altogether about 800 miles across some of the most difficult country in the world . . . Of course it was out of the question, even if the political side of it, which must have regard for the present friendship between Pakistan and Persia, were ignored. The Afghans are not even capable of keeping their own few roads in a fair state of repair—and this I knew from first-hand experience—much less could they afford to build a brand-new one ... But I had already come to the conclusion that this, unfortunately, is the way of thinking in this part of the world. When so much needs to be done, only the grandiose and the utterly impracticable is ever considered. I remembered that Lord Curzon mentions something about a plot he unearthed in the 1920s relating to Russian intentions to drive a corridor down to the sea here at Charbahar, and so gain an outlet to the Indian Ocean; I amused myself by wondering whether the Russians, who finance many of Afghanistan's projects, had anything to do with the alleged revival of this grotesque scheme.

It was pleasant after those four days of strenuous anxiety to relax once more in comparatively civilised surroundings, to drink morning coffee and eat European food, to lie out on the sand in the hot sun, and in the evenings to play chess and bridge, or poker ...

During these days I came to know quite well a young Dutch-man who was called Pierre. He told me that the Persians mystified him completely. He thought they were very strange people indeed, and in this I think I understood what he meant. He told me that not long ago he and a friend had been driving in a car through a desert not far from Shiraz. At one time they thought they were lost, and had been travelling across a stretch of wilder-ness apparently limitless when the wheels became stuck in the deep sand and they were forced to get out and dig them free. They had not been digging long when a Persian arrived trundling a wheelbarrow. What was particularly noteworthy about this was not so much the appearance of a man on foot in the middle of this desert but the contents of the wheelbarrow: it was full of sand; ordinary sand.

'Perhaps he was a lunatic,' I suggested.

'He might have been,' said Pierre. 'He made no sign of noticing us, and walked straight by. And we were so astonished that we said nothing to him at all. Certainly one of us must have been mad.'

But this was not all. No sooner had they dug themselves free of the sand than a man riding a bicycle passed. He had one hand on the handlebars and in the other he held an umbrella. 'Presumably,' said Pierre, 'because of the sun. It was midday.' These two events had made a deep impression on Pierre. Although, as he admitted, when described these incidents sounded merely ridiculous, he was convinced that for him at any rate they had some profound symbolic meaning. Especially the sand in the wheelbarrow.

Pierre and I usually partnered each other at bridge, and won substantially each time. I always played in a group where the bidding was in English, but I have never come across so many people who spoke so many different languages so well. David was unfortunate enough to get mixed up with the German-speaking party, and lost heavily; probably because he didn't speak German, and so confused all the suits. No one, as far as I can recall, ever spoke Dutch.

In the mornings Pierre would take a haversack and fill it with a great number of valuable instruments and go down to the beach where he would set up a pole and take a variety of bearings and measurements from other poles. When I had finished bathing I often came and sat near him, and we talked. I think the first subject we touched upon, besides the wonderful weather, was Zoroastrianism. He asked me if I had seen any Zoroastrians in Persia, and I told him that Yezd was one of the few remaining centres of this religion, but that as we had left Yezd sooner than we had intended, I had seen none at all. And the fire-temple? The one at Naksh-i Rustam has had its flame extinguished for centuries.

'Why on earth did they worship the sun when the sun can be such a menace in Persia?'

'Perhaps because it is like fire which, though it can destroy, also purifies. In any case sun and fire were only symbols for light, for the Good, Ahuramazda, floating over the heads of the Achaemenians and Sassanians at Persepolis and Bisutun.'

Pierre took a reading as he spoke.

'Then the smoke and the ashes from the fire must represent Darkness and Ormuzd.'

'The smoke at any rate,' I thought, but I wasn't sure about that and as neither of us knew much about Zoroastrianism we changed the subject to shellfish, of which there were many varieties scattered about the beach. Pierre was dark and short and had dreamy eyes. I enjoyed talking to him because he was always very straightforward, and liked the Persians; also he was the only Dutchman in the camp who refused to grow a beard.

When it came to Sufism, I could at least remember a little of what Ibrahim told me in the tea-house in Isfahan. *Suf* meant 'wool': the Sufis got their name because they were originally the ascetics of Islam, and wore nothing but a simple woollen cloak. They believed that a man could only learn to understand God by attaining the state of *fana*, the dying-of-oneself and the living-in-God; for God was everywhere and not least in each man's soul, if only he would see through the veil of himself and the world to the hidden truth within. 'I was a hidden treasure, and I desired to be known; therefore I created the creation in order that I might be known.' To 'know' God it was necessary to lead a blameless life of self-denial and contemplation.

'It sounds good to me,' said Pierre. 'One can only think clearly and to any purpose when one is alone for a long time. But what about the mystics, the poets like Hafiz and Sa'di, Rumi—I believe that their talk about the Beloved and Wine and Love is all symbols, it is allegory?'

So Ibrahim had said, but I think that it wasn't always so. I resolved to discover more from Ibrahim when I was in Isfahan again. As for Pierre, he also was determined to scratch the surface of this Sufism a little deeper. He was convinced that somewhere he would solve the riddle of that wheelbarrow full of sand in the desert, which seemed to have become so important to him.

❀

It had been difficult enough to reach Charbahar, but it appeared to be even harder to leave it. We could not encroach for much longer on the generous hospitality of the Dutch surveyors. A number of plans were considered, talked over with our hosts, and abandoned. Charbahar lay midway between Bandar-Abbas and Karachi. A dhow put in here about once a week, travelling to either port, and it was just possible that the car could be put on board. But there was no pier, and no 'capitan' was willing to beach his ship.

At one stage it seemed that our hopes might be fulfilled, and lengthy negotiations took place in the grubby office of the shipping agent. An exorbitant sum was asked, £100, to take the car the four-day voyage to Bandar-Abbas, an amount which we could not possibly afford and which was probably intended to be prohibitive. For although technically the plan to drive the car aboard when the ship lay stranded at low tide was feasible, the captain said that not all the beach was sand, there were concealed rocks. And there were also dangers of a sudden storm while the dhow lay in this defenceless position.

The Dutch-chartered dhow had come in and, though that ship was too small, we discussed the project with the captain. The two captains were brothers, and I think they must have been twins, for they looked exactly alike: bandy-legged and short, with immense broad shoulders and gnarled faces, blackened by sun and wind. They both wore very dirty headcloths and had several rings on their fingers. I learned from Pierre and his compatriots that their dhow-captain, for his intended two-month stay with the company in Charbahar, had contracted a temporary marriage—though he already had a wife and children at home in Bandar-Abbas. These Persian time-marriages had always interested me, and had even been wistfully considered, like so many delightful projects which one knows after all to be impracticable but nevertheless keeps happily in mind. For one thing, of course, we were never long enough in the same place. But on one score I was ruthlessly disillusioned by some of the members of the Dutch party who at Bandar-Abbas had gone into the whole matter with something more than academic interest. They had even seen some of the prospective brides, and once had been enough.

The time-marriage has been a feature of Persian life for centuries, and has always been regarded as a natural and almost inevitable part of it. When journeys were necessarily long and the caravans with their merchants were away for months, sometimes as long as a year, it is not surprising that a man should seek to continue his domesticated life in the city where for a considerable time he was forced to trade. A rented house, a wife to cook for him—no one can deny that in the interests of national stability and even of morality, there is something to be said for it. Now, however, when journeys are shorter, there is less need and therefore, perhaps, less excuse. But the authorities still sanction unions of this kind: one has but to find a bride, and a house, fix on the duration of the marriage and the sum to be paid, and sign a piece of paper. Naturally the price varies, depending on the length of the period: the shorter the more expensive, as a marriage of less than a month begins to carry with it the stigma of prostitution.

Temporary marriage has long been a subject of controversy between the rival sects of Islam, the Sunni and the Shi'ites, to which latter group the great majority of Persians belong. The Shi'ites believe that in the Koran there is no real pronouncement against the custom, and quote later traditions to support it; the Sunni, who include in their number most of the remaining Moslem world, interpret the Koran differently and find that it is forbidden. Differences like this one between the Shi'a and Sunni sects are not important. The basic difference is political, originating in the ancient dispute as to the succession of the spiritual leadership of Islam. The Shi'ites, or Persians, hold that this leadership passes from Mohammed not through his uncle and the Ommayad and Abbasid caliphs of Damascus and Baghdad, but through the Prophet's son-in-law Ali, and his murdered son Husein, to the Twelve Imams—the last of whom will return again at the end of the world.

The division had been widened and intensified by the Persian desire to become independent of the domination of the Arab world: there is a legend, therefore, that Husein before his death married a daughter of the last Sassanian king; and the founder of the Safavid dynasty, descended from the seventh Imam, was able to continue the tradition. By the time of Shah Abbas the Great the Shi'a sect was firmly rooted in Persia, and had become one with an instinctive Persian nationalism. Since 1500 Shi'ism, technically of the Jafarite sect, has been the national religion of the country.

The days were passing. We decided to call once more on the governor to see if perhaps his influence could sway the decision of the dhow-captain. The governor was polite, and offered to put his telegraphing system at our disposal, but regretted that he lacked the powers to requisition shipping for our personal use. . . . There were a number of people sitting in his office, the central figure being an unsmiling American, who was determined to remain undisturbed, quietly studying his papers, while a fierce argument raged over his head. He was an engineer commissioned by the authorities in Bandar-Abbas to prospect for the possible building of a school here. The news that an American engineer was coming had stirred the imagination of the inhabitants of Charbahar, and on being rowed ashore that morning the American had been surprised to find a delegation awaiting him on the beach, led by the village headman.

'They just wanted me to do a few little things for them while I was here,' the American told us drily. 'First they want a hospital. Also an electric plant. And a water-supply; a washing place; public lavatories. And I guess we'll give them a subway too.' He went back to his notes.

I saw the American once again, taking levels on a piece of sand behind the village. He was surrounded as before by a crowd of Persians all arguing at the tops of their voices. A group of children stood in the background, chanting unmelodiously. 'If these kind people would be quiet for a moment, I could do some work.' We

had come to thank him for the offer of his own dhow, provided
the captain was willing. But the captain had demanded £150 ...
He apologised for his inability to help and wished us luck.
We had decided, rather than stay in Charbahar for the rest of
our lives, to return to Zahedan if we could, by the gorge again.
The consequences of a possible breakdown on the route we already
knew were slightly less unpleasant than they might be somewhere
along the deserted shore of the Gulf of Oman. We thanked the
Dutch for their wonderful kindness and I said goodbye to Pierre.
I wished him luck with the solution of his sand-barrow riddle,
and suggested he call on Ibrahim in the tea-house, should he ever
visit Isfahan. As we drove into the hills the shadow of an aeroplane
passed overhead; the weekly mail-plane from Bandar-Abbas.
We stopped to look back, down at the little whitewashed
cottages on the edge of the bay, the dhow with sails furled
anchored on the glassy sea. Over at the camp a stream of half-
dressed Dutchmen were racing over the sand to the parked aeroplane, shouting and cheering at the prospect of their letters from
home.

Three days later we crawled through Khash. The gorge had
been easier than I expected. The river had shrunk to a trickle and
we found ourselves mounting dry rock ledges that before had
been white chutes of water. But all the time the rhythmic grinding
of the axle reminded us that our days were numbered; we drove
with a nervous caution. A lonely soldier lodged in a hut at the
edge of the gorge offered us dates and bread: he seemed sorry to
see us go. When, on the second day, the village of Ispakeh came in
sight, we made a wide detour to avoid passing too close. We
thought it might be unwise to renew our acquaintance with the
Sick Man, or his relatives. Should he have recovered we would
no doubt have been given a joyful reception; if he had not, had
even become worse ... then I suspected our reception would
have been joyful only in a particularly sinister way. At Khash we

also made no calls, preferring to sleep out rather than endure the deluge of sand; but other plans for us had been made. Scarcely a mile out of the village a hideous rending in the back, a lurch to one side, brought the car to a halt. The back wheel had fallen off. Burnt oil from the axle trickled black as pitch and bubbling on to the sand.

In a way we were lucky. There could have been no more convenient place for a breakdown of this magnitude. The military depot possessed the only powerful breakdown crane in the south of Persia. The Officers' Club once more became our home; we even saw the colonel. He was playing billiards with his officers, while a terrified soldier stood by with brush and pan, ready to step forward at intervals and sweep the billiard table free of sand. The next heavy military convoy left for Tehran in three weeks; we declined the offer with thanks: it was too long to wait. We chartered a private lorry from the village. Before we left we were asked once more about bandits—had we seen any? Of course not. I no longer believed they existed; they had been invented.

The scene was not without drama. The Land-Rover was suspended high above the lorry, while the engines of the breakdown truck thundered across the desert. A large section of the Khash population came out to watch. The crane swung round with its burden and began to lower it upon the lorry. At the last moment the lorry-owner lost his nerve. No, he couldn't do it. Why not? He had promised! Well, he had changed his mind.

We pleaded; we became very angry. The officers commanded him. No, he simply would not. A motor-cyclist was despatched to fetch the colonel, but the lorry-driver was off. He disappeared in the direction of Zahedan in a cloud of dust, and the car was left hanging pathetically in mid-air.

Two days later we had both returned to Zahedan by bus. The car was in the safe-keeping of the Khash depôt. David left by plane for Tehran, clutching the injured axle, carefully wrapped up in brown paper. In ten days, perhaps, he would be back, with the necessary new parts. In Zahedan they were still talking about bandits. It was not until two months later that I heard the news of the disaster. The four Americans must have made their fatal descent through the gorge about three weeks after we had come up it. The dead bodies of the three men were found near the car; the woman's was not recovered until later, when it was found some distance away among the rocks. Some people say that the bandits fired on the jeep, mistaking it for a police vehicle. The Americans had a weapon of some sort with them, and returned the fire. No one will know exactly what happened. My own guess is that they were mistaken for police; and I think that if they had had no weapon, or had not used it, no one might have been killed.

I walked out of the town across the hard channelled earth, out towards the line of bare brown hills whose sharp edges were outlined against the turquoise sky. It was warmer at last. I took off my coat and the sun burned comfortably into my shoulders.

I lay back against a rock and studied the town laid out below, flat roofs of mud-brick houses, lines of blue shadow marking the streets where men and women crawled like ants. The noise and clatter of the bazaar, dogs barking, drifted up across the desert. I turned to find myself looking at a flower sprouting miraculously by my hand. Farther away was another, blue and white, white and yellow, soft velvet petals triumphing for a moment in this iron wilderness of rock and sand. So it was true, the promise of a Persian spring, which I felt secretly had been a promise to myself alone, was being fulfilled.

I got up and walked back towards the town. I was thinking of a place where blue domes shine in the sun and scrolled minarets gleam against sky and mountain; a place where silver poplars line the streets, and pools lie as mirrors in the quiet courtyards of mosques; and a tea-house there, and faces in it that I knew. There would be a bus from Zahedan, and I would take it and go to Isfahan.

7

Return to Isfahan

❀

There is still something left of the old caravanserai romance, even in a bus-station. For in Persia it seems that only the method of travelling has changed: camels to motor-buses; to the Persian the spirit of the journey has remained the same.

Stand and watch in the corner of one of these bus-stations, in the evening, before the buses leave. Perhaps there will be a minaret, darkly pointing across the still-bright sky, a new moon balancing upon its topmost balcony. Below in the half-darkness of the yard there is all noise and confusion. The place is thronged with people talking and arguing, jostling round the heaps of luggage, round the waiting buses. They stand patiently these buses, monstrous coaches of tin and wood, painted the gayest colours that a Persian eye can demand: striped along each flank with crimson and green, turquoise and yellow, with the occasional rose of garish pink dropped as it were from heaven upon the bonnet. Men crawl like flies over them, hauling the boxes, bales of cloth and carpets up the ladders, cursing the skull-capped porters who struggle bowed under their loads through the press of people. Mechanics half hidden inside the bonnets make a last doubtful survey of the engines, tighten the last screws. Commands, counter-commands, expostulations . . . Stand back! someone is brandishing a starting handle . . . Voices are suddenly deafened by the first roar of the untried cylinders.

The beggars have turned out in strength, discreetly advertising their deformities. They stumble painfully among the crowd with arms outstretched, clinking handfuls of small coin, muttering their thanks to Allah for the alms received. Turbans and caps brush strangely together, long coats and flapping trousers with shabby Western suits; curled embroidered slippers knock delicately against cheap black shoes. In the corners huddle the women, blue-shawled and shrinking, only their eyes made bold by their inviolability. Especially attentive to them is the seller of charms and amulets, hideously illuminated Koranic texts . . . Buy one, or two, and you will be safe from the *djinns* of the desert, those malignant spirits always on the look-out to bewitch the unwary traveller. But doubtless you have already taken the necessary precautions.

One would think that the whole town was about to leave tonight. But for every traveller there is at least a half-dozen come to see him off; and besides, everyone is here to share the excitement. Those who are really going are easy to pick out. They pretend to shake off the endearments and encouragements of friends and relatives impatiently, as if to say, What's all this fuss about? If the family is travelling as well, their faces betray an added responsibility: the marshalling of the baggage (is it all there?), the women, children (keep together!). A mother, her face left unveiled in the urgency of the moment, clutches anxiously a child by the hand, a sack on her back, a baby trussed up in a bundle on her shoulder. The baby, if not stunned into wide-eyed amazement by the novelty of it all, is weeping hopelessly. Stop him crying! There is always the sweetmeat-seller ready at hand with his tray of sticky cakes and pink-and-green sugar-lumps . . . ragged boys pressing hungrily at his heels.

In the tea-houses opening into the yard, caverned deep in the mud-brick walls, the lights are on. Bare electric bulbs, hurricane lamps, charcoal fires blowing hot in the grates, cast out through the open doorways fierce broad beams of orange light, throwing huge shadows of men and buses across the yard, catching the flash of eyes or teeth, or painted metal. Along the benches against the wall the old men sit, sucking the long-stemmed bubble-pipes, sipping the inevitable glasses of green tea; looking on, wisely. A strange scent in the air: woodsmoke and water-pipes, petrol, oranges, the warm breath of spices from the ovens inside; all the smells of a city let loose in the evening air.

It is quite dark. Time for them to leave, any moment now. They are crowding noisily into the buses;—a driver has taken his seat and strikes the horn with authority. At last it is cool, a breeze chasing across the flat roofs, over the brown domes of houses edged faintly now with thin moonlight. Walk out in the road where the plane-trees rustle their dust-caked leaves. Follow the street, not far, and the houses stop, suddenly. Here, someone has dug a field of ditches. Beyond, the roads branch to all the compass-points, white ribbons swallowed immediately into the immense darkness. A bus thunders by, ablaze with light, rocking under its load upon the uneven surface. Someone is chanting the traveller's prayer: a chorus of voices shout the response, high above the muffled roar of the engine. Long after every sound has died away the bus's light is visible, a pinpoint moving far in the distance, dwindling, vanishing into a soundless gulf of stars. Turn your back quickly, walk back towards the warmth and light and comfortable noise of people. Your bus, the bus to Isfahan, leaves tomorrow.

From Azerbaijan and the Caucasus, south-east for a thousand miles to the deep waters of the Arabian Sea, stretches the plateau of Iran. On foothills based 4,000 feet above sea-level the mountains range across the bare tableland, chains of brown jagged peaks piercing a blue-brilliant dome of sky. In winter the mountains are white with snow, the peaks locked in conflict with the clouds; bitter winds sweep down from the north-east, ice-cold from the Turcman steppes. The deserts freeze. In spring the floods break loose. Bridges are washed away; buses and lorries plough axle-deep through mud, or lie abandoned in the fords. Week-end rivers, half a mile wide, swim suddenly across the desert, obliterating the roads, to disappear as suddenly as they came, leaving in their wake a brief riot of grass and flowers, in turn burnt up in the hot breath of summer winds. Time of wind-towers, craning above flat roofs to catch the faintest puff of air; of dust-devils, pillars of whirling sand dancing across the scorched plains; a time of boiling radiators, when buses carry chains and matting to fight the sand-drifts, when water is as valuable as life.

In Persia no one travels for pleasure. There must be a good reason for leaving the familiar surroundings of village or town: business perhaps, a visit to relations, or a pilgrimage to one of the holy cities, the tomb of some saintly Imam. When every journey is a long one, no journey can be undertaken lightly. Some of the dangers of Persian travel have lessened, some have changed their names. Banditry, on the main routes, is almost forgotten; even the legalised forms of robbery, the provincial tolls, have gone. Still, however, certain lawless gentlemen try to make a living in the south, where the wilderness of the terrain must always prove irresistible to the most apathetic outlaw. But the oldest enemy, the desert, remains; amd whether one travels by camel or by bus, the desert, and all the age-old terrors that belong to it, can never be long out of mind. Camels, it is true, may die; I had seen more than twenty in a single day, the sand blowing through their ribs, lining that old route across the wilderness of the Dasht-i-Lut, where no buses go. But buses also have a habit of breaking down; and every driver and his mechanic know that one day the engine will simply stop and die, perhaps a hundred miles from the nearest workshop. Though not this time, *Insha'allah*: God willing.

The ordinary Persian has turned his face inwards, away from the desert. He has learnt to ignore what he cannot comprehend: the power and the terror of this exterior world is of such magnitude as to become, in comparison with his own human efforts, almost meaningless. He lives absorbed in his self-contained community, prizing a fellowship made doubly dear by the relentless hostility on every side. What immediately concerns him, springing from out of the infinity around him, the sandstorms and the rain, he accepts. In the old days when a caravan appeared from over the skyline, and now, when a bus in a cloud of dust rumbles into the streets, the children run out to stare, the lounger sunning himself against the wall straightens up to gaze at the strangers dropped in for a moment from the outside world. Intruders, these travellers passing through; reminding him, with their glib talk of teeming bazaars and cities far away, of the narrowness and safety of his own quiet market-square. Names, names . . . tags at the end of that white track, forcing to the imagination distances so great as to defy calculation in terms of his own fields and hills—to be measured rather in *time*: a month to Shiraz, two months to Kazvin; and now that the camel-days are almost gone, in numbers of days. To travel . . . no; besides, 'God hateth him who roams'.

I was in Zahedan. It could be said that Zahedan marks the spot where the Kerman desert ends and the Baluchi desert begins . . . It boasts an airport, hardly more than a refuelling station between Tehran and Karachi, a bank and ten thousand people, and its mud-brick houses are as drab, the broad earth streets as rough, as those of any town in Persia. A colony of Sikhs in tight-woven pugarees, their beards carefully tied up in hair nets, have settled here as merchants; on certain days the narrow lanes of the bazaar are enlivened by the presence of white-turbaned Baluchi tribesmen, Afghans and a horde of Persian nomads in bright red-and-black rags. The Zahedani townsmen themselves are proud of the Western civilisation they are convinced they represent; but any feelings of superiority they might have towards their more backward visitors are confined to conversations among themselves, and evaporate before the actual presence of the tribesmen, particularly the Afghans. With sheepskins slung over their shoulders, these tall dark-bearded strangers from the mountains stalk through the streets not troubling to hide their contempt for the effeminate townsman in his shabby semi-European garb, who usually is miserably poor, and worse—takes no pains to conceal his poverty;

174

who appears to spend his time shivering in a blanket at street corners, or squatting in melancholy on the carpeted benches of the tea-houses, while his children in open shirts and patched fluttering trousers turn cartwheels in the open streets, to keep themselves warm from the icy wind.

One of these urchins, who preferred to call himself Johnny, attached himself to me and in fact came to regard me as his personal property. Like most Persian boys his hair was crew-cut, a useful custom: until they are old enough to do it themselves the mothers can the more easily remove the lice from their children's heads. Johnny's English was barely recognisable, and was confined to phrases such as: 'How are you, sirr? What a fine morning this day!' Nevertheless he was determined to improve, and each morning was let into my room in company with the breakfast and firewood, and while I was eating would systematically go through my possessions, trying on with undisguised pleasure the various articles of tattered clothing that still remained to me. He unearthed a hat which I had not yet worn, bought a year ago in a moment of weakness from a famous London store. 'I gather, sir, that you will be travelling east? In that case I have the very thing. This hat——' the assistant had leaned confidentially across the counter—'extremely fashionable in Baghdad just now, sir.' Tall-crowned, broad-brimmed and of the best grey felt, I had secretly admired myself in it; and though the ribald criticism of friends had to some extent undermined my confidence I had been certain that the time would come when, in favourable circumstances and in its proper locale, the hat would come into its own. Now, however, it seemed that I should not be visiting Baghdad, and besides the vicissitudes of travel had altered its shape: it was stained heavily with oil, smelt strongly of petrol. I presented it to Johnny.

His particular favourite was my silk dressing-gown, sole relic of better days. With this folded about his thin body and the Baghdad hat pulled rakishly over his eyes he would strike a theatrical pose and murmur with passionate intensity, 'How—are —*you*—sir?' Accompanied by Johnny (minus the dressing-gown, but proudly sporting the hat—which gave him a somewhat mushroom-like appearance) I would issue forth from the 'otal', stepping over the groups of cloaked men huddling over charcoal braziers, out into those brilliant cold mornings through the frozen streets of Zahedan, while a haze of mist and wood-smoke filtered upwards like some offering of incense into the the pale blue sky.

It was Johnny who steered me among the multitude of Persian notices at the post office, prevented me from buying twice too many stamps, and introduced me to the correct office at the Bank Melli, where two young clerks changed my traveller's cheque while I waited at the desk, drinking the tea they had immediately ordered. Somehow these two had acquired a ticket for a Maltese sweepstake, and they were anxious to have my opinion as to whether or not it was genuine. One of them spoke English, and I allayed his doubts as well as I could. A smile of happiness spread over his face: '*Certainly* will I win so much money?' I asked him what he would do if he won. It was all planned. First he would get out of Zahedan. Then, together, they would start a business. His friend would handle the Persian side of it while he, because of his English, would be the agent in England. How much money was needed to have an office in London? What sort of business? I asked. Carpets. 'You have seen the carpets of Kerman?' His eyes narrowed with pleasure as he caressed an imaginary rug. 'Ah—so beautiful! We shall have so many carpets ...'

I made it clear to Johnny that the sooner that I too left Zahedan the better. And so he took me to the bus station. By day the place was almost deserted. A few buses stood silent in the yard, and a mechanic half covered in oil was sitting on a petrol-can mending a puncture. We pushed open a door and discovered a man reading a newspaper while he picked his teeth, his feet up on the desk. '*Salaam aleikum ...*' Johnny began to explain his mission; the official listened with increasing interest. I began to grow impatient at this prolonged conversation over what was, after all, a very simple matter, and interjected the fundamentals of my request, Kerman—bus—when? He opened a drawer and laid out three rolls of tickets on the desk: white, pink, and a bilious green. Johnny stood back. It was up to me to choose,—no explanation of the significance of any of the colours was forth-coming from either of them. I picked the white, as being the least obnoxious. A groan escaped the official's lips and Johnny waved his hand emphatically, 'No, no!' I laid a tentative finger on the pink. The man slid back into his chair with a shrug of despair. I seized upon the green: the official beamed approvingly, and Johnny heaved a sigh of relief. I paid. And now it seemed that this absurd interview was over, except for one important detail: When did the bus leave?

I knew that the road to Kerman was flooded two weeks ago, and all communication in this direction had ceased; but now I understood the road had been repaired. The journey would take two days. To-day? I asked hopefully; the official shook his head. To-morrow, then? I *must* leave to-morrow. It was a mistake, I should have known, to press a point so determinedly. Impatience, to a Persian, is simply bad manners. The direct, 'European' method of approach is regarded not only as impolite, but little short of brutal. But a foreigner in all his crudity must be accepted, and, although most Persians are too polite to show their dislike for this sort of behaviour, they will meet it with a benign passive resistance, an apparent anxiety to please which renders every frontal assault futile. There is more than one doorway leading to the answer of every question: it is the side-entrance that is favoured in Persia. The official began to lose interest; Johnny seemed evasively acquiescent. It seemed that the bus left to-morrow.

The next afternoon I paid my hotel bill, after the usual wrangle over double charges and extras: an exhausting battle in which victory must go to whoever can display most convincingly the appropriate series of emotions involved in such a transaction. It is taken for granted that a foreigner is rich: how else could he have come so far from his own home? And 'every man according to his means' is, after all, only fair. But if one dislikes being cheated, or better still, cannot afford to be cheated, more than is absolutely necessary, then there is an ancient formula whose steps, ordained since time immemorial, must be faithfully followed. The bill is presented. I scan it and fix my eyes on the total. Have I read correctly? Surely there has been some mistake? No. Ha-ha! Then it is a practical joke, and a very good one. I congratulate the hotelier, we laugh heartily. The next stage follows on quickly. The bill is neither a mistake nor a joke. Instant payment is demanded. I refuse point blank. The demand is sternly repeated. I point out that the bill is a gross fiction, designed to cheat me of my last *rial*, and I pick out at random a few of the more flagrant over-charges. The hotelier begins to get angry. He enlarges upon the excellence of his hotel, of the room, the food, of himself and of his reputation. He raves, gesticulates, his eyes flash. I wait patiently, guarding my strength: I too can flash eyes, wave arms, rave; all these things I have learned to do if not perfectly at least adequately. My turn will come . . . it has come: I begin. I point to the floor, it is never swept; to the roof, it leaks; to the beds, they are dirty, uncomfortable. I describe the quality of the food: revolting; and the squalor, the incomparable squalor of himself, his guests and his 'hotel'. I appear furious, bitter, almost uncontrolled. (It is true: by this time, I am.) Finally we are finished: each of us has descended, spent, from his tower of ire: we face each other again as ordinary men. It is time to be reasonable. I take him by the arm, and suggest that we make out the bill again, item by item. We compare the total with the original, and find that it has shrunk to half. The hotelier is surprised, shocked: there had indeed been a mistake. He apologises; we both apologise. I pass across the money with a generous tip. We shake hands and almost fall on each other's necks; and we part—friends.

It is important to notice that throughout this entire gamut of emotional stages not once should either party be sincere. Unfortunately only too often the anger (on my part) is inclined to be genuine. But this is a pity. Because it must be possible to discard and replace each emotion at will; and to find that one is still angry at a moment when in fact one should be conciliatory . . . is not only upsetting, it destroys the structure of the bargaining process, tilts a delicate balance with unsatisfactory results. Sometimes I feel that I am being unfair, as a foreigner is not expected to dispute a bill, and is usually in too much of a hurry to waste time arguing; but although I could always subscribe to the thoroughly un-Persian habit of always being in a hurry, I was never in the enviable position of being able to afford being cheated overmuch. Of course I have still paid too much, probably twice too much; but not three times . . .!

I was surprised when Johnny did not come to say goodbye; perhaps he would be at the bus-station. But the big wooden gates in the archway were closed. I left my baggage on the ground and hammered on the doors. The bus to Kerman! I shouted. It might have gone: already it was getting dark. An old man sat hunched and shivering against the wall, his eyes covered by a corner of his cloak. He jerked his head backwards and stared at me disapprovingly. '*Jomeh*', he said. Friday! The Persian Sunday. No wonder Johnny hadn't appeared.

The next afternoon Johnny arrived punctually and beaming. I thought it pointless to bring up the affair of the previous evening, but tried to make my feelings plain by a certain coldness in my manner. I tried to think of an excuse for his behaviour. No doubt he must have thought that everybody knew nothing happened on a Friday; by 'to-morrow' he had naturally meant 'the first day something *could* happen'. Obviously, faced with my stubbornness, he and the ticket-official had not thought the point worth arguing . . . We walked to the bus-station in silence. The place had changed overnight. We passed from the quiet street between the open gates into the courtyard, into another, an older world.

It was still early, but dusk; the west still bright with the traces of sunset: that strange blue half-light when faces are hard to recognise, when there is an unreal feeling of being cut off and at the same time blended with one's surroundings. As yet no bus had left, but two had taken up positions facing the archway;

a little boy had escaped his mother's arms and was making a wild scramble across the bonnet: only just as he reached out for the slender arm of the windscreen-wiper, a flurry of excited hands including the driver's, his mother's and those of various onlookers dragged him back. I made my way towards the office and found an empty place on the benches against the wall. The warmth of the stove was pleasant after the frosty air outside. Behind the counter the bus official, my acquaintance of two days ago, was defending himself vigorously against the verbal onslaughts of a family of would-be travellers who were pressing in on him, brandishing a bunch of tickets—white ones, I noticed. I watched the official's unsuccessful attempts at explanation without sympathy. Apparently it is the custom to issue more tickets than in fact there are seats. This ensures that every bus leaves full, but the system has its obvious drawbacks, from the passengers' point of view . . .

A number of men had in curiosity collected around me, and a young man who introduced himself as Ahmed took upon himself the job of interpreting the inevitable questions. 'Do you like Persia?' 'Which is bigger [and therefore better], Tehran or London?' 'Why don't you travel by Iran Airways?' Johnny, who was annoyed at finding someone who spoke English better than himself, sat on my suitcase in a sulk. They took from their pockets paper bags crammed with every kind of eatable, and offered me boiled sweets, bread, nuts, lumps of brightly dyed sugar, even a packet of cloves. I retaliated by bringing out my biscuits. It is worth knowing that Persian custom insists that something offered, even a cigarette, must out of politeness be refused at least twice before it can be accepted. Ignorance of this may lead to scenes of acute embarrassment, especially for a stranger like myself, who does not know the correct tone to imply a genuine refusal. Often I have had recourse to feigning illness, by laying my hand tenderly on my forehead or stomach and giving out a slight moan. Sometimes this has the desired effect; usually it only serves to redouble the attentions of my sympathetic acquaintance, who fishes out some infallible and often unpalatable panacea for my imagined ills. But I blush with shame when I remember the occasions when, unaware of this particular item in the Persian code of manners, I have offered someone an English cigarette—always a rare and highly prized object—and on their first and natural refusal, have calmly lighted one myself, returning the packet to my pocket.

Ahmed followed me out into the crowded yard, talking volubly into my ear. He said he was going back to his wife in Kerman. I congratulated him, but the gloomy expression on his face showed that my pleasure on his behalf was misplaced. What he wanted was sympathy. 'No, this is trouble,' he said, 'I married too early.' This seemed quite possible. I looked at his thin face with its short crop of black hair, the large dark eyes that alternately glowed with a short-lived vivacity or gazed with a sort of deep sadness as if all the world pained him unutterably ... or was it in-difference? He could not have been more than twenty, and had been married nearly three years. We were standing aside from the main press of people to make ourselves heard above the babble of voices, the throbbing of the motors. At our feet in the shadow of a bus, huddled in the darkness against the wall I made out the shapes of four women, veiled from head to foot, crouching beside a heap of sacks and boxes. They spoke not a word, but simply waited. A little girl, her face buried in a roll of carpet, moaned softly to herself.

'But your wife', I said, 'she must be beautiful.' 'Yes, ah yes!' exclaimed Ahmed excitedly; and then, after a moment's struggle with himself and a sidelong glance at me, as if to say 'Well, I might as well confess all', he sighed deeply and admitted: 'No. She is so not.' 'Well, then, why did you marry her—if you don't like her?' But really, I knew the answer. Persians very rarely 'marry': they are married. The match is arranged by the parents when the two children are very young; much later comes the ceremony, or rather two ceremonies, and the bridal couple who may well not have seen each other until that moment, except for a few ritual words, are pushed together for the start of a new life, if they are lucky in a house of their own, more often to live with one of their in-laws. The system has always had its apologists, and no doubt many happy marriages are arranged this way. But often it means that the husbands spend little of their time at home, passing their free hours in the masculine society of the streets or tea-houses. Women are kept sternly in the background, their presence in bed and at table taken for granted. Attempts to emancipate women by legislation, in Turkey by Mustapha Kemal, in Persia by Reza Shah and in Afghanistan by Amanullah have all met with near-failure. The women themselves are obstinately against it. Instinctively they prefer to hold what privileges their present life, however much in the background, confers on them, rather than risk all in an attempt to live contrary to the way their religion and traditions have prepared for them. Ahmed listened with horrified sympathy as I briefly outlined to him the contrasting position in Europe and America, with its increasing tendency towards matriarchy.

Sounds of high argument from across the yard drew us towards the gateway where a man stood declaiming his wrongs to a circle of attentive listeners. He was a mechanic, his bare muscular arms, smeared with oil, waved over his head. Apparently he had not been paid for a month. He had a wife, children, he worked hard. So much was clear. He stood in the glare of the headlights, eyes flashing, spitting his accusations from between white teeth. A dramatic performance, that held his audience tight-bound in sympathy. His boss was a tyrant, a miser! Furthermore he was going to stand it no longer, he was going to see his boss, *now*. He looked round his audience for support: they were behind him, to a man. With a last menacing gesture of his oily fist he made for the entrance, the crowd surging eagerly behind. The 'boss', it seemed, lived only a few houses from the bus-station. The mechanic beat upon the rickety wooden door. Perhaps he was drunk. Everybody beat on the door. Suddenly, and to everyone's surprise, the door was flung open, and the mechanic overbalanced into the darkness beyond. The door was slammed behind him. Sounds of confused altercation reached the listeners outside. At this moment a policeman appeared, and dispersed the unresisting spectators. The excitement was over: they were no longer interested.

During this incident I had lost Ahmed in the crowd. Back in the bus-yard I dived into a tea-house, and sat with legs drawn up upon the carpeted bench, sipping at a little glass of scalding tea while the noises of preparation outside were reduced to a distant hum. Nothing had been done to disguise the primitive structure of the room; nails, on which were hanging strings of onions and bunches of dried dates, jutted from the plain mud-plastered wall; pieces of straw stuck out from between the bricks. On a ledge covered with sacking knelt a man saying his prayers, bowing up and down, murmuring gently to himself. There were three others sitting in the shadows, their stolid faces lit by the glow of charcoal braziers. No one moved, no one spoke. The samovar hissed on the stove, the fire crackled in the grate, relieving the gloom with sudden darts of flame.

My bus was already two hours late, for no particular reason. It was just late. I could see out through the low open doorway into the yard, a confused movement of people round the buses. Somewhere, very near me, a baby was crying; the mother with soft tones trying to soothe it. One of the buses seemed to be starting: the bus to Meshed, a three-day journey, filled with pilgrims to the holy city. The noise of engines and voices, the wail of women and children, reached a new pitch. If I wanted to, I could be with Amin and Ghani again, in two or three days . . .

A breathless figure burst into the tea-house: Johnny, in my Baghdad hat. 'Ah, sir, at last! The bus is to leave!' We stood beside the bus and looked up at the tiers of luggage roped on the roof. The height of the bus had been increased easily by half. It looked as if it would overbalance, and surely bring down the arch over the gateway. I could just make out the corner of my belongings crushed under an enormous tin trunk. A crate of screeching chickens was being pushed into place; a couple of bicycles crowned the whole. I shook Johnny warmly by the hand. He seemed sorry to see me go, almost tearful. 'Ah, sir, you have taught English so greatly!' I made a final adjustment to the brim of his hat; yet I felt that the assistant who had sold it me in London would not have approved.

Somebody gave a signal: there was a rush for the door. In the muddled darkness of the interior I could see that the gangway had been entirely choked with luggage. Sacks of flour, thick wool cloaks and blankets, rolled carpets and huge cotton bags stuffed with clothes and food for the journey were piled waist-high between the narrow seats. To reach my own, somewhere at the back, I had to crawl perilously balanced on hands and knees the length of the bus, rough hands helping me on, until I was safely wedged in my place. I was aware of close breathing around me, across the gangway the outline of women's shawled heads. At my elbow a half-moon face was examining me curiously, humming a strange wail of song under his breath as he peered.

On the roof the last knot had been tied. The bus shook: the engine burst into power. The driver shouted something out of the window that was lost in the uproar of last prayers and fare-wells. Inside the lights went on, the headlights blazed across the yard, putting to rout the groups of startled travellers, the ragged women with their babies, the limping beggars who forgot to limp. We were off—under the old brick arch that bends under the stars, out past the hotel and the rows of shuttered shops, turning down the blind high-walled streets of Zahedan until suddenly there was nothing, and the windows turned in on us, and it seemed that we travelled almost soundlessly, engulfed in a great darkness that was the desert.

We were alone, making for ourselves a tiny world in motion, a world safe in the familiarity of talk and warmth and the close-ness of each other, while the cold wind tore at the canvas roof-covers and the bus, defiant with noise and light, drove back the darkness ahead. A glimpse of lit windows, close-packed heads, a smell of dust—and we were gone, and the night and desert closed up behind. '*Allah humma sala a'le Mohammat . . .*!' Everyone joined. The *Salavat*, traveller's prayer, intoned in a triumphant sing-song chant, one man taking the lead, the rest following with the chorus. The prayer is sung at the start of every journey, whenever in fact the bus begins to move, even after a brief halt. Anyone can take the lead, and in this bus the response was always general and full-hearted. Later when I had travelled in smarter and swifter coaches, where most of the passengers were clerks or students or business-men, the custom had been almost wholly abandoned: sometimes an old peasant would start up in a quavering voice, but the lack of response would chill the words in his throat. Then, if I had only known the words, I would have shouted them out!

I began to take stock of the bus and its contents. My attention was first drawn to my companion, who had the place next to the window, and who seemed to be taking up more than his fair share of the seat. His name was Mansur, and he offered me a sweet. His face was perfectly round, and the top half of his head was enclosed in a circular turban which once had been white, but with no centre; so that when I stood up—no easy thing to do—I could see the dome of his shaven head protruding. That he possessed immensely broad shoulders was no comfort to me in our painfully restricted position. He was dressed in a most original fashion, having simply bought a large grey blanket and had it cut into a long coat, without lapels or lining, which reached to his knees. What was left over had been used for a waistcoat. Mansur loved to hear himself sing, in that wailing nasal treble that is so admired in Persia. At first I was foolish enough to praise his voice, which later I regretted. Overjoyed at finding an audience as attentive as himself, he sang for most of the night, and whenever my attention appeared to wander, would bring me back to consciousness by putting his mouth close to my ear . . . Not that I could really become angry with him. He told me he was born in Kerman, and was now returning from a pilgrim-age to Meshed, the tomb of the martyred Imam Reza, one of the greatest saints of Shi'ite Islam. As a pilgrim with this journey to his credit he was entitled to be called *Mash'adi*; there was no doubt that he was justifiably proud of himself. He never seemed to run short of religious texts, verses, prayers, any of which he would bring out on the slightest pretext. He would roll his black eyes, wrinkle his short snubbed nose, and, putting back his head, emit the most heart-rending notes.

There was some rivalry in the bus as to who should lead these communal travelling prayers, on each and every occasion that the bus stopped or started. Mansur considered himself worthy of this privilege, not only because of his fine voice but also because of his late religious experience. But somewhere in the front of the bus there sat an elderly peasant with white whiskers, who wore the green turban that distinguishes those descended from the Prophet himself: and this illustrious gentleman considered it was his inalienable right to lead the prayers ... One would have thought that Mansur would gracefully surrender to this grey-bearded *seyid*, but no, the battle was to be contested to the bitter end. At first it seemed that the green turban would win the day; his years and his descent carried the support of the majority of the passengers. But Mansur was indefatigable, and went about the task of silencing his rival in the most unscrupulous way. He began to start his singing a fraction *before* the bus started, or would peer out of the window and give tongue as soon as the bus even slowed up ... Devices which quite put out the greybeard in the front. Even—and this I could not approve, though out of loyalty to my bench-companion I often lent him my moral if not vocal support—he would begin his own singing when the old man had already got under way, calculating that a few sleepers in the back would be suddenly woken and follow the nearest and loudest voice. In this pre-supposition he was usually correct, but it was an unworthy tactic which always resulted in a hideous and most unholy babel.

Besides his voice, his broad shoulders and high spirits, there was one further disadvantage of having Mansur as a close companion on a long and tiring journey. He was afflicted with a most unpleasant open sore on the side of his face, which he was forced to dab continually with a filthy piece of wadding. Whenever the discharge became too much, he would wipe the wadding on the window pane ...

Across the gangway, which was piled with luggage up to my

chin, sat two women with their daughters aged about ten and fourteen. All four were enveloped from head to foot in *chadors*, the dark-blue shawls commonly worn by Persian women. I began to notice that the two girls, with shawls drawn close under their eyes, were regarding me intently. Whenever I happened to glance in their direction they would snatch their heads away and whisper diabolically into their mothers' ears. The mothers stirred uneasily. I was irritated at this: I was being framed. I had visions of these two worthy matrons suddenly denouncing me as a seducer of innocent Moslem maidens and demanding instant vengeance: I could almost see myself left to die, battered with stones by the passengers inflamed with religious and other prejudices . . . I resolved to remove every possible misunderstanding. The next time I glanced that way, to find the two pairs of velvety black eyes fixed malevolently upon me, I frowned, I scowled. An immediate panic followed, a flutter of shawls and whispers, which resulted in the transfer of the two girls to the seat beyond. In some ways I was rather upset at finding myself so successfully horrific: my face, after all, though having nothing in particular to recommend it, was at least—so I had always thought—quite inoffensive. Perhaps they thought that I had the 'evil eye': anyone in Persia whose eyes are coloured with any resemblance to blue is said to be invested with this unwelcome power. Or else it was my hat, unusual enough in this part of the country, of Caucasian fleece, with ear-flaps. On the other hand, when I looked at the variety of headgear—turbans, skull-caps, peaked furs, felts —worn by those about me, I realised that mine could not have excited more than a moment's notice. The two girls, now safely beyond my baleful sphere of influence, composed themselves to sleep.

The young ladies were not the only persons intrigued by my presence in the bus—or perhaps 'intrusion' was the better word. But Persians are some of the best-mannered people in the world, and, unlike most Turks, Afghans, Indians, are prepared to make an effort to conceal their curiosity. I suffered the usual rounds of sweets and cakes. I admitted that I was English; but when

Return to Isfahan

Mansur wondered, diffidently, as to what was my *purpose*, what was my reason for being in Persia, I found myself at a loss to give an adequate reply. No, I was not on business; no, I had no connection with Oil, or Roads, Surveys or Country Planning. I was beginning to find the subject as absorbing as it was to them. What was I? Why was I travelling by night in a Persian bus, why was I in Persia at all? Two elderly men were muttering together, casting an occasional discreet glance in my direction. Ahmed leaned back from his seat farther up the bus and called back to me.

'Sir, they say you are *sayyah*. In English, what is *sayyah*?'

'Something like . . . *pilgrim*,' I answered.

It seemed that the question of my identity, at least as far as my companions were concerned, had been satisfactorily solved. I was a *sayyah*: a pilgrim. Very well, then, a pilgrim, but a most uncertain one, with no definite goal in mind; travelling, but towards no particular shrine. After all, there are so many to choose from; and how could I be certain as to where I was going until I arrived? I would have liked to have gone to sleep with this enigmatic thought circulating drowsily in my head, but sleep was almost out of the question.

Nothing could have been more uncomfortable than the seating of this bus. The benches were so narrow and so close together that to put my knees down I had to sit bolt upright. The backs were too short for any head rest. There was a bar in front of me on which I tried to rest my forehead, but even when this was well padded with my hat, the continual bouncing and bumping of the bus threatened to give me a black eye. Every possible position was therefore of exquisite agony. I tried to resign myself to what must be my fate for the next two nights and a day. As the bus tore on through the darkness some of the lights were turned off, and most of my fellow-travellers, perhaps more adaptable to conditions of this sort, seemed to drop off to sleep. I began to notice that the interior of the vehicle was decorated in bright pink-and-white paint, with silken tassels and fringes of pale green hanging from the ceiling. The attempted luxury, the silk and colours, made a macabre contrast with the real condition of the bus, which seemed to be on the point of falling to pieces. In many places rust had eaten through the paint, revealing in brown patches the scarred and decaying metal. I remembered the battered appearance of the outside, especially the front: the dented bumpers and beaten-out wings—evidence of the bus's long and stormy life. Before the driver's seat I could just make out a gallery of lurid religious prints and paintings plastering the cab, charms and Koranic texts, beads, and even a bunch of spring flowers stuck in front of the wheel.

At times I must have dozed, to be rudely awoken by the bus grinding to a standstill before some solitary mud cottage. We would clamber out into the fresh air, shivering in the cold and silence, and disappear into the darkness for a while before entering the warmth of the tea-house, where from crowded ledges round the walls a flood of talk would be loosened by glasses of hot tea, while the drowsy and tousled proprietor busied himself with the eggs over a blazing fire.

Dawn came unawares, lighting the sky behind us, gradually withdrawing the horizon until the distant chains of mountains were revealed in softest shades of blue and purple, and the sun winked over the skyline, turning the desert to gold. We came to our first and only obstacle. The floods of three weeks ago had sent a sudden sea of water down from the hills which had swept the road into oblivion, making for itself a six-foot channel 800 yards wide across the plain. The water had gone, but the road had still to be rebuilt, and traffic must cross this belt of fine soft sand. A number of lorries were waiting their turn, and we drew in behind them. Only one vehicle could cross at a time, as the roadmenders had only a few planks to bridge the sand. The planks were thrown down in front of both sets of wheels and the bus would move slowly over them; another set was meanwhile hurled down ahead, and so with a great deal of running and shouting, a steady if ant-like progress was made across the river bed.

Some of the passengers took the halt as an opportunity to say their midday prayers. They removed their hats and shoes, and spreading cloaks or blankets upon the ground, knelt down

unselfconsciously, facing south-west. I noticed that only two
prayer-rugs were produced. One was faded and moth-eaten, the
colours hardly distinguishable; the old gentleman with the green
turban, however, unrolled a much better piece, though this too
was old and somewhat worn. I caught a glimpse of rich dark
reds, blue and a splash of yellow, before the voluminous folds
of the old man's white pantaloons hid the rug from my sight.

I walked over to where a rescue party was digging out the
washed-up remains of a lorry that had been caught in the flood.
It was a remarkable sight. The force of the water almost entirely
buried it in the sand, which when soaked had acted like quick-
sand, sucking the lorry under. A fifteen-foot-deep pit had been
made in order to dig out the lorry, which was prevented from
sinking further by chains and hooks suspended from a wooden
structure erected over the pit; the water that remained at the
bottom was being drawn out by pumps. Ahmed joined me at the
pit-head and together we sat watching the operation, spitting out
date stones into the water. In a way I was glad that Ahmed's seat
in the bus was some rows ahead of mine: the strain of keeping
up a continuous conversation in pidgin-English would have been
unbearable. I asked him when we should arrive at Kerman. To-
night perhaps, he said; very late. And Isfahan? I would have to
take another bus (a much better one) from Kerman: it was another
two days' journey to Isfahan. We got up to leave; the driver was
shouting from across the river bed that all was ready again, when
one of the hooks on the lorry suddenly broke, and the lorry was
tipped over sideways into the water, immediately sinking six feet
into the mud. We left to the sounds of the engineer's frenzied
cursing, as he seized a piece of brushwood and leapt down into
the pit to belabour the unfortunate coolies digging in the water.

It was becoming very hot. The sun fastened down upon the
tin roof, burning inwards upon the bus's close-packed cargo
of bodies. A few windows were forced open, and every now
and then someone would take off his hat and brush it free of its
coating of white dust. Mansur drew from his pocket a brown-
paper envelope; with great care and pride he took out a pair of

dark glasses which he ceremoniously stuck on his nose. Whenever we stopped the glasses were carefully returned to the envelope. He was surprised that I had none. In Persia, as elsewhere in the East, dark glasses are the hall-mark of a certain urbanity, and therefore of superiority: the larger the lenses the more sophisticated the wearer. It is the same with the quality of shoes. My own shoes should have been discarded long ago; but they were better than Mansur's, which, as I discovered when I walked behind him into a tea-house, had no soles.

The relief offered by those wayside halts was welcome to everyone. Besides the refreshment of tea, there was always the opportunity of having bread and eggs, fruit, and a delicious bowl of *sar-schir*—slightly soured cream taken with sugar. Behind the tea-house there was always fresh water, either an open flowing *quanat* or a water-tank. The passengers would line up, taking turns to pour over each other's heads quantities of the cool water from graceful metal jugs or jars of painted earthenware.

As the afternoon drew on the western horizon was gradually filled with the blue shapes of mountains: to the right the first foothills of the great Kerman range, which five months previously David and I had succeeded in crossing, a short cut to the edge of the Lut desert beyond. We were nearing the town of Bam. Columns of whirling sand nearly a hundred feet high danced in company with us across the desert: I have always imagined that it was in these dust-devils that the dervishes originally found inspiration for the rapid gyrations of their dance.

Sometimes we passed through the remains of villages, derelict shells of houses with crumbling walls and gaping doors, with often a little crenellated mud fort, its towers and arches collapsed in ruin, overlooking the plain. Sometimes these villages seemed only just abandoned: I almost expected to see the last remnants of the villagers trailing out of the far gateway laden with their possessions even as we entered, but always they were quite deserted. Gusts of wind sent the dust scurrying along the empty streets; dust-devils whirled desultorily in the courtyards. Strange places, where I felt I would not like to be left alone. We never stopped. I once asked Mansur the cause of this sinister abandonment. He simply rolled his eyes and raised his hands, palms upwards. Allah alone knows. Perhaps it was that the buildings, made solely from mud, had been washed away beyond repair in a particularly rainy winter; more likely it was the failure of the water supply, the collapse of the *quanats*, underground channels that brought water from the mountains, upon which the life of these villages depended.

The town of Bam came in sight. Groves of palm trees waved their feathered leaves against a background of tawny hills, shimmering in the heat; beyond, the mountain-tops glittered with snow. Bam was once an important fortress, defending the main road from India; the battlemented walls and bastions still stand, but the city gates no longer open and close. We drove through the broken wall into the main street. Many of the passengers had reached their destination, and we were to have at least half-an-hour's halt; besides, there was something wrong with one of the wheels.

I had become friendly with the driver of the bus, Mohammed, and with his mechanic, Akbar, and already I had been promised a more comfortable seat in the front, once the bus emptied a little. Mohammed was short and square, with a reserve and sense of powerful confidence that must be necessary for one who is responsible for piloting a bus across Persia. Anyone who can drive is much respected by the ordinary Persian, and a bus-driver holds a quite exalted position. He has taken the place of the elected leader of the caravan of days gone by, and once the journey is begun his word is law. Any intransigence among his passengers he will deal with firmly and often high-handedly: he knows that the rest of the bus will support him. Besides the fact that I was a foreigner, and therefore an object of some interest, I earned Mohammed's regard somewhat when he found that I too possessed a vehicle, a 'mosheen', though admittedly mine was left for the moment wrecked in Baluchistan. Because I was a stranger and was travelling in his bus Mohammed felt responsible for me, and often without a word to me he would stride into a tea-house and make quite certain with the proprietor that I was not being overcharged. He had a sense of humour, but spoke very little—except to chaff his mechanic, Akbar, a much younger man, tall and well built with a gay and often diabolic expression in his eyes. Akbar abounded with energy and strong good humour, which was directed to practical joking; as when, after a halt by a stream, he filled the old man's green turban with sand . . . a joke which was not, as a matter of fact, taken too well, and which brought on him Mohammed's stern reproval. Akbar never boarded the bus until the last moment, when running alongside he would leap aboard with a shout, swinging the doors shut behind him. Several of the passengers suffered from his clowning and banter, but generally he was popular, as anyone will be who can relieve the monotony of a long journey.

We left Bam as the sun was setting, and before turning north-west, drove for some time straight into the red eye of the sun, blazing over the black ridges of the hills. The desert had turned a fiery crimson, the palms and hills in shadow the deepest black. It seemed that we were moving in the glow of a mighty furnace, an illusion quickly dispelled by sudden gusts of cold air that blew in through the open windows.

The bus was half empty now, and the atmosphere was at once more informal and more cheerful, with everyone joining in the conversation, joking and laughing together. The descendant of the Prophet had got off at Bam, and so Mansur was left in un-disputed control of the religious proceedings, an opportunity of which he took the fullest advantage, stretched out in comparative comfort in the back. I sat in the place of honour, next to Moham-med. Behind me a large smiling woman, who no longer took the trouble of veiling herself, held two cherubic babies in her vol-uminous lap. It was plain that Mohammed and Akbar were old friends and understood each other perfectly: a friendship born of long association on numerous desert journeys such as this. There was a photograph stuck on the panel showing the pair of them at a wedding feast, clean and shaven, in smart double-breasted suits, arm in arm. The smooth smiling faces in the photograph bore little resemblance to the swarthy three-day-bearded figures beside me—a contrast I pointed out, and which drew a great hoot of laughter from Akbar. He invented an amusing game in which I played a leading role, and which kept the passengers behind convulsed with laughter. He would sing a verse of a Persian song and I would imitate him as exactly as I could, keeping to the tune and producing sounds as similar as possible to his own. The show was a great success. We nearly ran into a camel half blinded by the headlights who was browsing by the roadside, doubtless surprised to see this strange and monstrous meteor of thundering engines, bursting with light and shouting and singing, shoot past him in the night.

I was surprised when Akbar insisted that I follow him in the chanted prayer-call of the muezzin—'God is Great, There is no god but Allah, and Mohammed is his Prophet ...' but the passengers behind roared with laughter. I thought back on the astonishing contrasts of religious feelings I had noticed in Persia: the cynical indifference of the suave Tehrani; the jealous fervour and prejudice of crowds at holy cities like Qum or Meshed—or indeed at Yezd, where it was really dangerous for unbelievers to trespass on sacred ground; and finally the attitude of the uneducated people of the countryside, where religion is taken as a natural and integral part of living; where a man may kneel down and pray in the middle of a group of friends or strangers without disturbing himself or those talking over him, and where faith is so deeply and unquestionably founded that unmalicious humour on the subject is accepted without concern, simply because it could do no possible harm.

We stopped in a village where everyone except the tea-house owner was asleep, and where Mohammed treated me to tea and a water-pipe. There also we picked up the postman. He was a little squirrel-like man with clothes and a turban many sizes too large for him. He had short grey hair and little watery eyes, and carried a bulging sealed mailbag which was deposited carefully by the door. An hour later Akbar had to get out and crawl under the bonnet with a screwdriver: Mohammed was having difficulty with the steering. Not long after, the little postman nudged Mohammed and pointed to the place where the mailbag should have been, and no longer was. Akbar was detailed to search for it: it was probably under a seat, or mixed up with the other luggage in the gangway. With the bus still in furious motion Akbar began his search, climbing over the passengers, digging out the strangest assortment of bales, sacks and boxes. It soon became quite clear that the mailbag was no longer with us. We drove on in silence, thoughtfully. Suddenly the postman became hysterically alive: he wailed, beat his breast and called upon the saints. He would lose his job, poor fellow, if the mail were not delivered in Kerman that morning. We were all very sympathetic. A *djinn* had whisked the thing away, possibly in punishment for his sins. Eventually Mohammed was prevailed upon to turn round. Miles back we picked up the mailbag in the light of the headlamps, lying forlornly in the middle of the road. The postman continued the journey silent and thankful, the bag clutched like a child in his arms.

There was a last halt at Mahun, where we wolfed hot stew and flaps of hard bread. I had a few words with Ahmed, who was becoming increasingly depressed as the distance between himself and his wife decreased. It was well after midnight and everyone was very tired. A silence fell on the bus as we climbed the long col south-east of Kerman; a dark mass of mountains reared close over us, the jagged tops silhouetted against the stars. It had become bitterly cold. My blanket had been borrowed to wrap up the silent babies behind me, and an icy draught was concentrated upon my unprotected shoulders. Mercifully my feet were kept warm by the engine. Mansur set up a howl of thankful prayer as the lights of Kerman finally came into view, sparkling far away at the end of the valley; he was answered by the rest with a momentary burst of enthusiasm, but our hopes were short-lived. I had often thought of the unwisdom of thanking the Almighty in advance; here we were properly caught; for the chorus had hardly died away before the steering failed completely, and Mohammed spun the wheel helplessly in his hands.

A little tinkering with a spanner and a coil of wire by the resourceful Akbar, and we were off again, crawling drunkenly and at a snail's pace along the earthen track. Two hours later we were cruising down the silent streets of Kerman, and had at last come to rest in the deserted bus-station. Ahmed wandered sadly off to his wife, his bag on his shoulder; Akbar to stay with friends. The rest of the passengers dispersed after mutual and sleepy farewells and congratulations. Most of the baggage was left on the bus: it was too late to pull it all down. Mohammed made certain that there was room for me to sleep upstairs, before shaking hands and going off to his family. I climbed the stairs above the bus-yard and found a room full of sleeping figures stretched on the floor. A place was free and, rolling myself in my blanket, I lay down and was asleep before I could remember.

A bus-station in the early morning is a desolate place, something like a fairground after a carnival night. The stamped earth floor is littered with pieces of coloured paper, sacks and cases, orange-peel and half-collapsed stalls. Coming down only half awake from my upstairs dormitory I found a hunchback leaning on a broom surveying the chaos. I persuaded him to sanction the unloading of the bus, and finally retrieved my case. I wandered into the office and stumbled over the still-prostrate body of one of the officials asleep on a couch behind the door. The bus to Isfahan! I shook him. No. Yes. A bus left to-day—or was it to-morrow? But not from here. It appeared that Kerman boasted more than one bus-station. I presented him with a packet of English cigarettes. Very well, he would telephone: his brother possessed a taxi.

A few minutes later I was being raced through the streets of Kerman. Most of the town was still asleep. A few water-carriers were about, with huge brown earthen jars balanced on their donkeys' backs, whose noses were bound with blue beads. We seemed to be making for the open country, and at full speed, the tyres screeching round the corners. Suddenly we turned sharply, twice, and—we were heading the way we had come: he was mad! And then I saw. Round the corner came into view the great blue-and-yellow bus. The car swerved across the road to head it off; the bus hooted irritably, the taxi snorted, we waved. I think the bus would not have stopped if my driver—admirable man—had not smartly reversed the car and planted it firmly across the bus's path. Fortunately the bus braked in time. I ignored the abuse that issued from the cab window, and in a moment I had stuffed the taxi-driver's hand with notes, my luggage was stowed away, and I was safely settled in the only remaining seat, at the back. I sensed that my irregular and forced intrusion was not approved. I looked out of my window and waved at the taxi-driver. We left him there grinning, standing in a cloud of dust by his car in the middle of the road.

This bus was very different from the last. It was not so old and travelled much faster. It subscribed to the theory, on the whole a true one, that the faster it went over the hard corrugated dust surface of the road, the smoother the general impression of progress it gave. The seats were better spaced. Unfortunately I was in the extreme back—the only vacant place—and every ten minutes or so the bus would leap a little higher over some more unusual obstruction with the result that I would be hurled into the air and my head would knock smartly against the roof. Although it was hot I kept my hat on to ward off the worst belabourings of my skull. I realised why this seat had had no takers.

The bus cleared a little before midday, and I was able to find a less dangerous seat. I fell into conversation with a quiet young man dressed in a neat dark-blue suit who sat next to me on the other side of the gangway. We talked over the head of a little boy who rocked on a little stool set up between us, who had, when the bus hit a particularly severe pothole, to be forcibly held down to prevent him from being seriously injured. My friend was an Inspector of Roads, and was returning to Tehran to 'make a report'. He talked easily of plans to metal all the roads in the country within a few years, but I was not so sure that this was a good idea. There is a beautiful piece of tarmac stretching west from Tehran under the Elburz Mountains, which is being gradually and successfully extended. On the other hand I had driven on tarmac from Hamadan towards Kazvin on a road that had been metalled in the early part of the war, but was now in such a state of disrepair, so full of gaping holes that wore larger every year, that corrugated earth was infinitely preferable. I told him that the roads generally were not up to the standard of the Turkish, but were incomparably superior to anything in Afghanistan. In a country the size of Persia the problem of keeping up communications across such vast distances and in such extremes of climate will always be an expensive one. Unless the government can really afford the equipment and skilled labour not only to make the roads but to keep them in good repair I felt it would be wiser to be less ambitious. At the moment the earth-road system is almost adequate. Each province keeps in employment teams of road-workers, hard-bitten peasants mostly, whom one comes across every now and then labouring furiously with spades and pickaxes. Whenever a cloud of dust on the horizons heralds the approach of a car, these people set to work frenziedly, shovelling sand across the road, smoothing out the surface. So keen and determined do they appear that often they narrowly escape being run down, as they refuse to leave the roadway until the last moment. Besides coping to some extent with the roads, the work offers to thousands of peasants the chance of employment with a bare living wage which otherwise they would be hard put to find.

The Road Inspector shared his seat with a Persian whose name or profession I was never able to discover. To my mind he looked like a retired heavyweight boxer, an enormous hulk of flesh surmounted by a particularly craggy and powerful face. The brutality of his appearance was in contrast to the mildness of his manners and the gentle expression of his eyes. When the bus stopped for refreshments the three of us would sit together, blowing on the scalding tea in our saucers. Any conversation between the boxer and myself was dutifully translated by the Road Inspector.

198

Return to Yezd

That afternoon we came in sight of Yezd—Yezd of unhappy memory for me—against a backcloth of hazed blue sky and brown spiky mountains, the strange outline of minarets and wind-towers, flat-roofed houses and walls, matching the lion-coloured desert on every side.

We were lodged in a cheap hotel near the bus-station. There was a room with three beds in it, opening onto a balcony that overlooked a crowded main street. I said that I was going out to have a look round, but the Inspector, who seemed to feel great anxiety on my behalf, insisted that he accompany me, and the boxer thought he would come along too. It appeared that neither of them had been in Yezd before, and so it fell to me to act as guide, a novel position which struck me as amusing. I suggested that we should see the Friday Mosque, whose magnificent portal topped with twin minarets I had recognised from afar on the road, and which I had not had time to look at properly the last time I was here. . . . We set off down the street in the direction of the mosque, the boxer and the Inspector deep in conversation. Whenever the boxer had something important to contribute he stopped dead in his tracks, in order I suppose to deliver his views with an undistracted mind, while the Inspector took his arm and tried to drag him on. During this rather unsteady progress I saw that nearly every plane tree lining the road was festooned with washing hung out in the sun to dry, a fantastic array of shirts and trousers, blue shawls and coloured turban-cloths that gave the main street the appearance of a fête.

We stood under the magnificent pointed arch, a hundred feet high, that guards the entrance of the Friday Mosque. I was glad to be looking at it again, and glad also that I was in the company of two of the Faithful—though I did not trouble to tell them my memories as I followed them into the mosque. We left our shoes in the court and stepped up to the *mihrab*. The boxer grunted with appreciation: there was nothing like this in *his* village. It was almost dusk, and I went back again to look at the great portal arch. Fortunately, perhaps, I had no camera with me. The tiles, enscrolled with blue and yellow, were still warm to touch;

the colours glowed dully in the fading light. It was the last night of the journey: tomorrow, *insha'allah*, my travelling would be over.

❄

We left Yezd early the next morning, on the last stage to Isfahan. Before midday we passed through Nain. I saw the mosque from a long way off, the dome a strange and lovely pale blue, patterned in the shape of diamonds. I was beginning to understand how it must have felt in the old caravan days, with the camels strung out over this burning wilderness, day after day to move on across these great bare distances where the eye is held by no more than a brown twisted peak of mountain, or the fantastic shapes of rocks distorted on the shimmering horizon to the size of towers. How wonderful it must have been suddenly to make out the thin pencil of a minaret, dark patches of trees—cypress, chenar, palm—and best of all the blue dome of a mosque flashing in the far haze. Blue—the perfect Persian blue, which holds for the desert traveller all the promises of paradise, coolness and shade and running water, rest after the long journey.

I looked to the west where black clouds were massing over the mountains. A sudden chill dried the sweat on our foreheads; in the pass a snowstorm struck the bus, buffeting with white flakes the painted metal that two hours before had been too hot to touch. As we descended, the snow left off: we would be in Isfahan before sunset. The valley was opening out, unfolding like a patchwork quilt: fresh spring greens, fields of new corn studded with low cottages and groves of white-stemmed poplars. Rain had turned the earth a rich dark brown. I made out the mass of the city below, a glint of the Zayand river winding beyond. A low shaft of yellow light pierced the clouds and touched for an instant the tall minarets of the Madraseh, pointing a gleam to the dome of the Shah's Mosque, dark blue astride a sea of rooftops. Isfahan! For a moment that sudden vision of the city fulfilled all the dreams and hopes, all that I had read or heard of it: the ghosts and spirits, conjured by its name, were ready to be touched alive, were waking again before me. If, as they had said, I was *sayyah*, a pilgrim, then it was so; and if every *sayyah* must have his goal, then Isfahan, I knew, was mine.

From the bus-station I took a carriage, one of those shabby but exotic vehicles that still ply the streets. I felt I deserved some luxury after my journey of 800 miles. The driver looked down at me sprawled over the faded pink cushions. Where to? Hotel Kasbah! We jogged up the great avenue of the Charbagh, scattering the promenaders who strolled arm-in-arm under the trees, gazing in at the shop windows. A little boy took a jump at the footboard. 'Baksheesh, Agha!' We were passing the antique shops. A figure standing before his shop door called out to me. 'Meester Carroll, sir!' Jacob, the old rascal. 'I have something very nice to show you—come to-morrow!' I nodded and waved: Of course! I recognised a familiar figure, striped-shirted and collarless, Hassan, pushing aside the bead-curtained doorway of the tea-house. I would be with him in an hour.

8

Epilogue : Tea-leaves

❋

There is a garden at the back of the tea-house, not much of one, but Persian for all that: a bare earth courtyard with a blue pool in the centre to match the one within, though in the garden there is no fountain, but a tap. There are no flowers and no grass; but these are rarities in Persia. Yet the main ingredients that make a Persian garden—*firdaus*, where stems our word *paradise*—are here: the high surrounding walls, shutting out the rest of the world; water, from the pool; and shade, shade from four chenars tall and slender whose boles gleam white against the blue sky. An almond tree pink with blossom stands in one corner, and they are trying to grow peaches against one wall. At the far end there are two poplars which seem to have got cut off from their comrades on the other side of the wall, where the garden there is full of poplars rustling their plumed heads in the sky. Now that it is warmer I go and sit in the tea-house garden in the afternoons, when the sun has climbed high over the wall and poplars and shines down on the bench and the two trestles with a carpet on each of them that are set up by the pool. Besides the tea-boy, who comes out occasionally to refill my glass, my only company is usually a family of cats, who prowl about among the broken tea-cases that litter the yard, or sit with heads on one side wondering at their reflections in the pool.

I have been thinking of those worm-eaten pillars in the tea-house, and they seem so old that surely they might once have

been part of one of the great noblemen's houses that lined the
Charbagh in the days of Shah Abbas, built 'of many Stories,
distinguished by Balconies and which advance upon the Course:
Their fronts are embellished with Paintings, & enriched with
Leaves and Flowers of Gold, in *demi-Relievo* . . .' Ibrahim wasn't
sure about this, but he thought it quite likely. Perhaps the tea-
house may have been the very mansion where Pietro della Valle
stayed and complained about the shortage of fish in Isfahan, and
the consequent 'inconvenience of keeping Lent here'; or even
where Father Sanson came to write his detailed observations of
Safavid court life.

Certainly the wall at the end of the garden must have marked
the limits of the vast palace enclosure, which included the harem
gardens and pavilions, stretching beyond the poplars and the
Chihil Sutun down to the Ali Kapu and the Maidan. That the
wall did in fact divide me from the old gardens of the harem
was proved to me incontestably when one afternoon, falling
asleep over my writing, I heard quite clearly girls' voices from
over the wall, voices raised in laughter and the sound of light
steps running between the trees. Ghosts from three centuries? A
blue rubber ball sailed over the wall and descended into the
branches of the almond tree, showering my notebook with petals.
Dismayed silence. I picked out the ball and threw it back. I heard
it land the other side and the sound of a scuffle followed by confused giggles. In a few moments the ball came over again, and
when I returned it it got stuck in one of the poplars. I could
hear the girls arguing helplessly on the other side. They were
going to get the gardener, and a ladder.

Father Sanson was greatly interested in Persian women, and
especially sympathised with the enforced seclusion of those of
the Shah's court: 'The close encloistering of these Ladies in the
Haram would be insupportable, if they did not altogether banish
Idleness, and take care to sweeten their Solitude with diverting
Exercises; they are there taught to Ride, to draw the bow, to
fire the Fusil, to course Deer, & in fine, to Paint, Dance, Sing, &
play upon all sorts of Music. They also learn there Poetry, History,

and the Mathematicks. In short everything that may become 'em to render their Retreat the more agreeable.

'These Ladies are very Amazons; they know how to manage and spur a Horse as well as the greatest Jockies: they can run down great Beasts and dart 'em with Arrows when they have done, and which they level with wonderful dexterity. They follow the King with Hawkes upon their Fists, and which they flip when he commands them, and ride full speed when they see them mount; and when they have a mind to recall 'em, they beat a sort of little Drum, which they carry on the Pommels of their Saddles . . . But if they strike any Game they come immediately and show it to the King: if they be Cranes they have killed, the King pulls out the Feathers, and divides 'em amongst them, and of which they make Feather Caps . . .'

As to the women's gorgeous apparel the worthy Jesuit demonstrates the keenness of his observation by his detailed descriptions. He noticed also that '. . . they have a sort of Red Powder with which they paint the Palms of their Hands, the Soles of their Feet, and the Ends of their Nails; also they black their Eyes with Tuty. Blew, Gray, and Ash-colour'd Eyes have no esteem with them; the Black only are priz'd.' Unfortunately Father Sanson, in spite of his other-worldly profession, was never allowed to see any of their faces. What with mullahs ogling his women from the tops of minarets, Shah Abbas and his descendants knew well the dangers of allowing priests and women to mix.

When Ibrahim can escape his class he comes and joins me in the sun, and of course Hassan—who by this time, I would have thought, should have developed tea-poisoning, if there is such a thing—was never far away. Since I had last seen him Ibrahim had changed a little. For one thing he no longer wished to leave Isfahan. He was getting old, he said; his wandering days were over. He had become more thoughtful and seemed to talk less, but when I questioned him more on the subject of Sufism he was eager to tell me something of what he knew. Sufism had been occupying him particularly of late.

Hassan still felt guilty about not being able to produce his dervish, like a rabbit out of a conjurer's hat, for my closer inspection, but once when Hassan was not there Ibrahim told me that he doubted very much if Hassan's dervish was as holy as he seemed. If he was, then he was a remarkable exception from the general run of modern dervishes. Apparently my fiery tea-house sermoniser belonged to one of the Sufi Orders, of which there are many in Persia, whose members are notorious for their methods of preying upon the superstition and credulity of the masses, living off alms received from the poorest people, and selling them charms and talismans for magic protection against evil spirits. I was surprised that a way of thought such as Sufism, which had seemed to me in its origin to be so pure and with such lofty ideals, could have degenerated to such an extent; but I suppose there are almost identical parallels elsewhere in the world, not least of all in the West.

If you seek the untainted source of Sufism, said Ibrahim, then you must go back to the old teachers, to the poets and mystics like Rumi, a native of Khorassan who died in Konia, Turkey, in 1273, having founded the Mevleveya sect of 'whirling' dervishes, or Hafiz, the poet of Shiraz who died in 1391, who have expressed in their verses Sufi philosophy at its truest and best.

'What makes the Sufi?' asks Rumi in one of his poems, and answers, 'Purity of Heart.' The true Sufi, by rigorous self-discipline and contemplation, tries to efface himself, to lose his own identity in the love of the Pure Being—'Beauty', 'The Beloved'—and so becomes one with God. He tries to learn to distinguish between Reality, and the shadow of it, which is all the world; by learning to love, first the Reflection and then the Light itself, he will attain the Ideal, *fana*, the mystery of Divine Union.

The language of earthly love employed by the mystic poets seems now to be generally regarded as allegorical: the ecstatic experience of Ideal Love, for instance, has as its symbol, Wine;

the place of pure Unity, the Tavern. But there is still some doubt
in many cases, and some poems are thought to possess a *double*
allegory—Love both human and divine; while others are even
held to mean no more than what they say. My first thought is
of Omar Khayyàm, in whose *Rubaiyat*, taken as a whole, I find
it hard to believe there is much mystical symbolism. I was interested to see that Ibrahim is quite indifferent to this poet, and
Amin, in Meshed, although he had given me a *Rubaiyat* as a
farewell present, did so only because he knew of Omar Khayyàm's exclusive European reputation. Amin, like most Persians,
loved the poems of Hafiz best, and considered Hafiz without
equal. The two poems of Hafiz, translated by Nicholson, that
follow seem to me to be good examples of the mystical love-
allegory.

THE BELOVED*

Mortal never won to view thee,
Yet a thousand lovers woo thee;
Not a nightingale but knows
In the rose-bud sleeps the rose.

Love is where the glory falls
Of thy face: on convent walls
Or on tavern floors the same
Unextinguishable flame.

Where the turban'd anchorite
Chanteth Allah day and night,
Church-bells ring the call to prayer,
And the Cross of Christ is there.

REVELATION*

My soul is the veil of his love,
Mine eye is the glass of his grace.
Not for earth, not for heaven above,
Would I stoop; yet his bounties have bowed
A spirit too proud
For aught to abase.

* *Translations of Eastern Poetry and Prose* by R. A. Nicholson (Cambridge
University Press).

This temple of awe, where no sin
But only the zephyr comes nigh,
Who am I to adventure within?
Even so: very foul is my skirt.
What then? Will it hurt
The most Pure, the Most High?

He passed by the rose in the field,
His colour and perfume she stole.
Oh twice-happy star that revealed
The secret of day and of night—
His face to my sight,
His love to my soul!

According to Ibrahim the greatest of the Persian mystics and poets was Rumi, who lived a century before Hafiz. I would like to quote a few quatrains and parts of quatrains translated by Professor Arberry, because I do not believe that the eternal desire of so many people for this union with the infinite or God, which is expressed in so many religions and is the central part of the Sufi philosophy, has ever been put more perfectly by any man:

As salt resolved in the ocean*
I was swallowed in God's sea,
Past faith, past unbelieving,
Past doubt, past certainty. . . .

*　　*　　*

The Fount of Immortality
In Love is found;
Then come, and in this boundless sea
Of Love be drowned . . .

*　　*　　*

I sought a soul in the sea
And found a coral there:
Beneath the foam for me
An ocean was all laid bare.

*　　*　　*

* *Persian Poems* translated by Professor R. J. Arberry (J. M. Dent, Everyman Library).

Epilogue: Tea-leaves

Into my heart's night
Along a narrow way
I groped; and lo! the light,
An infinite land of day.

*   *   *

Happy was I
In the pearl's heart to lie;
Till, lashed by life's hurricane,
Like a tossed wave I ran.

*   *   *

The secret of the sea
I uttered thunderously;
Like a spent cloud on the shore
I slept, and stirred no more.

London, March 1959

I have had several letters from Persia. Amin has asked for more information about English universities, and adds that Ghani is still the terror of all Meshed carpet-dealers. I wrote to Martin insisting on my paying for the broken lavatory, but in his reply he politely avoids the subject, and instead stresses that the gold-fish are well, but for a slight tragedy: he gave a party in the garden and a Very Important Person fell into the pool, killing one of the fish. They are laying eggs now. Ibrahim wrote, with a beautiful hand, in green ink. He suggests I return to Isfahan and that together we try and write a book about Shah Abbas. As for Hassan, his pension has stopped. He wants to know whether it is true or not that if he comes to England he can draw another pension, because of his old age. He promises to send me more *kalian* tobacco when I need it. Jacob also wants me back in Isfahan, but I suspect his motives.

An interesting letter has come from Pierre, the Dutchman I met at Charbahar. He passed through Isfahan at the end of the year and called in at the tea-house as I had suggested, and met

A Curtain of Blue Beads

Ibrahim. The mystery of the wheelbarrow—which up to that time had remained unsolved—was promptly expounded to him. It was very simple. If your car is stuck in sand in the middle of a sand desert, and a man comes by, walking, with a wheelbarrow full of sand—it can only be taken as a divine signal revealing the futility of finite action, the vanity of earthly attachments. Now that he knows and understands, or thinks he does, Pierre is even more worried: such a hint, so clearly and personally given, will be difficult to ignore.

Soon in Persia it will be *No-Ruz* again; and in Isfahan the people will be crowding the tiered alcoves of the bridges watching the spring water flow under the arches; water from the mountains that ring the city with their barren slopes, mountains that range across Persia dividing desert from desert without end, brown spikes under a glittering blue dome of sky. And on that day Isfahan will be quite empty, the streets deserted; and only ghosts and dust-spirals will promenade the Charbagh, and Shah Abbas will be able to hold court again, undisturbed, in the throne-room of the Ali Kapu, while his noblemen play polo in the Maidan below. In the tea-house the pool will be still, the blue-bead curtain across the doorway quite motionless; and most people would say, if they were asked, that there was no one in the tea-house at all.

❈

Also available from Tauris Parke Paperbacks

Passenger to Teheran
Vita Sackville-West

In 1926 Vita Sackville-West travelled to Iran to visit her husband, Harold Nicolson, who was serving as a diplomat in Teheran. Her route was deliberately slow-paced – she stopped in Egypt, where she sailed up the Nile to Luxor; and India, where she visited New Delhi and Agra before sailing across the Persian Gulf to Iraq and on through bandit-infested mountains to Teheran. She returned to England in an equally circuitous manner and despite travelling under dangerous circumstances, through communist Russia and Poland in the midst of revolution, her humour and sense of adventure never failed. *Passenger to Teheran* is a classic work, revealing the lesser-known side of one of the twentieth century's most luminous authors.

Paperback, 160pp, 82 black and white illustrations
ISBN 978 1 84511 343 8

> *'It's awfully good... The whole book is full of nooks and crannies, the very intimate things one says in print.'*
> Virginia Woolf

> 'Passenger to Teheran *is utterly different from a returned traveller's lecture... It gives pleasure because it describes pleasure, illuminated by what Winifred Holtby called 'the lucid tranquility of her lovely prose'. She could describe a scene, a person, an emotion with enviable spontaneity, plunging her hands into the treasury of the English language as greedily as into the jewel-chests of the Shah. It is a glittering book.'*
> Nigel Nicolson, in his introduction to
> *Passenger to Teheran*

TPP
www.taurisparkepaperbacks.com